Treatment and Care
in Old Age Psychiatry

Treatment and Care in Old Age Psychiatry

Edited by

RAYMOND LEVY, ROBERT HOWARD

*Section of Old Age Psychiatry,
Institute of Psychiatry, London, UK*

and

ALISTAIR BURNS

*Department of Old Age Psychiatry,
University of Manchester, UK*

WRIGHTSON BIOMEDICAL PUBLISHING LTD
Petersfield, UK and Bristol, PA, USA

Editorial Office:

Wrightson Biomedical Publishing Ltd
Ash Barn House, Winchester Road, Stroud,
Petersfield, Hampshire GU32 3PN, UK
Telephone: 0730 265647
Fax: 0730 260368

British Library Cataloguing in Publication Data
A catalogue record for this book is available from the British Library.

Library of Congress Cataloging in Publication Data
Treatment and care in old age psychiatry/edited by Raymond Levy,
Robert Howard, and Alistair Burns.
     p.   cm.
   Includes bibliographical references and index.
   1. Memory disorders in old age. 2. Depression in old age.
3. Alzheimer's disease. 4. Mentally ill aged--Legal status, laws,
etc. I. Levy. Raymond. II. Howard, Robert, 1961-   , III. Burns,
Alistair S.
   [DNLM: 1. Mental Disorders--in old age. 2. Mental Disorders-
-therapy. 3. Geriatric Psychiatry. WT 150 T7838 1993]
RC451.4.A5T725 1993
618.97'689--dc20
DNLM/DLC
for Library of Congress   93-3405
                                                                 CIP

ISBN 1 871816 17 3

Composition by Scribe Design, Gillingham, Kent
Printed in Great Britain by Biddles Ltd, Guildford.

Contents

Contributors

Gordon R. Ashton, *Gedye & Sons, Solicitors, Main Street, Grange-over-Sands, Cumbria LA11 6DR, UK*

Alistair Burns, *Department of Old Age Psychiatry, University of Manchester, Withington Hospital, West Didsbury, Manchester M20 8LR, UK*

David Challis, *Personal Social Services Research Unit, Cornwallis Building, University of Kent, Canterbury, Kent CT2 7NF, UK*

B. Costall, *Postgraduate School of Studies in Pharmacology, University of Bradford, Bradford BD7 1DP, UK*

Thomas H. Crook III, *Memory Assessment Clinics, Inc., 8311 Wisconsin Avenue, Bethesda, Maryland 20814, USA*

A.M. Domeney, *Postgraduate School of Studies in Pharmacology, University of Bradford, Bradford BD7 1DP, UK*

Graham Dunn, *Department of Biostatistics and Computing, Institute of Psychiatry, De Crespigny Park, London SE5 8AF, UK*

Ian Hindmarch, *University of Surrey, Milford Hospital, Godalming, Guildford GU7 1UF, UK*

Robert Howard, *Section of Old Age Psychiatry, Institute of Psychiatry, De Crespigny Park, London SE5 8AF, UK*

R.G. Jones, *Department of Health Care of the Elderly, Medical School, University Hospital, Nottingham NG7 2UH, UK*

Cornelius L.E. Katona, *Department of Psychiatry, University College London, Middlesex Hospital, London W1N 8AA, UK*

M.E. Kelly, *Postgraduate Studies in Pharmacology, University of Bradford, Bradford BD7 1DP, UK*

vii

Raymond Levy, *Section of Old Age Psychiatry, Institute of Psychiatry, De Crespigny Park, London SE5 8AF, UK*

Simon Lovestone, *Section of Old Age Psychiatry, Institute of Psychiatry, De Crespigny Park, London SE5 8AF, UK*

Elaine Murphy, *Department of Psychogeriatrics, Guy's Hospital, London Bridge, London SE1 9RT, UK*

R.J. Naylor, *Postgraduate Studies in Pharmacology, University of Bradford, Bradford BD7 1DP, UK*

Brice Pitt, *Department of Mental Health of the Elderly, Community Health Unit, St Charles Hospital, Ladbroke Grove, London W10 6DZ, UK*

Patrick Rabbitt, *Age and Cognitive Performance Research Centre, University of Manchester, Oxford Road, Manchester M13 9PL, UK*

Charles Twining, *Clinical Psychology, Whitchurch Hospital, Whitchurch, Cardiff CF4 7XB, UK*

Gordon K. Wilcock, *Department of Health Care of the Elderly, University of Bristol, Frenchay Hospital, Bristol BS16 1LE, UK*

David G. Wilkinson, *Old Age Psychiatry, Moorgreen Hospital, Botley Road, West End, Southampton SO3 3JD*

K.W. Woodhouse, *Department of Geriatric Medicine, University of Wales College of Medicine, Cardiff Royal Infirmary, Cardiff CF2 1SZ, UK*

Preface

For some years the Institute of Psychiatry has held a series of short courses focusing on recent progress in psychiatry of the elderly. The first was a general view of advances covering the broad range of the field, and the second coincided with the 125th anniversary of the birth of Alois Alzheimer. The third one concerned itself entirely with affective disorders. The chapters in this current book are largely based on contributions to such a course entitled 'Treatment and Care in Old Age Psychiatry' held in July 1992. A clear demand on the part of the audience for a rapid publication led us to believe that this sort of book would be of interest to the increasing numbers of people of different disciplines currently contributing to old age psychiatry. Our aim has not been to cover the well-trodden path of standard descriptions of well established treatment which may be obtained elsewhere. Rather we have attempted to concentrate on advances or potential advances in treatment of common conditions, on subjects which have been of topical interest and controversy and on certain issues which are less frequently discussed. We have not attempted to cover treatment and care comprehensively but have instead adopted the approach usually associated with the rubric 'recent advances'. It has been our intention to ensure reasonably quick publication in a field which is in part typified by very rapid developments and we are grateful both to our contributors and to the publisher for having made this possible.

In many ways, successful publication of such a volume can be likened to the reproductive process in which the editors play a paternal role: a certain amount of effort at the moment of conception, anxious pacing outside the delivery room and distribution of cigars when all is over. We were fortunate enough to have an excellent literary obstetrician in Judy Wrightson and as dedicated midwives Lee Wilding, Institute of Psychiatry Conference organiser and Margaret Derrick, secretary in the Section of Old Age Psychiatry. To each of these, for their expertise and uncomplaining hard work, we are truly grateful. We hope our 'child' delights others and that siblings will soon be forthcoming.

THE EDITORS

Alzheimer's Disease

Treatment and Care in Old Age Psychiatry
Edited by R. Levy, R. Howard and A. Burns
©1993 Wrightson Biomedical Publishing Ltd

1

Nerve Growth Factor and Other Experimental Approaches

GORDON K. WILCOCK

Department of Care of the Elderly, University of Bristol, Frenchay Hospital, Bristol, UK

INTRODUCTION

The brain utilizes a formidable array of neurotransmitters, some of which are known to be depleted in Alzheimer's disease (AD). It is not necessarily clear whether, in all instances, neurotransmitter loss is responsible for the clinical presentation of AD rather than acting as a marker for the disease process. In order to make some sense of the deranged biochemistry, especially in relation to therapeutic strategies, it is convenient to classify the neurotransmitters into intrinsic and extrinsic groups relative to the cerebral cortex. Intrinsic neurotransmitters are those that are synthesized predominantly within the cerebral cortex and, to some extent, are a marker for the integrity of cortical neurones. The extrinsic group are synthesized elsewhere and are transported to the cortex along projection pathways. It is this latter group which appear to be most significantly depleted in AD, and some authorities believe that their relatively long projection pathways may go some way towards explaining why there is an apparent predilection for the pathology to affect these particular systems. The most important are usually considered to be acetylcholine, noradrenaline and serotonin (5HT). As the reader will be aware, the cholinergic hypothesis forms a cornerstone to present neurotransmitter related strategies for the treatment of AD and this has led to extensive research into the physiology of the cholinergic system within the brain. It is now firmly established that neurones in the cholinergic system appear to be, at least to some extent, dependent upon one or more trophic factors if their functional and structural integrity is to be preserved. This knowledge forms the background to the development of therapeutic strategies based upon neurotrophic factors, which will be discussed below. In addition this chapter will briefly touch upon several other aspects of the molecular pathology of Alzheimer's disease that may yield potential therapeutic benefit.

NEUROTROPHIC FACTORS AND ALZHEIMER'S DISEASE

The most extensively explored neurotrophic factor in relation to AD is of course nerve growth factor (NGF). This was first identified by Levi-Montalcini 40 years ago when she and her co-workers discovered that mouse sarcomas transplanted into chick embryos induced innervation by sensory and sympathetic fibres. They isolated the factor responsible, and the term nerve growth factor was invented to describe it. This area is well reviewed more recently by Levi-Montalcini (1987).

Nerve growth factor is a dimeric molecule that is widely conserved in nature and has been cloned from a number of different species. The sequence of the protein structure is very similar in each case indicating a central role for NGF in the development of the central nervous system, in evolutionary terms.

There are now many studies that have confirmed that NGF is a trophic factor for peripheral sympathetic and sensory fibres. Peripheral target tissues release NGF which interacts with specific receptors and is then transported back to the neuronal perikaryon whence it enters the nucleus. More recently NGF has been shown to be present in the central nervous system where a transport mechanism has also been confirmed, e.g. NGF that has been radioactively labelled and injected into the hippocampus or cerebral cortex in experimental animals leads to the labelling of cells at the cholinergic sub-cortical sites, i.e. the septum, the diagonal band of Broca and the basal nucleus of Meynert (Seiler and Schwab, 1984).

Receptors for NGF have been found on neurones of the sub-cortical cholinergic sites, e.g. the medial septal nucleus and the basal nucleus in laboratory animals, especially the rat, and also on fibres in the cortex and hippocampus. It has also been shown that the majority of cholinergic basal forebrain neurones express NGF receptors, by staining alternate sections with antibodies to a cholinergic marker (ChAT) and the NGF receptor (Dawbarn et al., 1988). This co-localization of NGF receptor and cholinergic marker staining further suggests that there may be a trophic interaction between NGF and sub-cortical cholinergic neurones. In addition, many research groups have now shown that application of NGF to these neurones, either in vitro or in vivo, upregulates cholinergic function, further confirming a potential functional interrelationship.

Although there is no good animal model for Alzheimer's disease, many attempts have been made to mimic certain aspects of AD by chemically or physically manipulating neurotransmitter systems in laboratory animals. One such model involves lesioning the fimbria-fornix pathways which will cause degeneration in sub-cortical cholinergic neurones (Gage et al., 1988; Hagg et al., 1988). NGF shows protective properties in such models.

Ageing rats and primates develop atrophy of cholinergic neurones associated with impairment of spatial memory. Administration of NGF into the brains of these ageing mammals has apparently improved such memory impairment and at least partially reversed some of the neuronal atrophy (Fischer et al., 1987; Tuszyinski et al., 1990).

Turning now to the human brain, investigation of the distribution of NGF receptors confirms the animal findings, i.e. that NGF receptors are synthesized by cholinergic sub-cortical neurones (Allen et al., 1988; Mufson et al., 1989). Furthermore, comparison of the number and size distribution of basal forebrain neurones expressing these receptors is similar in AD and aged-matched normal brains (Allen et al., 1990). It is probable that earlier reports of a significant cellular loss of neurones from the basal nucleus and other sub-cortical sites in Alzheimer's disease exaggerated the degree and extent of neuronal decay because small shrunken cholinergic neurones are indistinguishable from background glia. Although there is indisputably neuronal loss from cholinergic sub-cortical sites, it is probably not so marked, particularly in elderly subjects, as was previously reported.

The binding characteristics of NGF in the human brain have also been explored using radiolabelled NGF. No significant differences were discovered in the mean K_d or the B_{max} in Alzheimer brain tissue compared with age matched normal subjects (Treanor et al., 1991). This relates however only to the low affinity receptor.

What happens to NGF levels in the Alzheimer brain? Using a modification of a two site ELISA to measure the NGF content in AD brain compared with normal age-matched controls, no reduction was found in four cortical regions and the hippocampus (Allen et al., 1991). This implies that cortical synthesis of NGF is unimpaired, and that measurement of sub-cortical NGF levels is essential to decide whether or not the sub-cortical sites are deprived of NGF, e.g. as a result of a breakdown of intraneuronal transport systems, possibly related to the formation of neurofibrillary tangles. Even if NGF synthesis is not reduced in AD, and is adequately transported to the sub-cortical sites, this does not preclude a potential therapeutic role as it has well described neuroprotective effects, some of which have been referred to above. It may be however that NGF will prove to be more relevant to the so-called normal memory loss associated with ageing, rather than specifically in relation to the treatment of Alzheimer's disease, and that other trophic factors are more important in AD. This is an area for further exploration.

OTHER NEUROTROPHIC FACTORS

It has become clear over the last three or four years that there is a whole family of neurotrophic factors, of which NGF is only one. These are all structurally related with a significant degree of homology within the family. Other neurotrophic factors include brain derived neurotrophic factor (BDNF), neurotrophin-3 (NT-3), NT-4 and NT-5. Of these, the distribution of mRNA for BDNF correlates most closely with that seen for NGF in the rodent brain, with a particularly strong association in the cortex and hippocampus, and a similar distribution in the human hippocampus (Phillips *et al.*, 1990). BDNF exerts a neuroprotective effect on rat septal neurones grown in culture (Alderson *et al.*, 1990) and the effects of BDNF and NGF on ChAT activity are additive.

At least three of these neurotrophic factors, NGF, BDNF and NT-3, bind equally to the low affinity NGF receptor, but with different specificities for high affinity receptors which have been identified as tyrosine receptor kinases. Of the three, NT-3 is least specific at the high affinity receptor binding level, with some binding ability to the high affinity receptors of both NGF and BDNF, as well as its own receptor.

Clinical experience with trophic factors is limited to the report by Olson *et al.* (1992) of possible benefit when NGF, derived from mouse salivary gland, was injected into the ventricular system over three months in a 69 year old lady with severe Alzheimer's disease. It is difficult to extrapolate from a single case, particularly in the presence of severe disease, but it would appear that there was some evidence of physiological benefit, and possibly a minor degree of improvement in the clinical condition.

In summary, the physiological role of neurotrophic factors in the brain, and also of their receptors, is proving far more complex than was initially envisaged. It is nevertheless an area of active research interest and may well produce new substances of potential therapeutic benefit, although there are technical problems that will have to be overcome if a therapeutic role is confirmed.

AMYLOID RELATED STRATEGIES

The presence of amyloid in the centre of the senile plaques and also within the walls of some of the blood vessels in many sufferers with Alzheimer's disease has of course led to speculation that this may itself be neurotoxic, although this is disputed by some. As the reader will be aware, it is formed by the reassembly of a small portion of a precursor parent protein, amyloid precursor protein (APP), into the amyloid protein itself, nowadays usually referred to as the amyloid β-protein. The sub-unit of APP involved in the β-protein synthesis is a little over 40 amino acids long.

Yankner *et al.* (1990) have shown that a synthetic sequence involving amino acids 25–35 is trophic to developing neurones at low concentration *in vitro*, but at higher concentrations is very toxic to mature neurones; significantly more so than glutamate, one of the more potent neurotoxins. This amino acid sequence has some homology with the tachykinin neuropeptides and the neurotrophic and neurotoxic effects can be mimicked by tachykinin antagonists, and reversed by tachykinin agonists including substance P. Interestingly substance P neurones are reported as depleted in the hippocampus in Alzheimer's disease.

Using an *in vivo* rat model, Kowall *et al.* (1991) injected β-amyloid into the cortex and reported neuronal loss and degeneration as a result. In addition the Alz-50 antigen was induced in some of the neurones in the surrounding area. These changes were prevented by the co-administration of substance P, whether this was undertaken locally or systemically.

In summary therefore, tachykinin neuropeptides appear to be able to block the neurotoxicity of amyloid, which may be of therapeutic benefit if the latter is indeed at least partly responsible for the Alzheimer's pathology. Furthermore, attempts at preventing the deposition of amyloid are also under exploration. This has been particularly stimulated by the finding that one of the forms of the amyloid precursor protein contains a protease inhibitor sequence. Evidence has also emerged recently (Koh *et al.*, 1990) that amyloid may increase the vulnerability of neurones to excitotoxic damage from glutamate, *N*-methyl-D-aspartate and kainate. In other words, β-amyloid, or part of its protein sequence may be indirectly neurotoxic in addition to or instead of the direct toxicity reported by others. This may result from destabilization of calcium homeostasis, as it has been shown (Mattson *et al.*, 1992) that synthetic β-amyloid peptides corresponding to amino acids 1–38 or 25–35 also impaired the ability of human fetal neurones to reduce intracellular calcium levels to normal limits. The neurotoxicity caused by excitatory aminoacids and potentiated by the synthetic peptides did not occur in a calcium deficient culture medium.

Although an exciting area of research, much more work is required to settle many of the controversies surrounding the apparent toxicity of the amyloid molecule.

CYTOKINES

Cytokines consist of a vast number of multifunctional proteins and glycoproteins which act as local and/or systemic intercellular regulatory factors. As is the case for many other diseases, the interleukin family has been particularly investigated in relation to AD. A small body of evidence is emerging suggesting that they might potentially play a role in the development of some of the pathology. Interleukin-1 for instance has been shown to induce over-expression of the APP gene (Donnelly *et al.*, 1990). This of course does not mean that there is an increase in amyloid production itself but further circumstantial evidence exists, e.g. that interleukin-1 mRNA is increased in AD. Certainly there is evidence that a receptor antagonist for interleukin-1 inhibits local cerebral damage in an apparently unrelated condition, i.e. focal ischaemia, if the antagonist is administered centrally. This is of interest because ischaemia may produce an accumulation of APP, which can also be prevented by the administration of an interleukin-1 receptor antagonist. Although the relationship between interleukin-1, APP, and Alzheimer's disease is speculative, largely resting on circumstantial evidence, it is possible that therapeutic trials of a recombinant interleukin-1 receptor antagonist may be a practical possibility since such trials are already underway for the treatment of other conditions, e.g. rheumatoid arthritis.

SUMMARY

A number of novel therapeutic approaches to the treatment of Alzheimer's disease are under investigation. Some are closer to potential clinical trial than others, and some remain speculative requiring further investigation. Of these, three of the more important areas have been described in this chapter. If any of them should prove a practical and reliable therapy for Alzheimer's disease they will probably not be available for some time. Meanwhile it is important that the role of neurotransmitter related strategies, e.g. the aminoacridines such as THA, is not overshadowed. One must remember that most of the strategies for the future are aimed at preventing or retarding cell death and other pathology. By the time the diagnosis is made, the very fact that the patient is suffering with symptoms implies that there may still be a role for neurotransmitter related therapy and similar approaches for the treatment of the patient's existing symptoms. Neuroprotection, whether via neurotrophic substances or amyloid related strategies, etc., is unlikely to reverse the illness, but rather to prevent further progression.

REFERENCES

Alderson, R.F., Alerman, A.L., Barde, Y-A, and Lindsay, R.M. (1990). Brain-derived neurotrophic factor increases survival and differentiated functions of rat septal cholinergic neurons in culture. *Neuron*, **5**, 297–306.
Allen, S.J., Dawbarn, D. and Wilcock, G.K. (1988). Morphometric immunochemical analysis of neurons in the nucleus basalis of Meynert in Alzheimer's disease. *Brain Res.*, **454**, 275–281.

Allen, S.J., Dawbarn, D., MacGowan, S.H., Wilcock, G.K., Treanor, J.J.S. and Moss, T.H. (1990). A quantitative morphometric analysis of basal forebrain neurones expressing β-NBF receptors in normal and Alzheimer's disease brains. *Dementia*, **1**, 125–137.

Allen, S.J., MacGowan, S.H., Treanor, J.J.S., Feeney, R., Wilcock, G.K. and Dawbarn, D. (1991). Normal NGF content in Alzheimer's disease cerebral cortex and hippocampus. *Neurosci. Lett.*, **131**, 135–139.

Dawbarn, D., Allen, S.J. and Semenenko, F.M. (1988). Coexistence of choline acetyltransferase and B-nerve growth factor receptors in the forebrain of the rat. *Neurosci. Lett.*, **94**, 138–144.

Donnelly, R.J., Friedhoff, A.J., Beer, B., Blume, A.J. and Vitek, M.P. (1990). Interleukin-1 stimulates the beta-amyloid precursor protein promoter. *Cell Mol. Neurobiol.*, **10**, 485–495.

Fischer, W., Wictorin, A., Bjorklund, A., Williams, L.R., Varon, S. and Gage, F.H. (1987). Amelioration of cholinergic neuronal atrophy and spatial memory impairment in aged rats by NGF. *Nature*, **329**, 65–67.

Gage, F.H., Armstrong, D.M., Williams, L.R. and Varon, S. (1988). Morphological response of axotomised septal neurones to nerve growth factor. *J. Comp. Neurol.*, **269**, 147–155.

Hagg, T., Manthorpe, M., Vahlsing, H.L. and Varon, S. (1988). Delayed treatment with nerve growth factor reverses the apparent loss of cholinergic neurons after acute brain damage. *Exp. Neurol.*, **101**, 303–312.

Koh, J.Y., Yang, L.L. and Cotman, C.W. (1990). Beta-amyloid protein increases the vulnerability of cultured cortical neurons in excitotoxic damage. *Brain Res.*, **533**, 315–320.

Kowall, N.W., Beal, M.F., Busciglio, J., Duffy, L.K. and Yankner, B.A. (1991). An *in vivo* model for the neurodegenerative effects of beta amyloid and protection by substance P. *Proc. Natl Acad. Sci. USA*, **88**, 7247–7251.

Levi-Montalcini, R. (1987). The nerve growth factor: Thirty-five years later. *Eur. Mol. Biol. Org. J.*, **6**, 1145–1154.

Mattson, M.P., Cheng, B., Davis, D., Bryant, K., Lieberburg, I. and Rydel, R.E. (1992). Beta-amyloid peptides destabilize calcium homeostasis and render human cortical neurons vulnerable to excitotoxicity. *J. Neuroscience*, **12**, 376–389.

Mufson, E.J., Bothwell, M., Hersh, L.B. and Kordower, J.H. (1989). Nerve growth factor receptor immunoreactive profiles in the normal, aged human basal forebrain: colocalization with cholinergic neurones. *J. Comp. Neurol.*, **285**, 196–217.

Olson, L., Nordberg, A., von Holst, H., Backman, L., Ebendal, T., Alafuzoff, I., Amberla, K., Hartvig, P., Herlitz, A., Lilja, A., Lundqvist, H., Langstrom, B., Meyerson, B., Persson, A., Viitanen, M., Winblad, B. and Seiger, A. (1992). Nerve growth factor affects 11C-nicotine binding, blood flow, EEG and verbal episodic memory in an Alzheimer patient (case report). *J. Neural. Transm. Park. Dis. Dement. Sect.*, **4**, 79–95.

Philips, H.S., Hains, J.M., Laramee, G.R., Rosenthal, A. and Winslow, J.W. (1990). Widespread expression of BDNF but not NT-3 by target areas of basal forebrain cholinergic neurons. *Science*, **250**, 290–295.

Seiler, M. and Schwab, M.E. (1984). Specific retrograde transport of nerve growth factor (NGF) from neocortex to nucleus basalis in the rat. *Brain Res.*, **300**, 33–39.

Treanor, J.J.S., Dawbarn, D., Allen, S.J., MacGowan, S.H. and Wilcock, G.K. (1991). Nerve growth factor receptor binding in normal and Alzheimer's disease basal forebrain, *Neurosci. Lett.*, **121**, 73–76.

Tuszyinski, M.H., U, H.-S., Amaral, D.G. and Gage, F.H. (1990). Nerve growth factor

infusion in the primate brain reduces lesion-induced cholinergic neuronal degeneration. *J. Neuroscience*, **10**, 3604–3614.

Yankner, B.A., Duffy, L.K. and Kinchner, D.A. (1990). Neurotrophic and neurotoxic
effects of amyloid beta protein: reversal by tachykinin neuropeptides. *Science*, **250**,
279–282.

Treatment and Care in Old Age Psychiatry
Edited by R. Levy, R. Howard and A. Burns
©1993 Wrightson Biomedical Publishing Ltd

2

Baseline Changes in Cognitive Performance with Age

PATRICK RABBITT

Age and Cognitive Performance Research Centre, University of Manchester, UK

To understand age-related pathologies of memory we must identify the changes in cognitive performance that occur with age in normal populations. This is of some practical importance. For example, in order to assess the value of putative 'nootropic' drugs which are claimed to improve memory in the aged it is essential to be able to relate treatment effects in clinical trials against adequate normative baseline data, which can only be obtained by screening very large populations of elderly people. Since 1982 we have screened over 6000 individuals aged from 50–96 years on two different batteries of cognitive tests. This has not only given us precise information about average levels of performance at different ages but, more importantly, has revealed the extent of variation between and within individuals that determines the boundaries of normal limits of ability. The most interesting insight into age changes that we obtain from screens of such large populations is not the rate at which average levels of performance change across age decades but the enormous increase in variability in performance between individuals on the same tasks, and within individuals across different tasks with the ages of the cohorts that we study.

Data from screenings of very large populations are liable to many biases, both those introduced by the tests used and by the ways in which volunteers are recruited. One of the constraints on tests is illustrated by distributions of scores on the AH 4(1) IQ test obtained from 964 individuals aged from 50–86 years and plotted in Figure 1. We see that changes in average scores with increasing age largely reflect a progressive skewing of distributions for successive age groups. As sample ages increase from 50–59, 60–69 and then to 70+ years, although a diminishing number of individuals can still attain maximum scores an increasing number cluster at the lower end of the distribution. This

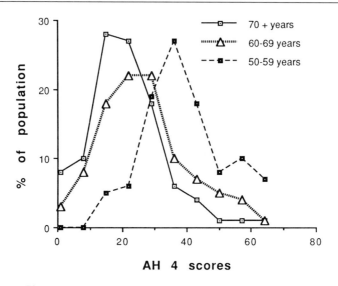

Figure 1. Distributions of IQ test scores for 934 persons.

raises the interesting possibility that cognitive ageing occurs at different rates in different individuals. Figure 1 makes the further point that as cohort age increases so does the proportion who are unscorable on the AH 4(1), (Heim, 1968), a rather simple IQ test. This means that task difficulty imposes an artificial 'floor' to the performance of the less able members of older cohorts. Figure 2 shows data from the same subjects compared on the much simpler task of recalling as many items as they can from a list of 30 words. Here average levels of recall decline with age but, because all subjects achieve non-zero scores, variability between individuals is no longer truncated by 'floor effects' and slightly, but significantly, increases with group age. In other words, for a test to be an efficient measure of cognitive changes in an ageing population it must have both a high 'ceiling' and a very low 'floor'; i.e. it must allow both very able and very frail individuals to be assessed along precisely the same continuum of performance. In practice this is usually a very difficult constraint to meet.

The patterns of data we obtain from cross-sectional studies can also be affected by the ways in which we recruit our subjects. It is very difficult to recruit large samples of volunteers who constitute a truly representative sample of their age groups in the population at large. A large proportion of people in their 70s, and most of those over 80, are institutionalized or housebound so that it is logistically difficult and expensive to contact, visit and test them. The alternative we have been obliged to adopt, of media advertisements for individuals willing to come to a centre for testing, results in an

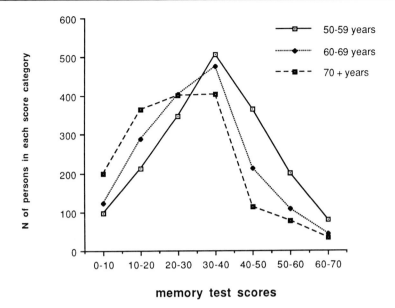

Figure 2. Digit spans, means and standard deviations by age group.

'elite' sample of atypically mobile, motivated, well-educated and intelligent older people. These selection biases become steadily more severe with increasing sample age so that, for example, our 80 and 90 year olds are probably truly exceptional members of their generations. These selection biases obviously reduce the estimates of cognitive change that we observe on our tests and so limit generalizability of our results. On the other hand they ensure that our estimates of the amounts of change are conservative and that the marked age-related increases in variation in ability between individuals that we have found must greatly underestimate an even larger true variation in the entire population. From a practical point of view the fact that our tests detect changes in the most able members of the elderly population also means that they are sensitive indices of the minimal impact of cognitive ageing and provide very conservative baseline estimates of its actual extent.

Having made the point that ageing increases variance in ability between individuals in memory, as in all other cognitive functions, we can go on to ask whether age also increases variance between different cognitive abilities within the same individual; that is whether some cognitive skills, such as memory, decline faster than others so that the difference between people's best and least maintained skills increases as they grow old. A first approach is to inspect correlations between scores on tests of specific cognitive abilities, chronological age and scores on the AH 4 (Heim, 1968) and Cattell

Table 1. Correlations between scores on 13 tests age between 50–86 years (N = 386) and unadjusted scores on the Cattell Culture Fair IQ Test.

	Age	CFIQ
Cattell culture fair IQ test	-.447	—
Wais vocabulary	-.149	.497
Baddeley 'silly sentences' (Sp)	-.314	.484
Visual search speed	-.325	.593
Letter/letter coding (Sp)	-.367	.331
Memory for code (from above)	-.2	.012
Rate of improvement in L/LC	-.018	.302
Immediate free recall of words	-.336	.362
Delayed free recall of words	-.359	.362
Memory for people	-.251	.349
Memory for object names	-.411	.407
Memory for locations of objects	-.221	.183
Memory for symbol location	-.364	.549

Culture Fair IQ tests. Table 1 shows such correlations from one of our longitudinal screening batteries. Tests are grouped into sub-sets dealing with memory and information processing speed. Correlations between chronological age and performance on all of the tests are very modest, though because of the large numbers of observations they are significant in all cases. Chronological age, *per se*, does not account for more than 16% of the total variance between individuals on any task. In contrast, correlations between scores on individual cognitive tests and on IQ tests are significantly larger. Indeed, when the contributions of IQ test scores to individual variance are partialled out chronological age has no additional effect on performance of any other task.

This obviously does not mean that age has no effect on cognitive performance but rather that nearly all age-related changes in ability on our tests are completely picked up by changes in IQ test scores. This result has been so often replicated in the literature that it has led Salthouse (1982, 1985, 1991) to propose a 'single factor' theory of cognitive ageing that assumes that all cognitive changes are secondary consequences of an age-related decline in a single performance index which is sensitively assessed by tests of fluid intelligence, (g_f). Because there are modest but robust correlations between IQ test scores and performance on information processing tasks, such as digit-symbol coding, Salthouse suggests that declines in scores on IQ tests and on tasks involving most other cognitive skills, including memory, are consequences of the well-documented slowing of information processing speed in old age; (Birren, 1965; Birren *et al.*, 1979; Cerella, 1985). Salthouse's argument curiously does not acknowledge earlier suggestions by Anderson (1992), Brand and Deary (1982), Eysenck (1982, 1986), Jensen (1982a,b,

1985), Nettelbeck and Brewer (1981); Nettelbeck and Lally (1981), Vernon (1985) and Vernon and Jensen (1984) among many others that information processing rate is a 'master' performance parameter which entrains ability on most other tasks and so may be taken as a 'biological', or at least a 'functional', basis of human intelligence. This theoretical context sets the main question for our discussion; whether age-related changes in memory efficiency are, functionally, secondary reflections of changes in information processing rate, and so proceed at the same rate as all other cognitive changes driven by this single master parameter, or whether memory ability may rather change in different ways, at different times and at different rates, in different individuals.

In evaluating the single-factor theory of cognitive ageing it is important to stress that it need not account only for individual differences in rates of cognitive change with increasing chronological age but can also explain changes associated with other factors, such as health. Table 2 compares scores on a variety of cognitive tests obtained from non-insulin dependent diabetics and their closely matched healthy controls. It is evident that non-insulin dependent diabetes depresses cognitive performance on all tests including all memory tasks. However, just as in the case of chronological age, when the effects of IQ test score are taken into account in a stepwise regression, diabetes, on its own, accounts for no additional variance. That is to say, we cannot discount the hypothesis that the change in memory efficiency brought about by diabetes is a secondary consequence of its effect on a single master variable, g_f, which is most sensitively detected by simple IQ tests.

To test the single-factor theory we need to discover whether, as a population ages, patterns of correlations between performance indices change and, in particular, that IQ test scores begin to predict less of the individual variance between scores on all other cognitive measures. In one respect this is easy to demonstrate because it has long been known that while age markedly reduces performance on most novel tasks it has little effect on performance of tasks that depend on a lifetime's acquisition and use of data and procedures; (Horn and Cattell, 1966; Horn, 1982, 1986). As an example

Table 2. Means and standard deviations of scores for elderly diabetics and controls on the AH 4 IQ test and on four memory tasks.

	Diabetics	Healthy controls
AH 4 part 1	23.8 (11.9)	28.0 (11.6)
AH 4 part 2		
(Spatial test)	22.5 (11.2)	26.9 (11.0)
Cumulative learning	37.5 (9.6)	39.9 (9.3)
Free recall	6.6 (2.7)	7.8 (3.3)
d' for picture recognition	84 (0.5)	0.99 (0.5)

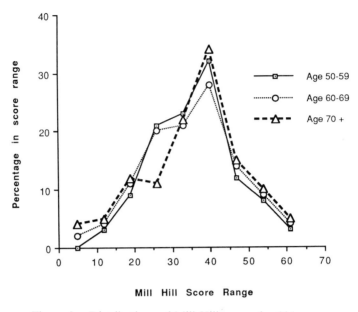

Figure 3. Distributions of Mill Hill scores for 934 persons.

Figure 3 shows distributions of scores on the Mill Hill vocabulary test obtained from the same subjects whose distributions of AH 4(1) scores are plotted in Figure 1. In marked contrast to their AH 4 scores, not only the averages but also the distributions of Mill Hill scores are identical for all age groups. This and other similar phenomena documented by Horn (1982, 1986) and Rabbitt (1993) are relevant to our study of memory changes with age because, of course, all our knowledge of language, as of the world in general, must be stored in long-term memory. Horn (1982, 1986) suggests that the massive bodies of knowledge about language and the world, which we have spent a lifetime acquiring and continue to use even late in our lives, comprise a conceptual toolkit of data and problem solving procedures which he terms 'crystallized intelligence' (g_c). This body of remembered information remains resistant to age-related changes in the central nervous system that markedly affect 'fluid' abilities, such as information processing speed, efficient allocation of attention, working memory capacity and ability rapidly to cope with novel information and problems. These, in Horn's model, comprise our fluid intelligence, (g_f). Bahrich and his associates use an equally engaging metaphor to capture their finding of substantial bodies of retained information such as High School Spanish, retention of knowledge of the topography of a town known in youth or information about once famous people (Bahrick, 1979, 1983, 1984; Bahrick et al., 1975; Bahrick and Phelps, 1987).

They found that if such bodies of information are not regularly used and rehearsed they show marked decrement over a period of two or three years followed by decades of little further loss. They suggest that this residual information has attained 'permastorage', after which further decrement is unlikely. Such metaphors as 'crystallization' and 'permastorage' covertly convey the speculation that long acquired and continually practised memories enter into a distinct state of functional representation, which is different from, and much more robust than that in which more recent and less rehearsed information is held.

Neisser (1984) challenged this assumption, pointing out that we have as yet no grounds for believing that older and more practised memories undergo any change of representational state, and that Bahrick's findings might be explained by the fact that longer established memories have become more highly 'schematized' by acquiring richer patterns of associations. Conway *et al.* (1991) examine this possibility by studying retention, over periods of up to 10 years, of information acquired during an Open University course in Cognitive Psychology. They conclude that because different *kinds* of information show different amounts and rates of decline we must assume that duration and efficiency of retention and rate of loss are very strongly influenced by qualitative differences in the degree of schematization to which these different kinds of 'knowledge' are susceptible. Until direct neurophysiological evidence is available the most parsimonious hypothesis is that continued accessibility of information in memory depends on the informational architecture of the data stored rather than on differences in changes in its neurophysiological representation. Rabbitt and associates have recently extended this in a different context showing that the extent to which practice or experience determines recall varies directly with task complexity (Rabbitt, 1993). Thus the extent to which the level of a cognitive skill depends on practice, rather than on intrinsic individual differences such as those associated with age, will be determined by the complexity of task demands. We may recall that Horn based his distinction between g_f and g_c on the outcomes of principal components analyses in which chronological age and scores on performance IQ tests turned out to load on the same factors as scores on relatively simple tasks, on which levels of performance were relatively little affected by practice, but not on relatively complex tasks, such as vocabulary tests, on which levels of performance are predominantly determined by a lifetime's learning and use. In view of Rabbitt's (1993) results and discussion this dichotomy is best interpreted as a straightforward consequence of differences in the rates at which different performances can be mastered rather than as evidence for a change in the nature of functional representation of data in memory which results in the robust, age-resistant, 'crystallization' of stored data and procedures.

As Bahrick (1979, 1983, 1984) and Conway *et al.* (1991) have shown, acquired information can remain available for decades even with little or no intervening rehearsal. However in everyday life it is rare for information never to be rehearsed or re-encountered over a period of many years. Studies of the very long-term recall of information such as the names or faces of individuals who once were briefly famous face the obvious drawback of reminding by media 'retrospectives', or by recapitulation during conversations with contemporaries. However, allowing for these difficulties, the accuracy of recall has been shown to decline with the duration of the period since it was first encountered. The age of first encounter is also a factor since older people suffer the double handicap of gradually forgetting information acquired in their youth and also of becoming increasingly less accurate and efficient both at recalling and at acquiring new information. This is true whether, as in the case of names of public figures the information is systematically acquired and linked with historical, cultural or sporting events or with personal life history (Stuart-Hamilton *et al.*, 1988) or whether it is encountered only incidentally, such as recollection of the TV programmes linked to particular theme tunes which are used to cue subjects' recall (Maylor, 1991).

It is also important to distinguish between the ultimate availability of information in memory, and the relative ease with which it can be accessed. For example access to vocabulary which, as we have seen, appears to be very well preserved, is markedly affected by advancing age. Figure 4, taken from

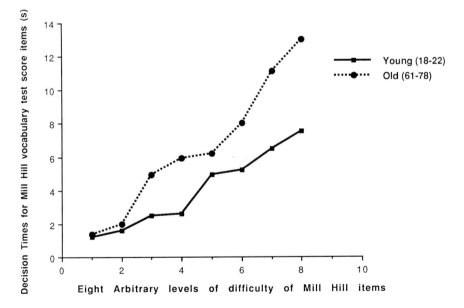

Figure 4.   Decision times for young and old subjects on the Mill Hill vocabulary test.

Bryan (née Core) (1985) shows that as people age they take increasingly long to retrieve the correct names of objects from memory. Similarly, Perfect (1989) measured the times people take to recall answers to 'trivial pursuit' questions. He identified young and elderly people who were 'experts' on some topics, in the sense that they recalled a great deal of accurate information about them, but who were also 'novices' on others, in the sense that they had some, but not much, knowledge about these. He found that all individuals recalled information more rapidly on their 'expert' than on their 'novice' topics, that all elderly people took much longer than young adults to answer questions on both their 'expert' and on their 'novice' topics. Further, just as in the case of names of rare objects illustrated in Figure 3, the less familiar the piece of information recalled the greater was the relative lag in retrieval by old as compared to young adults. Data of this kind make the 'single factor' theory hard to challenge since they illustrate a marked effect of increasing age on information retrieval time even for errorless recall.

As memories become older they take longer to retrieve and eventually may become entirely inaccessible. However the availability and accessibility of memories can be enhanced by rehearsal and Winthorpe and Rabbitt (1988) found that frequency of recent rehearsal was the most potent factor in guaranteeing accessibility of life events. They compared spontaneous recall of life events by active community resident volunteers and of intellectually intact residents in a nursing home with whom they were precisely matched for scores on the AH 4(1) IQ test. The two groups recalled similar total numbers of life events but while most of the events recalled by the community resident volunteers were from their very recent pasts, nursing home residents tended to recall remote events from periods of their lives when they were adolescents or young adults. Holland and Rabbitt (1991a,b) took this as evidence that the relative availability of memories depends on the particular uses made of them. The mental lives of individuals who are actively engaged in the world tend to be concerned with plans for their immediate futures. Recollection of the immediate past is crucial for this purpose. In contrast, life in residential care is relatively uneventful and recollection of more entertaining incidents from the remote past becomes the staple of conversations and reverie. Especially in old age the accessibility of memories is directly dependent on the recency and frequency with which they have been accessed and this, in turn, depends on the particular uses to which individuals put their memories. Since the total number of incidents that subjects in either group could recall was well predicted by their current AH 4(1) IQ test scores these findings do not yet challenge the idea that memory efficiency is determined by the degree of integrity of a single 'master factor' which involves speed of information processing and is sensitively assessed by tests with high loadings for Horn's factor g_f. However it does make the point that, in practice, the precise nature of the information that older people can remember depends more on their current everyday preoccupations than on the rate with which they can process information. In this sense it also shows that the integrity and availability of our conceptual tool kits of 'crystallized intelligence' (Horn's g_c) depend on their continued maintenance and updating by everyday use as strongly as on the amount of effort and time we put into their initial acquisition.

At first sight the most convincing demonstrations that memory efficiency may depend on a single factor of information transmission rate, and that age decrements are directly related to loss of information processing speed come from studies of the acquisition of new information. Relationships can be shown to be especially direct in the case of immediate memory. Waugh and Barr (1980) showed that the accuracy with which people can recall words is directly related to the time for which they are allowed to study each item in a list. Given sufficiently long study times older individuals can be brought to the same levels of performance as young adults though, of course, young adults gain proportionately more benefit when their study times are also extended. Craik and Lockhart (1972) have made the point that the amount of new material that people of any age can remember depends on the degree to which they have been able to elaboratively encode it, for example by making associations between new information and data that they have already mastered, or with their general stock of information about the world. It follows that individual differences in efficiency of acquisition must markedly depend on the speed with which new information can be processed and useful associations retrieved. As we have seen people become increasingly handicapped in both these respects as they grow old; Holland (née Winthorpe) (1986) reports particularly clear demonstrations of the relationship between richness of recall and information processing speed. She compared people of different ages and IQ test score attainments on recall of brief stories. Older individuals, and those with lower IQ test scores, recalled the main points of all stories as well as did the young and the more gifted, even when the difficulty of the material was increased by introducing two separate and independent themes. However the more able individuals were, the greater the number of subsidiary details they recalled. As in most other memory tasks chronological age, *per se*, had no effect once variance associated with individual differences in current IQ test attainment had been taken into account. A sufficient explanation for these and many other results is that all individuals successfully attempt to structure their recall by identifying the theme of an event or episode that they are required to remember. Without this prioritization they would be left struggling to recall a mass of disconnected detail. However the more rapidly individuals can process information the wider the range of details that they can identify and relate to the main context of the episode, and so the more of this subsidiary information they can recall.

A very clear example of the relationship between information processing speed and memory capacity occurs in models for working memory which were devised to explain individual variability in memory span for spoken words. It has long been known that immediate memory spans are limited by the total number of syllables (rather than words) presented for immediate recall, and that individual differences in span directly depend on the rates with which people can articulate or read aloud. The most satisfactory model to explain this relationship was proposed by Baddeley and Hitch (1974) who suggest that syllables decay at a constant rate unless refreshed by circulation around an 'articulatory rehearsal loop'. The number of syllables that can be held in memory is jointly determined by this decay rate and by maximum rehearsal rate. Goward (1987) analysed data from individuals aged from 50 to 80 years, all of whom had been scored on the AH 4(1) IQ test and assessed for articulation rates and reading rates. As in all of the many studies of this relationship described by Baddeley (1986) there was a linear relationship between individuals' spans and their articulation and reading rates (i.e. their individual information processing rates). The linear functions relating spans and processing rates for all age and IQ test score groups were parallel, and differed only in terms of their intercepts. This means that while, as expected, individuals who processed information faster had longer spans, there was no evidence that the rates at which items in the articulatory loop decayed over time varied with age or with IQ test scores.

Many other experiments in our laboratory confirm modest but robust positive relationships between information processing rate and immediate memory capacity. However, in contrast, most of our studies do not find any change in rates of forgetting with age or IQ test score. Yang Qian and Rabbitt (unpublished) have recently found that the amount that people recall in continuous serial recognition tasks is jointly, but quite independently, limited by their rates of acquisition and rates of forgetting; that is, it seems that forgetting rates are not well predicted by learning rates. It seems that individual differences in memory efficiency are determined by individual differences in both of these two independent performance parameters. Individual differences in memory efficiency cannot be determined by a single 'master' performance parameter, such as information processing rate, which reduces with age and increases with IQ test score attainment.

In spite of Salthouse's (1985, 1991) persuasive arguments we should not find this surprising because in terms of even the most simplistic current simulations of how hypothetical neural networks process information and learn to make connections it is certainly clumsy, and perhaps impossible, to conceive how all of the different performance indices we measure in laboratory tasks can all depend on a single performance parameter. Even an elementary schematic shows that the efficiency with which a net performs its most elementary tasks will usually be determined jointly by several different

performance parameters. For example the rate at which information can pass
through the net must be constrained by the minimum delay required for one
unit to excite another, but will also depend on other quite independent
properties, such as the degree of connectivity of the network or the extent
to which the system is free of internal random noise or external interference.
A second elementary performance parameter of any network must be the
speed with which it can learn to make new discriminations or transforma-
tions. This will be partly determined by factors which also affect maximum
information processing speed, such as the number of units and connections
in the network, and so the degree to which parallel processing is possible, or
the level of random noise in the system. However the rate at which the net
can learn must also critically be determined by the rate at which units alter
their activation thresholds as a result of repeated mutual activity. The rate
at which the network loses information (i.e. 'forgets'), whether as a result of
the simple passage of time or in response to interference from new tasks,
must also be determined by several different functional properties, some of
which will also affect its information processing rate and learning rate while
others may not. So, in a simple network correlations between indices of information processing rate, learning rate and forgetting rate may well be robust,
because all of them partially depend on the same performance parameters,
but they will also be modest, because each performance index also depends
on particular performance parameters that do not affect the others. It follows
that when we empirically explore unknown systems, measuring joint and
independent changes in their performance indices in the hope of deducing
the performance parameters that set limits to their efficiency, we will usually
find pervasive, positive but modest correlations between information
processing rate and learning rate or between memory accuracy and memory
retrieval rate. It would be a mistake to conclude from this that the information processing rate of a network is invariably a 'master' performance parameter that alone determines the level at which it can carry out all the tasks we
may set it.

This elementary discussion is certainly not intended as a serious speculation as to how the brain actually works. It is merely intended to illustrate
that the single factor theory is logically untenable even if we make the
extreme and unlikely assumptions that the central nervous system is undif-
ferentiated and unspecialized, that any part of it may potentially subserve
all basic cognitive functions and that all its performance parameters may be
altered by diffuse insults from ageing or benefits from favourable individual variability. It allows us to recognize that even in this unlikely limiting
case it does not logically follow that all performance parameters of the
system will be equally degraded by age or enhanced by the factors promoting 'intelligence'. Further, even if, against probability, we assume that this
is the case, and we insist that the single factor theory is valid, it still does

not follow that changes in information processing rate will alter all of the various performance indices that we may measure in the same direction and by precisely comparable amounts.

In reality we know that the brain is a highly differentiated system in which distinct anatomical structures, neurochemical pathways and neurophysiological sub-structures support quite different cognitive functions. Evidence accumulates that the ageing of the brain is not completely diffuse and global, but rather affects, to different degrees, separate sub-systems and so, presumably, the cognitive functions they support. In particular, more than a century of research on amnesia suggests that loss of memory efficiency is diagnostic of localized rather than of global brain damage, in particular damage to the temporal lobes of the cortex and to associated deeper structures such as the hippocampus and mamilliary bodies. Following this, and other equally well established 'modular' mappings of cognitive processes on to underlying neurophysiology, it is reasonable to ask three successive and contingent empirical questions. The first is whether, across the population at large, performance on different kinds of tasks which are known to be associated with different brain structures do, in fact, cluster, so that for example, people's performance on some memory tasks predict their performance on other memory tasks better than they do on IQ tests or on tests of information processing speed. If we find that this is the case we can ask the second question whether people's performance declines faster on some clusters of tasks than on others as they grow old. Finally, given the evidence that rates of ageing vary markedly both between different individuals and between different cognitive skills within the same individuals we can go on to ask whether the disparity in rates of change of cognitive functions with age is greater in some individuals than in others.

As part of our longitudinal study we administered a battery of tests including two that we assumed tested information processing rate, two tests that we assumed tested memory ability, the Catell Culture Fair IQ Test, the WAIS Vocabulary test and chronological age. The matrix of Pearson's rank-order correlations across these tasks is given in Table 3. The generally low but significant correlations between scores in Table 3 support the assumption that, in general, levels of performance are similar across tests, and that age affects all

Table 3. Matrix of correlations between test scores.

	C Fair sum	SS sum	Cod sum	Fr first	Corr objs	Vocab	Age
C Fair sum	1						
SS sum	.49	1					
Cod sum	.59	.63	1				
Fr first	.3	.27	.31	1			
Corr objs	.4	.35	.41	.41	1		
Vocab	.49	.47	.44	.26	.23	1	
Age	-.44	-.32	-.37	-.34	-.42	-.14	1

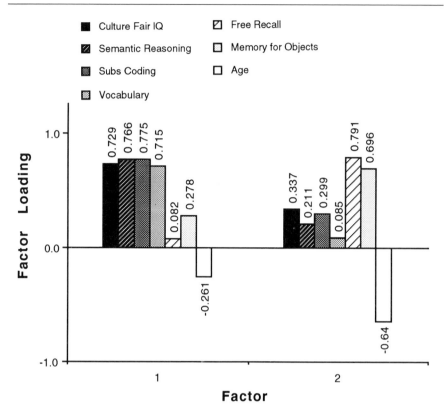

Figure 5. Principal components analysis of TB2 data from 286 volunteers aged 50–86 years.

of them to a similar extent. However cluster analysis showed that although correlations between all measures were generally significant, and although each task within each sub-set made distinctly different demands, tasks that involve memory and learning fall into a separate cluster from those that measure information processing speed, and from IQ test scores.

With this reassurance a principal components analysis was carried out. Figure 5 shows the factor loadings. In agreement with earlier findings by Salthouse (1985, 1991) and suggestions by Eysenck (1986), Jensen (1982, 1985) and others, there is a dominant first factor which accounts for about 26% of the variance and includes IQ test scores and measures of information processing rate. However contrary to expectations from Salthouse (1985, 1991) chronological age is less strongly associated with IQ test scores and information processing speed than with scores on tests of memory and learning. Note that while this finding does not agree with the general theoretical position that

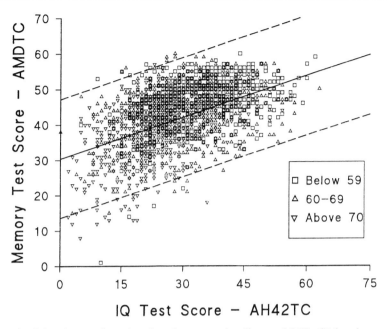

Figure 6. Manchester data showing the regression line and 95% CI for the memory test score.

Salthouse derives from other batteries, in which memory tasks were not included, it does not contradict any of his published data since he examined somewhat different sets of tasks.

The same patterns of dissociation between scores on memory tasks and on information processing tasks, and the same association of chronological age with a second 'memory factor' rather than with the dominant 'intelligence and information processing' factor occur in data from three other test batteries that we have used. Given this evidence that cognitive change with age may be patterned rather than uniform it is natural to proceed to our third question, whether some individuals may show exceptionally large disassociations between scores on memory tests and on IQ tests and measures of information processing rate and whether the incidence of individuals with these marked performance disassociations becomes more common as the age of the population we examine increases.

To test this we normalized scores on all memory tests and summed these transformed scores to obtain a composite 'memory test score' for each individual. Figure 6 shows a plot of individuals' memory test scores against their scores on the AH 4(1) IQ test. We found that a linear regression fitted the data better than any other and so could identify individuals whose

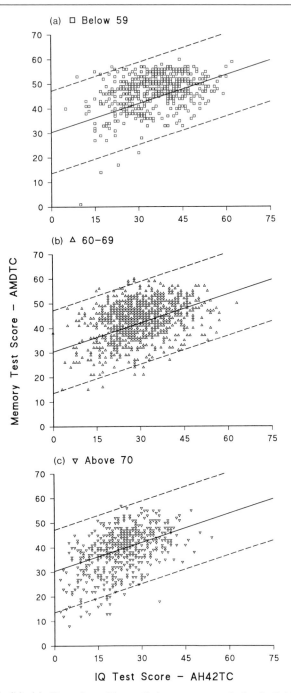

Figure 7. (a), (b), (c). Data from Figure 7 shown separately for individual volunteers.

composite memory test scores were 2 sd worse than we would expect from their current IQ test scores. Figure 7(a), (b) and (c) shows these plots separately for volunteers aged from 50–59, 60–69 and 70+ years.

The number of individuals whose memory test scores were more than 2 sd below expectation from their current IQ test scores steadily increased with the age of the group sampled. There were three such individuals in the 50 to 59 age group, seven in the 60 to 69 age group and 19 in the 70+ age group. It seems that within a large population of fit elderly people the probability of a large disassociation between memory efficiency and IQ test scores increases with age.

Holland (1986) screened a group of 72 'memory poor' individuals who had been identified in this way by our longitudinal screening batteries. She eliminated 36 with various pathologies. The remaining 36 healthy individuals, as we might expect, scored much more poorly than their closely matched controls on a battery of neuropsychological tests which are used in clinical practice to detect signs of amnesia consequent on temporal lobe damage. Holland (1986) also compared these 'memory poor' individuals and their controls on a battery of clinical tests designed to detect cognitive impairments associated with 'frontal' damage but found no differences between them. Nettelbeck and Rabbitt (1991) have recently published a comparison between these individuals and their matched controls on a further battery of tasks including measures of information processing speed. Both in a large random sample of normal elderly people and in individual matched controls for the 'memory poor' subgroup, scores on laboratory measures of information processing speed (CRT and tachistoscopic recognition threshold) correlated modestly but significantly with scores on memory tests. However within the 'memory poor' sub-group these measures did not correlate. This is further evidence for a functional disassociation between two classes of performance measures, efficiency of memory and information processing rate. Principal components analyses such as those illustrated in Figure 5 show disassociations between the relative levels of scores obtained by people of different ages on indices of IPR and on IQ tests scores on the one hand, and memory test scores on the other. The data presented in Figure 6 and those discussed by Nettelbeck and Rabbitt (1992) show a parallel disassociation within subjects; the incidence of individuals with marked disassociations between memory test scores and IQ test scores, or between memory test scores and information processing rate (IPR) measures, increases with the age of the sample tested.

CONCLUSIONS

As with cross-sectional comparisons of all other cognitive skills age-related decline in average memory efficiency is less interesting than the striking increase in the variance between individuals as sample ages increase. This increased variability is at least in part due to increases in the incidence, in older samples, of illnesses which depress cognitive function. The most widely accepted model for loss of memory efficiency has been that a steady decline in information processing rate in old age has secondary effects on all other cognitive functions. This theory is applicable to age changes in recall of information acquired over a lifetime since, although there may be little or no apparent increase in errors of recall, there is a very marked increase in the time needed to retrieve correctly remembered material. However factors quite other than age, such as the uses to which remembered information is put and, consequently, the frequency with which it is rehearsed, also determine both accuracy and speed of its retrieval.

However the single factor theory of memory change is less satisfactory when data from large test batteries are analysed by cluster analysis and principal components analysis. These procedures show that while measures of information processing speed in association with IQ test scores do account for the largest proportion of variance between individuals, measures of memory efficiency and chronological age cluster together in a factor distinct from that in which IQ test scores and information processing rate are represented.

REFERENCES

Anderson, M. (1992). *Intelligence and Development: A Cognitive Theory*, Blackwell Scientific, Oxford.

Baddeley, A.D. (1986). *Working Memory*, Clarendon Press, Oxford.

Baddeley, A.D. and Hitch, G.J. (1974). Working Memory. In: Bower, G.H. (Ed.), *The Psychology of Learning and Motivation. Advances in Research and Theory (Vol. 8)*, Academic Press, New York.

Bahrick, H.P. (1979). Maintenance of knowledge: Questions about memory we forgot to ask. *J. Exp. Psychol. Gen.*, **108**, 296–308.

Bahrick, H.P. (1983). The cognitive map of a city: fifty years of learning and memory. *Psychol. Learning Motivation*, **17**, 125–163.

Bahrick, H.P. (1984). Semantic memory content in permastore: Fifty years of memory for Spanish learned at school. *J. Exp. Psychol. Gen.*, **113**, 1–29.

Bahrick, H.P. and Phelps, E. (1987). Retention of Spanish Vocabulary over 8 years. *J. Exp. Psychol.: Learning Memory Cognition*, **10**, 82–93.

Bahrick, H.P., Bahrick, P.O. and Wittlinger, R.P. (1975). Fifty years of memory for names and faces: A cross-sectional approach. *J. Exp. Psychol. Gen.*, **104**, 54–75.

Birren, J.E. (1965). Age changes in speed of behavior: its central nature and physiological correlates. In: Welford, A.T. and Birren, J.E. (Eds), *Behavior, Aging and the Nervous System*, Charles Thomas, Springfield, Ill.

Birren, J.E., Woods, A.M. and Williams, M.V. (1979). Speed of behavior as an indicator of age changes and the integrity of the nervous system. In: Hoffmeister, F. and Muller, C. (Eds), *Brain Function and Old Age*, Springer-Verlag, New York.

Brand, C.R. and Deary, I.Z. (1982). Intelligence and Inspection Time. In: Eysenck, H.J. (Ed.), *A model for Intelligence*, Springer, New York, pp. 133–148.

Bryan, J. (née Core) (1986). *Old Age and Memory for Complex Material*, Unpublished D.Phil thesis, University of Durham.

Cerella, J. (1985). Information processing rates in the elderly. *Psychol. Bull.*, **98**, 67–83.

Conway, M., Cohen, G. and Stanhope, N. (1991). On the very long term retention of knowledge acquired through formal education: twelve years of cognitive psychology. *J. Exp. Psychol. Gen.*, **120**, 395–409.

Craik, F.I.M. and Lockhart, R.S. (1972). Levels of processing: a framework for memory research. *J. Verbal Learn. Verbal Behav.*, **11**, 671–684.

Eysenck, H.J. (1986). The theory of intelligence and the psychophysiology of cognition. In: Sternberg, R.J. (Ed.), *Advances in the Psychology of Human Intelligence. Vol. 3*, Erlbaum Assts., Hillsdale, NJ, pp. 1–34.

Goward, L.M. (1987). *An Investigation of the Factors Contributing to Scores on Intelligence Tests*, Unpublished Ph.D. thesis, University of Manchester.

Heim, A. (1968). *The AH 4 IQ Test*, Nelson, NFER, Slough.

Holland, C.A. (née Winthorpe) (1986). Unpublished Ph.D. thesis, University of Manchester.

Holland, C.A. and Rabbitt, P.M.A. (1991a). Ageing memory: use versus impairment. *Br. J. Psychol.*, **82**, 29–38.

Holland, C.A. and Rabbitt, P.M.A. (1991b). The course and causes of cognitive change with advancing age. *Rev. Clin. Gerontol.*, **1**, 81–96.

Horn, J.L. (1982). The theory of fluid and crystalised intelligence in relation to concepts of cognitive psychology and aging in adulthood. In: Craik, F.I.M. and Trehub, S. (Eds), *Aging and Cognitive Processes*, Plenum, New York, pp. 237–278.

Horn, J.L. (1986). Intellectual Ability Concepts. In: Sternberg, R.J. (Ed.), *Advances in the Psychology of Human Intelligence*, Erlbaum Assts., Hillsdale, NJ, pp. 35–75.

Horn, J.L. and Cattell, R.B. (1966). Age differences in fluid and crystalised intelligence. *Acta Psychol.*, **26**, 107–129.

Jensen, A.R. (1982a). Reaction time and psychometric "g". In: Eysenck, H.J. (Ed.), *A Model for Intelligence*. Springer-Verlag, Heidelberg, pp. 93–102.

Jensen, A.R. (1982b). The Chronometry of Intelligence. In: Sternberg, R.J. (Ed.), *Advances in the Study of Human Intelligence, Vol. 1*, Lawrence Erlbaum, Hillsdale, NJ.

Jensen, A.R. (1985). The nature of the black-white difference on various psychometric tests: Spearman's hypothesis. *Behav. Brain Sci.*, **8**, 193–219.

Maylor, E.A. (1991). Recognizing and naming tunes: memory impairment in the elderly. *J. Gerontol. Psychol. Sci.*, **46**, 207–217.

Neisser, U. (1984). Interpreting Harry Bahrick's discovery: what confers immunity against forgetting? *J. Exp. Psychol. Gen.*, **113**, 32–35.

Nettelbeck, T. and Brewer, N. (1981). Studies of mental retardation and timed performance. In: Ellis, N.R. (Ed.), *International Review of Research on Mental Retardation, Vol. 10*. Academic Press, NY.

Nettelbeck, T. and Lally, M. (1981). IQ put to test. *Nature*, **290**, 440.

Nettelbeck, T. and Rabbitt, P.M.A. (1992). Age, information processing rate and intelligence. *Intelligence*, **18**, 234–248.

Perfect, T.J. (1989). Unpublished Ph.D. thesis, University of Manchester.

Rabbitt, P.M.A. (1993). Does it all go together when it goes? The 19th Bartlett lecture to the Experimental Psychology Society. *Q. J. Exp. Psychol.*, in press.

Salthouse, T.A. (1982). *Adult Cognition: an Experimental Psychology of Human Aging*, Springer-Verlag, New York.

Salthouse, T.A. (1985). *A Theory of Cognitive Aging*, N. Holland, Amsterdam.

Salthouse, T.A. (1991). *Theoretical Perspectives on Cognitive Aging*, Erlbaum Assts., Hillsdale, NJ.

Stuart-Hamilton, I.A., Perfect, T. and Rabbitt, P.M.A. (1988). Remembering who was who. In: Gruneberg, M.M., Morris, P.E. and Sykes, R.N. (Eds), *Practical Aspects of Memory: Vol. 2: Clinical and Educational Implications*, John Wiley, Chichester.

Vernon, P.A. (1985). Individual differences in general cognitive ability. In: Hartledge, L.C. and Telzrow, C.F. (Eds), *The Neuropsychology of Individual Differences: A Developmental Perspective*, Plenum, New York, pp. 125–150.

Vernon, P.A. and Jensen, A.R. (1984). Individual and group differences in intelligence and speed of information processing. *Personality and Individual Differences*, **5**, 411–423.

Waugh, N.C. and Barr, R.A. (1980). Memory and mental tempo. In: Poon, L.W., Fozard, J.L., Cermak, L.S., Arenberg, D. and Thompson, L.W. (Eds), *New Directions in Memory and Aging*, Lawrence Erlbaum, Hillsdale, NJ.

Winthorpe, C.A. and Rabbitt, P.M.A. (1988). Working memory capacity, IQ, Age and the ability to recount autobiographical events. In: Gruneberg, M.M., Morris, P.E. and Sykes, R.N. (Eds), *Practical Aspects of Memory Vol. 2: Clinical and Educational Implications*, John Wiley, Chichester.

3

Design and Analysis of Clinical Trials

GRAHAM DUNN

Department of Biostatistics and Computing, Institute of Psychiatry, London, UK

INTRODUCTION

Although the use of experimentation to evaluate various therapeutic techniques has a long history (Bull, 1959), it is only since the fundamental work by R.A. Fisher on the foundations of experimental design in the first half of this century (Fisher, 1942) that statistically valid procedures have been applied to clinical trials both in general medicine and in psychiatry. Fisher's ideas were adopted for use in the design and analysis of clinical trials by Sir Austin Bradford Hill (Hill, 1962) and their use is now well established (Pocock, 1983). Apart from the theoretical developments in experimental design, the motivation for the development of clinical trial methodologies at the end of the Second World War was the discovery and clinical use of antibiotics. Similarly, the discovery of tranquillizers and antidepressants in the 1950s and 1960s provided the impetus for the development of rigorous trial methodologies in psychiatry. The 1980s have seen the appearance of several potential 'antidementia' drugs and, again, their appearance has led to the demand for convincing controlled clinical trials.

The first psychiatrist to advocate the use of Fisher's ideas seems to have been Sir Aubrey Lewis (Lewis, 1946). In his article he criticizes the past use of small series of cases and 'the common lack of co-ordinated plan for the therapeutic experiment'. Of a controlled trial he concludes: 'An organized experiment would demand much that has not hitherto been practicable, including voluntary acceptance by independent hospitals and clinics of an agreed procedure for the selection, management, evaluation of mental state, and follow-up investigation of treated, as well as control cases. Such an experiment, as Fisher (1942) demonstrated, requires much forethought and self discipline on the part of those who carry it out'. He also adds: 'For most important psychiatric conditions, such trials are essential, unless we are prepared to go on taking decades to decide questions which could be settled in a few years'. The results of the first trial of the sort envisaged by Lewis in 1946 were published in 1965 (Medical Research Council, 1965). A similar trial was also undertaken in the USA at roughly the same time (Greenblatt *et al.*, 1964). Reviews of the methodological problems faced by the designers of clinical trials in psychiatry are provided by Johnson (1983, 1989). In the 1983 article he acknowledges that many trials have incorporated important design features such as the use of concurrent controls, random allocation to treatments and 'blindness' and goes on to consider other, equally important though neglected, aspects of trial design. These include entry criteria (including the problem of patient heterogeneity), patient accrual, and statistical power. All of these are, of course, important in designing treatment trials for dementia.

In this chapter I will not discuss the general problems of trial design but will concentrate on two statistical issues that appear to be particularly important for the design of future trials of the treatment of dementia. These are (1) the choice of experimental design and, in particular, the role of crossover designs, and (2) the methods of statistical analysis of repeated measures data containing missing values arising from patient withdrawal from treatment or death. A third problem, that of the development and use of appropriate outcome measures, will be left to another author (see Rabbitt, Chapter 2). Other issues have been discussed, for example, by Amaducci *et al.* (1990), Swash *et al.* (1991), and by the FDA (1990). Readers interested in trial methodologies in general are referred to Pocock (1983). A modern introduction to the theory of experimental design is provided by Mead (1988) and practical aspects of randomization are discussed by Pocock (1979, 1983) and by Mead (1988). *Bradford Hill's Principles of Medical Statistics* (Hill and Hill, 1991) provides an excellent start to those interested in the ethical issues in trial design.

TRIALS FOR DEMENTIA

Here we assume that the objective of the trial is to test the effectiveness of a drug or other form of treatment in slowing the rate of, say, cognitive decline, although the more optimistic investigators might be hoping to stop the decline altogether and even think of treatments (neuronal grafts, for example) which might reverse the previous loss of cognitive abilities or daily living skills. Typically, the outcome of treatment will be assessed by the use of serial measurements (i.e. a repeated measures design) of one or more cognitive abilities or skills, together with similarly repeated measures of, for example, daily life activities, quality of life, depression and, possibly, depression, stress and burden in carers and close relatives. To simplify matters, we will ignore this aspect of the data and discuss trials as if there is a simple univariate outcome which we will arbitrarily label as 'cognitive ability'. Having decided that the outcome of a trial is assessed by an estimate of a rate of change based on serial measurements, two further questions can now be addressed. They are: 'What is the most appropriate or efficient design for the trial' and 'How do we analyse and interpret the results?'

The design and analysis of such trials are discussed in the next two sections, respectively. Rather than attempt a detailed review or critique of the trials that have been carried out to date (a task which the present author is unqualified to carry out), two particular trials will be used to illustrate some of the points made. The first is a double-blind, placebo controlled trial of lecithin using a simple two groups design, without crossover (Little *et al.*, 1985); the second is a randomized, double-blind placebo controlled two-period crossover trial to evaluate the effectiveness of tacrine (Eagger *et al.*, 1991a). They were chosen for discussion simply because they were the first two that the author came across in the search for illustrative examples and the reader should not infer that their choice is a result of any methodological flaws or that they are regarded by the author as being either significantly better or worse than trials carried out by other research groups.

TRIAL DESIGN

Given a limited budget, access to clinical facilities and manpower, the trial designer is faced with the problem of the most efficient use of resources for the problem at hand. In a trial for the treatment of dementia, one is usually concerned with the estimation and comparison of rates of change. At its simplest, this can be achieved by measuring cognitive performance, for example, at the onset of treatment and again at the end of, or some time after the cessation of, a fixed period of treatment. The main disadvantage of this approach is that, if a significant proportion of the elderly patients die or are withdrawn from the trial before the fixed follow-up assessment, the design can be very inefficient and (if dropout is related to rate of progress or treatment allocation) potentially biased (see next section). The use of serial measurements increases the precision of the rate of change estimates in patients with complete follow-up and also enables the estimation of changes in patients who do not stay in the trial until the very end. If serial measurements are made then virtually all patients will contribute some useful information.

The next important concern is the length of the period of treatment. Longer treatment durations presumably lead to more precise estimates of treatment differences. They enhance potential problems caused by withdrawal, loss to follow-up or death, however, and there are several other practical and ethical reasons why one should not wish to extend the length of treatment indefinitely.

Finally, how many patients? Although both the duration of treatment and the number and quality of the outcome measurements influence the power of a trial, clearly one of the most important components is the number of patients taking part. Whilst statisticians appear to be always advocating larger and larger trials, clinicians, quite understandably and for several reasons, wish to keep trial size to the minimum necessary. For this reason crossover trials have become very popular in several areas of medicine and, in particular, in the assessment of potential antidementia drugs. The design most commonly used is the simplest, the two group period design — the 2×2 crossover trial (Hills and Armitage, 1979; Jones and Kenward, 1989). Eagger et al. (1991a), for example, employed a 2×2 design to compare the effects on cognitive performance of tacrine and a placebo control. There were two 13 week treatment periods, separated by a four week washout to reduce carry-over, and monitoring every two weeks. Subjects were randomly assigned to one of two groups. Group A received active treatment first, followed by the placebo. In Group B the order of treatments was reversed.

The rationale behind the use of the crossover design is that through the use of a patient as his or her own control (all patients having received all treatments, but randomly allocated to receive them in different orders) one can obtain increased power for a fixed number of patients (or get away with using fewer patients for any given level of power). The disadvantages of the 2×2 design in many settings, however, appear to outweigh its advantages. A critical review of the commonly used 2×2 crossover trial is provided in the recent book by Jones and Kenward (1989, pp. 84–88). There are two major statistical problems. The first is that one cannot distinguish the main effects of sequence group (order), treatment carry-over and the treatment-by-period interaction (in technical terms, they are said to be *aliased*). The latter interaction literally means that the difference between the two direct treatment effects depends on the period in which they are administered; a direct treatment effect being the effect of a treatment during the period in which it is being administered. The effect of a treatment that persists after the end of the treatment period is referred to as the carry-over effect. More important than the problem caused by the above aliases, however, is that the validity of the direct treatment comparisons rests on the assumption that all three aliased effects are, in fact, absent. Although one can test for the presence of the aliased effects, and one is often advised to do so (Hills and Armitage, 1979), the required significance test, unlike that for the main treatment differences, is based on a *between-patients* comparison and therefore usually lacks the required power — the size of the trial having been determined by the power of a within-subject comparison (Brown, 1980). Typically, the results arising from a 2×2 trial have been analysed using a two-stage procedure recommended by Hills and

Armitage (1979). First one tests for the carry-over effect (recognizing it to be aliased as described above). If there is no evidence of carry-over then the analysis proceeds via the estimation and testing of differences between treatments based on within-subject comparisons. If carry-over appears to be present then the analysis proceeds by a between-subject comparison based on the first treatment period only. Because of the problems arising from the lack of power of the test of the carry-over effect, and from other, more subtle objections (Jones and Kenward, 1989) the validity of the above two-stage procedure is now often questioned.

The analysis of the data in the trial by Eagger *et al.* (1991a) followed the above two-stage procedure. They first tested for a carry-over effect and, if one had been found, they would have based their remaining analysis on the first treatment period only. They found no evidence of carry-over, however, and proceeded to test for direct treatment differences using the standard within-patient comparisons. They found a highly-significant beneficial effect of tacrine over the placebo. In a follow-up paper by Eagger *et al.* (1991b), the authors acknowledge doubts concerning the interpretation of data arising from a 2×2 crossover trial and, in fact, present a reanalysis of their data using only the results obtained from the first treatment period (i.e. considering the trial as if it had been planned as a simple parallel groups design). The treatment effects were still highly statistically significant. These findings are, no doubt, reassuring to the clinicians but do prompt the question: 'Should the crossover design have been chosen in the first place?'. I would be inclined to answer 'No'. It does not appear to have been essential from the perspective of statistical power. More importantly, unless there are strong *a priori* grounds for believing that there will be no carry-over effects, the crossover design is probably best avoided. In most situations, the simpler parallel groups design is the method of choice. As a designer of a trial one is trying to produce convincing results. In particular, one is trying to convince the sceptics and, quite correctly, these sceptics will question every potential weakness in the authors' design, analysis and interpretation of the results. For this reason it might be wise to stick to the simpler watertight designs.

THE PROBLEMS AND CHALLENGES OF MISSING VALUES

There are several reasons why data might be missing from the results of a dementia trial. Patients might fail to turn up to certain follow-up assessments or may be temporarily unfit to complete the assessment procedures. Many patients might drop out of the trial without completion of the course of treatment. This might be completely unrelated to both their treatment or to their health status. On the other hand, patients might be withdrawn from treatment because of unpleasant or life-threatening side-effects. Finally they might die due to causes which may, or may not, be related to treatment or to the progress of their dementia. Where possible, investigators should attempt to get follow-up assessments on all patients, whether or not they are complying with, or have been withdrawn from, the treatment of interest. Eagger *et al.* (1991a), for example, report that of 89 patients included in their trial, 24 were withdrawn — 19 because of side-effects, four with other illnesses, and one for non-compliance. They chose to analyse data from only those subjects who completed all of the assessments. In an earlier parallel groups trial of lecithin in the treatment of senile dementia (Little *et al.*, 1985) subjects were randomly allocated to active treatment or placebo, monitored for a six month treatment period, and reassessed following a further six month, drug-free, period. Of the 63 patients allocated to the two treatments, 12 withdrew during treatment and three died during follow-up, leaving 51 patients who completed treatment (26 on placebo, 25 on lecithin) and 48 who completed the full year (24 in each group). Again, the analysis involved the use of data from only those patients who completed the study.

Ignoring data from patients who have not provided full information concerning treatment outcome would seem to be an inefficient use of available data. Investigators should aim to use all of the data at their disposal. Perhaps more importantly, restricting the analysis to only subjects with complete data may bias the results. Whether the traditional methods of analysis (based on complete data only) introduce lack of efficiency or bias, or both, depends on the reasons why the other data are missing. If, for example, the reason for the missing values is in no way related to the rate of cognitive decline then this would simply lead to loss of efficiency. If patients drop out of the active treatment group because of side effects (liver failure, for example) but their rate of improvement before withdrawal was typical of that of the others in their treatment group, then leaving the drop-outs out of the analysis would not lead to biases. On the other hand, if patients had died in the placebo group for reasons arising from their faster rate of cognitive decline, then the analysis of the data from those who had not dropped out or died would underestimate the placebo-active treatment differences.

In situations where drop-out, withdrawal or death are not related to the rate of progress in the trial, the statistical problem is 'simply' that of the efficient use of all available data. Over the last five–six years there have been many developments in both analysis of repeated measurements (see, for example, Crowder and Hand, 1990) and, in particular, incomplete data from repeated measures experiments (Laird, 1988; Schluchter, 1988; Gornbein *et al.*, 1992). The technicalities are well beyond the scope of this chapter but it is sufficient for the present purposes to point out that there are widely available and (relatively) user-friendly computer programs. In particular, the reader is referred to procedure 5V of the software package BMDP PC90.

In general, investigators should get into the habit of drawing progress curves for individual patients, whether or not they have provided full follow-up information. Leading from this, simple summary measures of progress could be calculated *for each patient individually*. These individual summaries could then be used to check various assumptions concerning the data (is rate of progress related to time of withdrawal or death, for example? — see Wu and Bailey, 1988), and they could also be used as the 'raw' data in a second stage of analysis. Such a two-stage analysis is likely to be much more informative than the methods which might have been used in the past. Readers are referred to the non-technical discussion by Matthews *et al.* (1990) and the more difficult treatment by Wu and Bailey (1988).

POSTSCRIPT ON DESIGN

A challenging implication of the development of the newer methods of handling subjects with missing data is that it enables the investigator to consider the introduction of data values that are *missing by design*. Consider, for example, the design for a simple parallel groups trial for which there are staff and facilities available for 3 years (ignoring the time required for the analysis of the data). It is intended to provide treatment and concurrent monitoring and assessment of each patient for a period of 2 years. In a traditional trial design one would only be able to recruit patients into the trial during the first year, patients recruited later would have incomplete follow-up. Knowing that one can now effectively analyse incomplete data one might now change the design to allow patient recruitment up to, say, six months before the end of the trial, i.e. recruitment over the whole of the first 2.5 years. Many patients would provide incomplete data but would contribute to the trial outcome in proportion to the amount of available follow-up information. The present author and his colleagues incorporated this design into the St Bartholomew's Head Injury Case-Management Study (in preparation) and similar examples can be found in Gornbein *et al.* (1992). Readers are left to consider for themselves other approaches to the deliberate introduction of missing values.

REFERENCES

Amaducci, L., Angst, J., Bech, P., Benkert, O., Bruinvels, J., Engel, R.R., Gottfries, C.G., Hippius, H., Levy, R., Lingjaerde, O., López-Ibor Jr, J.J., Orgogozo, J.M., Pull, C., Saletu, B., Stoll, K.D. and Woggon, B. (1990). Consensus conference on methodology of clinical trials of 'Nootropics', Munich. *Pharmacopsychiatry*, **23**, 171–175.

Brown, W.B. (1980). The crossover experiment for clinical trials. *Biometrics*, **36**, 69–79.

Bull, J.P. (1959). The historical development of clinical therapeutic trials. *J. Chronic Dis.*, **10**, 218–248.

Crowder, M.J. and Hand, D.J. (1990). *Analysis of Repeated Measures*, Chapman and Hall, London.

Eagger, S.A., Levy, R. and Sahakian, B.J. (1991a). Tacrine in Alzheimer's disease. *Lancet*, **337**, 989–992.

Eagger, S.A., Morant, N.J. and Levy, R. (1991b). Parallel group analysis of the effects of tacrine versus placebo in Alzheimer's disease. *Dementia*, **2**, 207–211.

FDA (1990). *Division of Neuropharmacological Drug Products: Draft Guideline for the Clinical Evaluation of Antidementia Drugs*, The Food and Drug Administration, Rockville.

Fisher, R.A. (1942). *The Design of Experiments (3rd edn)*, Oliver and Boyd, Edinburgh.

Gornbein, J.A., Lazaro, C.G. and Little, R.J.A. (1992). Incomplete data in repeated measures analysis. *Stat. Meth. Med. Res.*, **1**, 275–295.

Greenblatt, M., Grosser, G.H. and Wechsler, H. (1964). Differential response of hospitalized depressed patients to somatic therapy. *Am. J. Psychiatry*, **120**, 935–943.

Hill, A.B. (1962). *Statistical Methods in Clinical and Preventative Medicine*, Churchill Livingstone, Edinburgh.

Hill, A.B. and Hill, I.C. (1991). *Bradford Hill's Principles of Medical Statistics (12th edn)*, Edward Arnold, London.

Hills, M. and Armitage, P. (1979). The two-period crossover clinical trial. *Br. J. Clin. Pharmacol.*, **8**, 7–20.

Johnson, A.L. (1983). Clinical trials in psychiatry. *Psychol. Med.*, **13**, 1–8.

Johnson, A.L. (1989). Methodology of clinical trials in psychiatry. In: Freeman, C. and Tyrer, P. (Eds), *Research Methods in Psychiatry: A Beginner's Guide*, Gaskell and Royal College of Psychiatrists, London.

Jones, B. and Kenward, M.G. (1989). *Design and Analysis of Cross-Over Trials*, Chapman and Hall, London.

Laird, N.M. (1988). Missing data in longitudinal studies. *Statistics Med.*, **7**, 305–315.

Lewis, A.J. (1946). On the place of physical treatment in psychiatry. *Br. Med. Bull.*, **3**, 22–24.

Little, A., Levy, R., Chuaqui-Kidd, P. and Hand, D. (1985). A double-blind, placebo controlled trial of high-dose lecithin in Alzheimer's disease. *J. Neurol. Neurosurg. Psychiatry*, **48**, 736–742.

Matthews, J.N.S., Altman, D.G., Campbell, M.J. and Royston, P. (1990). Analysis of serial measurements in medical research. *Br. Med. J.*, **300**, 230–235.

Mead, R. (1988). *The Design of Experiments*, Cambridge University Press, Cambridge.

Medical Research Council (1965). Clinical trial of the treatment of depressive illness. *Br. Med. J.*, **1**, 881–886.

Pocock, S.J. (1979). Allocation of patients to treatment in clinical trials. *Biometrics*, **35**, 183–198.

Pocock, S.J. (1983). *Clinical Trials: A Practical Approach*, Wiley, Chichester.

Schluchter, M.D. (1988). Analysis of incomplete multivariate data using linear models with structured covariance matrices. *Statistics Med.*, **7**, 317–324.

Swash, M., Brooks, D.N., Day, N.E., Frith, C.D., Levy, R. and Warlow, C.P. (1991). Clinical trials in Alzheimer's disease. *J. Neurol. Neurosurg. Psychiatry*, **54**, 178–181.

Wu, M.C. and Bailey, K. (1988). Analysing changes in the presence of informative right censoring caused by death and withdrawal. *Statistics Med.*, **7**, 337–346.

Treatment and Care in Old Age Psychiatry
Edited by R. Levy, R. Howard and A. Burns
©1993 Wrightson Biomedical Publishing Ltd

4

Is there Life in the Neurotransmitter Approach to the Treatment of Alzheimer's Disease?

RAYMOND LEVY

Section of Old Age Psychiatry, Institute of Psychiatry, London, UK

The exciting recent advances in the molecular biology of Alzheimer's disease have thrown into sharp relief the role of the accumulation of β-A4-amyloid as the pivotal event in the causation of the condition (Hardy and Allsop, 1991) and highlighted the cascade of effects which follow with the abnormal phosphorylation of *tau* and its attendant formation of neurofibrillary tangles, the main discovery made by Alzheimer himself. The neurotransmitter changes are considered by most people as occurring 'downstream' from these basic neurobiological changes (see Fig. 1). This has led to a somewhat critical view of attempts to reverse the putative neurotransmitter changes in the condition. This chapter will (1) rehearse the criticisms of the neurotransmitter approach to treatment, (2) spell out the counter-arguments to these criticisms, (3) examine what we have learnt from the use of cholinesterase

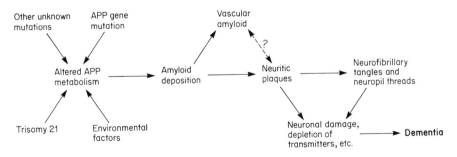

Figure 1. Suggested pathogenic pathway for the progression of Alzheimer's disease. (Reproduced with permission, from Hardy and Allsop, 1991.)

inhibitors with reference to tacrine, and (4) look at possible developments in the future both in the short term and in the long term.

THE NEGATIVE VIEW OF NEUROTRANSMITTER-BASED THERAPY

This view incorporates the following components.

(a) As pointed out above, neurotransmitter changes may occur very late in the sequence of changes leading to the symptoms of Alzheimer's disease and are not considered basic.

(b) The most determined attempts to treat the symptoms of the condition are based on the so-called 'cholinergic hypothesis' even though it is now clear that there are multiple neurotransmitter deficits in the condition which include noradrenergic and dopaminergic deficits as well as changes in neuropeptides and in excitatory amino acids. Attempts at treatment targeted to the cholinergic system may therefore only achieve a very partial effect.

(c) The effects of trials of medication based on the cholinergic approach whether by substrate loading, by the use of cholinergic agonists, or cholinesterase inhibitors have been 'disappointing' and have produced either completely negative results or only minor and not clinically relevant improvements.

THE POSITIVE VIEW

(a) Treatment targeted at the neurotransmitter system is the only practical approach at the moment since we are not in a position to do anything to reverse the accumulation of β-amyloid and/or *tau* and the attendant formation of plaques and tangles.

(b) Even if we were to get to the stage where this might be possible, it may still be necessary to correct neurotransmitter deficits in addition to doing something about the accumulations of amyloid.

(c) The fall in cholinacetyltransferase is still the most consistent change in the condition, and

(d) it is the only one which correlates closely with both the characteristic neuropathological changes and with the severity of the disease.

(e) Behaviour disturbances which are such a crucial part of the condition and usually the ones which are of most concern to carers and lead to medical referral are almost certainly neurotransmitter based. This probably applies both to the attendant depression which may be seen in approximately 40% of patients and possibly also to the other psychiatric concomitants of cognitive disturbance such as delusions, hallucinations, aggressive and other forms of destructive symptomatology. These generally respond favourably to antidepressants, tranquillizers and other forms of neuropharmacological interventions.

(f) The bold statement that clinical trials of cholinesterase inhibitors have been disappointing is incorrect in that it does not take account of the methodological problems of clinical trials and makes no distinction between well conducted and poorly conducted trials or between those which have used adequate doses and those which have not. Furthermore, one must question the expectations which lead to the use of the term 'disappointing'. It is unrealistic to expect a miraculous cure and what is currently being sought is a modest improvement in symptoms for periods of one to two years which may allow patients to function more adequately for a time and postpone major changes in living arrangements. This aim must be considered as both socially and economically worthwhile. Generally speaking, well conducted clinical trials of cholinesterase inhibitors in adequate doses have produced sizeable improvements in at least a proportion of patients (Eagger et al., 1991a; Murphy, 1992) and are therefore far from disappointing although there is of course great room for improvement.

WHAT WE HAVE LEARNT FROM TRIALS OF CHOLINESTERASE INHIBITORS

In the author's own clinical trial of tacrine (Eagger et al., 1991a) doses of up to 150 mg of the hydrochloride (or 120 mg of the base) were given in a placebo controlled situation for a period of three months followed by a washout phase of one month after which the opposite treatment condition was pursued. This produced highly significant changes in the Mini Mental State Examination (MMSE) either in a crossover design (Eagger et al., 1991a) or when the first three months' period was examined as a parallel group study (Eagger et al., 1991b). Ratings of activities of daily living employing the Lawton and Brody scale (1969) were subject to ceiling effects and were not significant. However, when carers' comments which were recorded in routine casenotes were transcribed and rated blindly by two independent raters, a high correlation was obtained between these raters and significant changes in favour of the drug were detected (Eagger et al., 1991b). This trial and others like it have shown that traditional scales for rating the activities of daily living which were developed for much more severely impaired patients than those which currently enter clinical trials are ill adapted to measure changes and throw into sharp relief the need for the development of new scales which should be geared to the higher functioning patients and

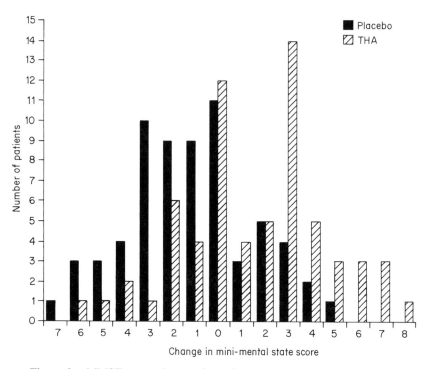

Figure 2. MMSE score changes in patients on the THA and placebo.

not be gender bound since many of the activities rated in such scales as the Lawton and Brody are difficult to rate in the case of male patients of this particular generation.

One of the most striking features of this trial was the extreme variability in response with patients showing improvements of up to 8 points in the Mini Mental State Examination and others showing either no improvement at all or a deterioration (see Fig. 2). Similar variability of response has been reported with velnacrine (Murphy, 1992). Unfortunately attempts to predict which patients might respond did not prove very successful although it is clear that those patients with dysphasia did not do well (Eagger *et al.*, 1991a). Patients who improved and elected to continue taking the drug on an open basis maintained their improvement for periods of one–two years, after which they showed gradual decline. As far as unwanted effects were concerned, the most frequent changes were elevations in liver enzymes but these did not prove as troublesome as we expected and no patients developed serious or irreversible liver damage. This lack of serious problems with liver toxicity may be a reflection of the relatively slow titration to a maximum dose over one month. Patients who were withdrawn from the trial because of unacceptable elevation of liver enzymes returned to normal within a short period and some were rechallenged with the drug with no apparent problems.

As far as this particular trial was concerned there was an overall mean improvement in the drug treated group which was roughly equivalent to a reversal of the decline which would have been expected over a period of six months. Thirty nine percent of patients showed an improvement by more than 3 points in a Mini Mental State Exam which represents a reversal of the decline which would have been expected over the year.

Comparison with other trials is difficult because of differences in doses, in the length of period during which the drug was given and in the methods of testing the patients. A subsidiary analysis (Eagger et al., 1992) however showed some factors which might account for differences between trials. For example, it is clear that the use of tests with no parallel forms which are repeated at too frequent intervals produces a practice effect which may disguise any influence of the drug. This analysis also showed that improvement only became significant at four weeks. Trials using such drugs for shorter periods would not be expected to show significant effects. We were also able to demonstrate that a four week washout period was sufficient to avoid the presence of any carry-over effect and that testing after withdrawal of the drug detected a cessation of treatment effect but no true drug rebound. The most widely quoted study reporting negative results (Chatellier and Lacomblez, 1990) suffered from the following problems. It was a three week crossover trial with no washout period, maximum doses were achieved over a period of one week thus producing serious side-effects and liver toxicity, associated centrally acting medication (10 patients on domperidone and 10 patients on benzodiazepines) although disbarred by the protocol appeared nevertheless to have been used. The inclusion of patients suffering from hypertension was at variance with the stated intention to include only patients who fulfilled the NINCDS/ADRDA criteria. An additional problem arose from the repeated use of the MMSE at three-weekly intervals thus introducing the possible emergence of practice effects outlined above. The otherwise well conducted trial by Gauthier et al. (1990) was also marred by its apparent use of the MMSE at two-weekly intervals on 19 occasions. There is also a question about whether the power was sufficiently high to detect a change since on many ratings the numbers were down to 25–35. In spite of these difficulties, the ratings and measures on tacrine were consistently higher than those on placebo and there was a significant difference in the MMSE at four weeks. Thus, the results may not be as negative as is often supposed.

Such detailed scrutiny of published trials and comparison with those currently being conducted, suggest that one of the most important benefits of clinical research in this area has been the development of better method-ology together with a consensus about trial design, key outcome measures, minimum length of treatment and length of washout period. These are incor-porated in the guidelines for the Food and Drug administration drafted by Leber (1990).

FUTURE TRENDS

As far as future trends are concerned it is convenient to distinguish between the short term and the long term. In the short term possibly the most urgent task is the convenient and early identification of potential responders to drug therapy. Trials of both tacrine and velnacrine suggest that approximately 40% of an already carefully selected group of subjects show a favourable response. It is important to try to find out the characteristics of these subjects. Unfortunately, relatively few data exist at the present time. For instance, the large multi-centred US study trial of tacrine (Wallace, 1992) employed an 'enriched design' and detailed information is not available on those patients who did not enter the full trial because no 'best dose' was identified. Although a similar design was adopted for trials of velnacrine, word has it that information on 'non-responders' was both recorded and analysed. It is assumed this will be published with the detailed results. In the absence of other information this chapter will therefore have to rely entirely on the symptom profile and other information from our own trial. Although this was large enough to show clear differences between drug and placebo groups, the numbers were probably too small to do more than identify certain trends within the total population. As far as cognitive symptom profile is concerned, the only clearly negative predictor worth mentioning was the presence of dysphasia. A prior prediction that dyspraxia would also identify non-responding patients was not borne out, but this finding could be subject to a type 2 error. More recently, follow-up and post-mortem data have become available on two responders. In both cases neuropathological examination revealed the presence of diffuse cortical Lewy bodies in addition to classical Alzheimer disease pathology although neither of the patients exhibited symptoms and signs which might indicate such pathological changes. The ability to tolerate moderate to large doses of the drug may also be of some importance in that there was a small but significant correlation between plasma levels of tacrine and its hydroxylated metabolites and changes in the Mini Mental State Examination score (Eagger et al., 1992b). These features are mentioned here as possible pointers for future research but can in no way be considered as definitive.

Functional imaging may in future prove to be a useful technique for the early identification of responders. For example the results of a small SPET study of tacrine (O'Brien *et al.*, 1992) and one on velnacrine (Hunter *et al.*, 1992) suggest that an early increase in cerebral blood flow in response to the drug may be useful in identifying potential drug responders.

In view of the fact that only some patients appear to respond favourably, another task which lies ahead is the widening of the range of response, possibly by the use of a combination of agents acting on the cholinergic system with those acting on other neurotransmitter systems. Here again, it would seem worthwhile to launch studies which would concentrate on trying to determine which patients require such a combined approach and what the appropriate combination might be. A third relatively short-term task is the improvement of the benefit to risk ratios. At the moment most, if not all potentially effective drugs have important unwanted effects, e.g. interference with liver function as evidenced by a rise in liver enzymes in the case of the aminoacridines. The production of molecules which achieve at least as great a therapeutic benefit with no change in liver enzymes would clearly be a very desirable development.

In the longer term, it is clear that current attempts to interfere with nerve cell death will prove to be of key importance. At the moment efforts are being concentrated on interfering with amyloid precursor protein (APP) metabolism in order to prevent the accumulation of β-amyloid (Lieberburg, 1992). Other efforts are being directed at interfering with the abnormal phosphorylation of *tau* and thus prevent the formation of tangles. This important research targeted at the basic and possibly the earliest changes in Alzheimer's disease will take some time to bear fruit. Bearing in mind current trends in drug developments and the time lag taken between the development of a potentially effective drug and its marketing, one cannot expect such substances to be available for widespread testing in humans before the next 10 years. In addition, even if these important aims were to be achieved, it is possible that the use of drugs targeted at the neurotransmitter systems will be required in addition. Thus the answer to the question incorporated in the title of this chapter must assuredly be 'yes'. In spite of any reservations one might have, the neurotransmitter approach to the treatment of Alzheimer's disease certainly has a future.

REFERENCES

Chatellier, G. and Lacomblez, I. (1990). Tacrine (tetrahydroaminoacridine; THA) and lecithin in senile dementia of the Alzheimer type: a multicentre trial. *Br. Med. J.*, **300**, 495–499.

Eagger, S., Levy, R. and Sahakian, B. (1991a). Tacrine in Alzheimer's disease. *Lancet*, **337**, 989–992.

Eagger, S., Morant, N. and Levy, R. (1991b). A parallel group analysis of the effects of tacrine versus placebo in Alzheimer's disease. *Dementia*, **2**, 207–211.

Eagger, S., Morant, N., Levy, R. and Sahakian, B. (1992). Tacrine in Alzheimer's disease: time course of changes in cognitive function and practice effects. *Br. J. Psychiatry*, **160**, 36–40.

Gauthier, S., Bouchard, R., Lamontagne, A., Bailey, P., Bergman, H., Ratner, J., Tesfaye, Y., Saint-Martin, M., Bacher, Y., Carrier, L., Charbonneau, R., Clarfield, A.M., Collier, B., Dastoor, D., Gauthier, L., Germain, M., Kissel, C., Krieger, M., Kushnir, S., Masson, H., Morin, J., Nair, V., Neirinck, L. and Suissa, S. (1990). Tetrahydroaminoacridine-lecithin combination treatment in patients with intermediate-stage Alzheimer's disease. *N. Engl. J. Med.*, 1272–1276.

Hardy, J. and Allsop, D, (1991). Amyloid deposition as the central event in the aetiology of Alzheimer's disease. *Trends Pharm. Sci.*, **12**, 383–388.

Hunter, R., Brown, D., Bach, L., Wyper, P., Patterson, J. and McCulloch, J. (1992). The effect of the anticholinesterase inhibitor Velnacrine on memory and regional blood flow in Alzheimer's disease. *Neurobiol. Aging*, **13** (Suppl. 1), S. 124.

Lawton, M.P. and Brody, E.M. (1969). Assessment of older people, self-monitoring and instrumental activities of daily living. *Gerontologist*, **9**, 179–186.

Leber, P. (1990). *Guidelines for the Clinical Evaluation of Antidementia Drugs*. Food and Drug Administration, Washington, D.C.

Lieberburg, I. (1992). Current therapeutic approaches. In: Copeland, J. (Ed.), *Alzheimer's Disease: Potential Therapeutic Strategies*. IBC Technical Services, London.

Murphy, M.F. (1992). Is the process as important as the product? The Hoechst experience in Alzheimer disease research. *Neurobiol. Aging*, **13** (Suppl. 1), S. 121.

O'Brien, J., Syed, G.S. and Levy, R. (1992). The effects of tacrine on regional cerebral blood flow in Alzheimer's disease. *Int. J. Geriatr. Psychiatry*, **7**, 835–838.

Perry, E.K. (1986). The cholinergic hypothesis ten years on. *Br. Med. Bull.*, **42**, 63–69.

Wallace, J.D. (1992). Tacrine: a review of clinical data. In: Copeland, J. (Ed.), *Alzheimer's Disease: Potential Therapeutic Strategies*, IBC Technical Services, London.

Treatment and Care in Old Age Psychiatry
Edited by R. Levy, R. Howard and A. Burns
©1993 Wrightson Biomedical Publishing Ltd

5

Treatment of Non-Cognitive Features of Dementia

ALISTAIR BURNS

Department of Old Age Psychiatry, University of Manchester, Withington Hospital, Manchester, UK

INTRODUCTION

Non-cognitive features in dementia (i.e. psychiatric symptoms and behavioural disturbance) are currently attracting research interest. Their importance is five-fold. First, they have a significant impact on carers and are often one of the main determinants as to whether an individual requires long-term care. Secondly, they may have diagnostic value in different types of dementia and, in Alzheimer's disease, may represent subtypes. There is some evidence in Alzheimer's disease that the presence of some symptoms and behaviours does reflect differences in cerebral structure and natural history which may reflect biological subtypes. Thirdly, their presence may be helpful in early diagnosis — it is likely that changes in personality and affect are among the earliest signs of dementia. Fourthly, their presence may shed light on the so-called functional psychoses. Fifthly, in the absence of an effective treatment for the cognitive deficits, non-cognitive features have been a fruitful area for therapeutic intervention.

There has been accurate documentation of the proportions of patients affected by these symptoms (Burns *et al.*, 1990; Cummings and Victoroff, 1990) and their significance with regard to carers has been outlined (Rabins *et al.*, 1982). Biological correlates of these symptoms have been sought with some success (Burns *et al.*, 1990; Cummings, 1985; Zubenko *et al.*, 1988).

Treatment of medical conditions usually predates a full understanding of their aetiology. Clinicians have been successfully controlling psychiatric symptoms and behavioural disturbances in patients with dementia for many years in the absence of full knowledge of their pathophysiology. In the light of current interest in non-cognitive features, it is a natural step to evaluate what treatments have been used for these features, how their efficacy has been assessed and what recommendations, in the light of current research, can be given for their rational use. Pharmacological intervention is the mainstay of most treatments and it is drug therapy on which this chapter will concentrate. It will start with an overview of psychiatric symptoms and behavioural disturbances followed (for the sake of completeness) by a brief mention of behavioural manipulation, an analysis of neuroleptic medication, non-neuroleptic medication and, finally, examples of an approach to particular symptoms and behaviours.

NON-COGNITIVE FEATURES — AN OVERVIEW

In this chapter, non-cognitive features is a term used to coincide with those psychiatric symptoms and behaviours which may accompany a dementia syndrome and consist of clinical features which are not attributable primarily to the cognitive deficits of amnesia, aphasia, apraxia, and agnosia. Cummings and Victoroff (1990) have suggested a categorization of non-cognitive features. These include delusions (persecutory, infidelity, theft, abandonment, parasitosis and syndromes such as Capgras' and de Clérambault's), hallucinations, mood changes, neurovegetative features (disturbances of sleep, appetite and sexual changes), psychomotor changes (wandering, agitation and aggression) and personality changes. Some have suggested a separate category of misidentifications (Burns *et al.*, 1990; Rubin *et al.*, 1988) to include misidentification of other people, the belief that someone is living in the patient's home, and misidentification of mirror image and television. The proportion of individuals affected varies from study to study depending on definitions of the symptom and the dementia, and the sample from which the patients are drawn. Broadly speaking, delusions occur in about 1/3 of patients, hallucinations in 1/5, misidentifications in 1/3, mood changes (especially depression) in 2/3 and neurovegetative and psychomotor changes (referred to by others as behaviours) in about 1/3.

Many studies have used unstandardized definitions of symptoms and behaviours but some instruments are available which have been standardized. These include the Sandoz clinical assessment — geriatric (SCAG) (Shader *et al.*, 1974), the BEHAVE-AD (Reisberg *et al.*, 1987) the Present Behavioural Examination (PBE) (Hope and Fairburn, 1992), the Psychogeriatric Dependency Rating Scale (PGDRS) (Wilkinson and Graham-White, 1980) and the Nurses Observations Scale (Nosie) (Honigfeld *et al.*, 1966). Each has its proponents and opponents and the choice of the individual scale depends on the preference of the investigator and type of behaviour/symptom to be assessed.

BEHAVIOURAL TREATMENT

This has been reviewed by Woods (1987). Most psychological treatments of dementia are aimed at improving memory loss and trying to rehabilitate the individual in general terms rather than being aimed at particular behaviours and symptoms. Behavioural management of specific features has been less extensively studied although some case reports are available. An emphasis on positive reinforcement is important, for example a subject with incontinence can be given rewards for dryness, and consistent toileting using a bell and pad method for nocturnal incontinence can be useful. It has been suggested that shouting is a form of self stimulation and tactile contact with the individual by, for example, rubbing their back may be helpful. It has been pointed out that behavioural management requires a significant degree of staff input.

PHARMACOLOGICAL TREATMENT

Neuroleptic treatment

Efficacy

There have been three excellent recent reviews on this subject (Tune *et al.*, 1991; Schneider *et al.*, 1990; Schneider and Sobin, 1993) to which the reader is referred for full details.

The fundamental question is 'Are neuroleptics effective in the management of dementia?'. This only becomes answerable when the symptomatology is defined at which the drugs are directed. The commonest form of behaviour at which neuroleptics have been directed is 'agitation'. Tune *et al.* (1991) found 30 studies and reported that all the open and double-blind trials and six of the seven double-blind placebo controlled trials showed a favourable response of a variety of symptoms to neuroleptics. These included agitation but also anxiety, overactivity, restlessness, self care, persecutory ideas and depressive symptomatology. It should be noted however that these improvements were noted on global scales of behaviour and, for example, it would be unwise to conclude that neuroleptics had a specific benefit on, say, depression.

Schneider *et al.* (1990) performed a meta-analysis of controlled trials and reported on seven which satisfied the criteria for double-blind placebo controlled, parallel group design containing subjects with diagnosed primary degenerative dementia or vascular dementia. These were published between 1960 and 1982 and the numbers of patients ranged from 18–61. Individually, X^2 analysis showed no significant change but taking the group as a whole showed that neuroleptics were more effective than placebo but there was a small effect size. The improvement rate in agitated dementia indicated that 18 of 100 patients benefitted from neuroleptics.

In seven separate studies, it was possible to compare the effects of thioridazine or haloperidol against another neuroleptic and it was shown that there was no difference in the response pattern. Symptoms which tended to improve included anxiety, aggression and agitation.

A novel way of assessing efficacy is to assess the effect of discontinuing neuroleptics. Barton and Hirsch (1966) found that three weeks after discontinuation of chlorpromazine, eight out of 50 patients showed a greater than 10% deterioration in their behaviour. Raskind et al. (1987) withdrew chlorpromazine from nine patients, two of whom deteriorated. Findley et al. (1989) withdrew thioridazine from 36 patients with Alzheimer's disease in a double-blind placebo controlled fashion. No differences were seen in outcome between the two groups.

Thus, it can be said that neuroleptics are generally effective with a number of symptoms in Alzheimer's disease but that this effect is small. No particular agent is superior and there is evidence that the doses are effective only in the short term as discontinuation of neuroleptics can be performed without serious side effects in the majority of patients.

Dosage

Generally, relatively low doses of neuroleptics are required, lower than those usually employed for the treatment of psychosis. There seems little advantage to increasing doses in most patients. Some studies (Gottlieb et al., 1988; Risse et al., 1987) have suggested that ultra low doses, e.g. 0.125 mg of haloperidol or 5 mg thioridazine are effective.

Side effects

These are not specific to demented elderly patients, although it may be that subjects with pre-existing brain damage may be more susceptible to or suffer from more severe side effects. Extrapyramidal symptoms occur frequently in the elderly and were universal at doses of 2 mg of haloperidol a day in the study of Steele et al. (1986). Tardive dyskinesia is seen in up to 50% of elderly psychiatric patients who have received neuroleptic treatment (Toenniessen et al., 1985) and appears to occur more often within the first two years of treatment. The relationship of tardive dyskinesia to different types of neuroleptics is uncertain and the relationship, in demented patients, between tardive dyskinesia and the atypical antipsychotics such as clozapine has yet to be investigated. Other common side effects include postural hypotension, agranulocytosis, liver and cardiac toxicity. Sedation appears to be mediated through blockage of histamine receptors and, presumably, results in beneficial effects in some aroused patients. Anticholinergic side effects are particularly troublesome and Steele *et al.* (1986) found detectable serum anticholinergic levels in patients receiving 100 mg or more of thioridazine.

In a follow up of the study by Steele *et al.* (1986), the same authors found that side effects occurred up to three months after stabilization on either thioridazine or haloperidol (Tune *et al.*, 1991).

Specific Agents

As mentioned above, there seems little to choose between specific antipsychotic agents and the choice depends on the preference of the prescribing clinician and previous response (or non response) to neuroleptics.

Non-neuroleptic medication

A number of medications have been tried for non-cognitive features of dementia and these are summarized in Table 1. The discussion here will concentrate on the use of antidepressants to control non-affective symptoms in dementia. Depression in dementia and its treatment with antidepressants is a large subject in itself and has recently been reviewed (Alexopoulous and Abrams, 1991; Burns, 1990). Theoretically, monoamine oxidase inhibitors may have special efficacy but traditional tricyclic antidepressants and ECT have all been shown to be effective.

Table 1.   Non-neuroleptic medications used in dementia.

Antidepressants
Tricyclic antidepressants
Trazodone
Monoamine oxidase inhibitors
Selective serotonin re-uptake inhibitors
Lithium
Anticonvulsants
Carbamazepine
Sodium valproate
Beta-blockers
Benzodiazepines
Psychostimulants
Specific agents
Buspiron
Chloralhydrate

Non-neuroleptic medications have recently been the subject of an excellent review by Schneider and Sobin (1991).

Monoamine oxidase inhibitors

Monoamine oxidase inhibitors (type A) have been used in two studies in cases of Alzheimer's disease with depression. Both showed marked improvement in the depressive symptoms. Four studies have looked specifically at L-deprenyl, a monoamine oxidase inhibitor, type B. Originally marketed for Parkinson's disease, some symptoms in Alzheimer's disease have been controlled with the drug. Memory and concentration, anxiety and depression have shown to be improved in double-blind placebo controlled studies as well as in one uncontrolled and one open trial. It may be that the drug was having an effect on general motivation and was shown, in at least two of the studies, to improve depressive symptoms.

Selective serotonin re-uptake inhibitors

Serotonin is currently receiving much attention as one of the neurotransmitters deficient in Alzheimer's disease. The re-uptake inhibitors are relatively new on the market and it is interesting to note that both the drugs tested have been done so in methodologically sound studies. (Neither drug is currently available in the UK.) Alaproclate improved aggression and irritability in one study but not in another. Citalopram was investigated in 98 patients with dementia and similar improvements in the Alzheimer's group were found. It is interesting to note that no changes were found in patients with vascular dementia.

Lithium

Lithium has been used in younger patients to control aggression in addition to its traditional role in the treatment and prophylaxis of bipolar affective disorder. Schneider and Sobin (1991) reviewed five studies looking at the effects of lithium in agitated demented patients. Two studies (one a case report, one with 10 patients) showed no improvement with lithium; another case report showed a rapid clinical improvement with a low serum level of the drug; another study showed that two patients out of nine improved and a final case report was suggestive of improvement but lithium had to be stopped because of side effects. It is likely that the high toxicity of lithium and the marginal, if any, benefit means that it is unlikely to be beneficial in the treatment of behaviourially disturbed demented patients.

Anticonvulsants

Carbamazepine has been reported in about 50 patients with Alzheimer's disease to control aggressive, agitated and wandering behaviour. The majority of these have shown a clinical improvement, in one case dramatic. There has been one placebo controlled study (which involved a crossover design) which showed no improvement in 19 patients with senile dementia. Indeed, carbamazepine resulted in slight deterioration of cognitive function. There was no evidence that the patients suffered from epilepsy although it is conceivable that outbursts of rage and aggression may have an ictal basis in some patients. Serum levels, when they are measured, appear to be at the lower end or lower than the normal therapeutic anticonvulsant dose. The use of sodium valproate is anecdotal.

Beta-blockers

It has been known for 15 years that beta-blockers are effective in controlling aggression. Reports contain information on about 125 patients most of whom had been unsuccessfully treated with other medication. Propranolol is the most commonly used agent, although nadolol, pindolol and metoprolol have all been used. Of those with a primary dementia, six patients showed an improvement in agitation and aggression in uncontrolled studies. More recently, pindolol has been used in dementia because of fewer reported side effects and a placebo controlled crossover trial showed it to be more effective than placebo in controlling agitation.

Benzodiazepines

The tendency for benzodiazepines to cause confusional states and dependence has meant that their prescription in the elderly has been very limited. Some trials have looked at their efficacy. In seven trials described by Stern et al. (1991) benzodiazepines were associated with diminution of symptoms of anxiety, tension and agitation. Oxazepam was found to be better than chlordiazepoxide, the latter being associated with side effects in 40% of subjects. Some studies have compared a benzodiazepine and a neuroleptic. Of three studies, two have shown a trend for improvement and one a statistically significant improvement in patients taking neuroleptics such as thioridazine and haloperidol compared with benzodiazepines.

It is likely that clinicians will favour antipsychotic medication and newer sedatives rather than benzodiazepines, but the drugs are effective in the short-term amelioration of some behaviours.

Psychostimulants

The rationale behind the use of these agents is that deficits of attention and vigilance result in some behaviours and that 'activation' of such subjects will result in improvement. Methylphenydate has been the most investigated but the effects have been shown to be beneficial only in open trials. With the advent of newer safer drugs it is likely that psychostimulants will not have a place in the treatment of behaviour disturbance in the future.

Specific agents

Buspirone. In view of its role in enhancing serotonergic function, buspirone has been reported in three cases of dementia, two of whom improved. To the author's knowledge, no proper trials of the drug have been published. It has been reported that a combination of trazodone and trypto-phan resulted in an improvement in aggression in subjects with dementia. Three case reports showed improvement (or demonstrated further improvement after addition of tryptophan). Two open trials have used the drug. One included only one patient with Alzheimer's disease in whom the response was equivocal and the others showed that four out of eight patients improved but these were on ratings of mood rather than behavioural disturbance.

RECOMMENDATIONS

Gottlieb and Piotrowski (1990) have suggested recommendations regarding antipsychotic medications in the elderly. These are as follows.

(1) A full assessment of an individual subject is essential for assessing both underlying medical and environmental factors which may affect the medical state.
(2) Simple and safe behavioural interventions should be considered before medication is tried. If such interventions are not successful and if the behaviour is severe, then prescription of medication may be necessary.
(3) Antipsychotic neuroleptics give reasonable control of severe behavioural symptomatology and should be reserved for patients with severe behavioural disturbance.
(4) It should be noted that no neuroleptic has been shown to be consistently better than any other.
(5) It may be worthwhile to consider the use of a specific non-neuroleptic drug.
(6) The clinician should make note of idiosyncratic reactions to drugs or past reactions to medication in an individual patient.

(7)   Generally speaking, medication should be given for a short time with tapering off of dose and discontinuation of the drug after resolution of the behavioural disturbance.

SPECIFIC BEHAVIOURS

To reorientate the reader away from a purely pharmacological approach, there follows a brief outline of the management of individual conditions. With regard to *depression*, the most difficult aspect of care is to make an accurate diagnosis. The symptoms of depression in dementia commonly overlap. If a clinician is satisfied that depressive symptoms severe enough to merit treatment on their own are present, then a conventional antidepressant should be prescribed. Drugs with lower anticholinergic effects might be theoretically more applicable to avoid worsening the cognitive deficit. *Delusions* which focus on an individual item may respond to reassurance and correction of a behaviour pattern, e.g. placing a patient's handbag in the same place very day if an individual is convinced it has been stolen. Sensory loss may exacerbate the beliefs. If part of a wider psychotic illness, neuroleptics are indicated. *Anxiety* may be related to the worry that a relative may not visit and the patient may have to wait around a particular door, waiting for the assumed visit. Consistent reminding, not only when asked by the patient, of the relative's visit will help to reassure. Anxiolytic medication may be helpful. *Insomnia* may be part of a dementia or may be manifestation of a confusional state. A regular schedule during the day, increased activity during the day, attention to factors which might cause the subject to wake (e.g. a diuretic at night) along with a short-acting hypnotic may be effective.

With regard to behaviours, *aggression* is particularly troublesome. It is important to assess the precipitants of aggression. Is it situational or spontaneous? Is it to everyone or only to certain individuals? Does the patient have a history of aggression? While containing the individual, the mainstay of control of aggression should be pharmacological, along the lines of the neuroleptics outlined above. Serotonin reuptake blockers with or without tryptophan and/or beta-blockers may also be of help. *Shouting* can often be a form of self stimulation and a behaviour programme to contain it (and not reinforce the behaviour) should be carried out. It is unlikely that medication would have much to offer. *Wandering* can be contained by a number of environmental constraints such as alarm systems, bracelets, judicious use of locked doors or double handled doors. Sedation for wandering behaviour is rarely effective and often people would have to be too heavily sedated for an effect. Finally, *agitation* (often with aggression) is the usual target behaviour for many of the compounds discussed above. Treatment is generally effective.

CONCLUSIONS

(1) Psycho-active drugs, in particular neuroleptics, are effective against non-cognitive features of dementia but individual patients and behaviours should be considered when prescribing medication. Some behaviours are not amenable to drug treatment.

(2) Neuroleptics are consistently better than benzodiazepines in controlling behaviour but no individual neuroleptic is better than another. Non-neuroleptics may be of help but lithium, buspirone, benzodiazepines and psychostimulants are probably of little benefit. Antidepressants relieve depression and may have an effect of agitation; anticonvulsants are effective at lower doses than the anti-epileptic levels, and beta-blockers appear to have an effect in aggression.

(3) Most research has been performed on patients with dementia and trials on subjects with rigorously diagnosed Alzheimer's disease should be carried out.

(4) There are often methodological flaws in studies and placebo controlled parallel groupings should be considered for all new trials.

(5) There is significant variability in symptoms, and ratings of symptoms in behaviours require a full description — existing rating scales often amalgamate a number of different terms which is misleading.

REFERENCES

Alexopoulous, G. and Abrams, R. (1991). Depression in Alzheimer's disease. *Psychiatric Clin. N. Am.*, **14**, 327–340.

Barton, R. and Hirsch, L. (1966). Unnecessary use of tranquillizers in elderly patients. *Br. J. Psychiatry*, **112**, 989–990.

Burns, A. (1990). Disorders of affect in Alzheimer's disease. *Int. J. Geriatr. Psychiatry*, **5**, 63–66.

Burns, A., Jacoby, R. and Levy, R. (1990). Psychiatric phenomena in Alzheimer's disease. *Br. J. Psychiatry*, **157**, 72–94.

Cummings, J. (1985). Organic delusions. *Br. J. Psychiatry*, **146**, 184–197.

Cummings, J. and Victoroff, J. (1990). Non-cognitive neuropsychiatric syndromes in Alzheimer's disease. *Neuropsychiatry, Neuropsychol. Behav. Neurol.*, **3**, 140–158.

Findley, D., Sharma, J., McEwen, J., Ballinger, B., MacLennan, W. and MacHerg, A. (1989). Double-blind controlled withdrawal of thioridazine treatment. *Int. J. Geriatr. Psychiatry*, **4**, 115–120.

Gottlieb, G. and Piotrowski, L. (1990). Neuroleptic treatment. In: Cummings, J. and Miller, B. (Eds), *Alzheimer's Disease: Treatment and Long Term Management*, Marcel Dekker, New York.

Gottlieb, G., McAllizter, T. and Gur, R. (1988). Depot neuroleptics in the treatment of behavioural disorders in patients with Alzheimer's disease. *J. Am. Geriatr. Soc.*, **36**, 619–621.

Honigfeld, G., Gillis, R. and Klett, J. (1966). Nosie-30. A treatment sensitive ward behaviour scale. *Psychol. Rep.*, **19**, 108.

Hope, A. and Fairburn, C. (1992). The present behavioural examination (PBE). *Psychol. Med.*, **22**, 223–230.

Rabins, P., Mace, M. and Lucas, M. (1982). The impact of dementia on the family. *J. Am. Med. Assoc.*, **248**, 333–335.

Raskind, N., Risse, S. and Lampe, T. (1987). Dementia and antipsychotic drugs. *J. Clin. Psychiatry*, **48** (Suppl. 5), 16–18.

Reisberg, B., Borenstein, J., Salob, S., Ferris, S., Franssen, E. and Georgotas, A. (1987). Behavioural symptoms in Alzheimer's disease. *J. Clin. Psychiatry*, **48** (Suppl. 5), 9–15.

Risse, S., Lampe, T. and Cubberley, L. (1987). Very low dose neuroleptic treatment in two patients with agitation associated with Alzheimer's disease. *J. Clin. Psychiatry*, **48**, 208.

Rubin, E., Drevets, W. and Burke, W. (1988). The nature of psychotic symptoms in senile dementia of the Alzheimer type. *J. Geriatr. Psychiatry Neurol.*, **1**, 16–20.

Shader, R., Harmatz, J.S. and Saltzman, C. (1974). A new scale for clinical assessment in geriatric patients. *J. Am. Geriatr. Soc.*, **22**, 107–113.

Schneider, L. and Sobin, P. (1991). Non-neuroleptic medications in the management of agitation in Alzheimer's disease and other dementia. *Int. J. Geriatr. Psychiatry*, **6**, 691–708.

Schneider, L. and Sobin, P. (1993). Treatment for psychiatric symptoms and behavioural disturbances in dementia. In: Burns, A. and Levy, R. (Eds), *Dementia*, Chapman and Hall Medical, London, in press.

Schneider, L., Pollock, D. and Lyness, S. (1990). A meta-analysis of controlled trials of neuroleptic treatment in dementia. *J. Am. Geriatr. Soc.*, **38.**, 553–563.

Steele, C., Lucas, M. and Tune, L. (1986). Haloperidol v thioridazine in the treatment of behavioural symptoms in senile dementia of the Alzheimer's type. *J. Clin. Psychiatry*, **47**, 310–312.

Stern, R., Duffelmeyer, B., Zemishlani, Z. and Davidson, M. (1991). The use of benzodiazepines in the management of behavioural symptoms in demented patients. *Psychiatric Clin. N. Am.*, **14**, 375–384.

Toenniessen, L., Casey, D. and McFarland, B. (1985). Tardive dyskinesia in elderly samples. *Psychopharmacol. Bull.*, **20**, 22–26.

Tune, L., Steele, C. and Cooper, T. (1991). Neuroleptic drugs in the management of behavioural symptoms in Alzheimer's disease. *Psychiatric Clin. N. Am.*, **14**, 353–373.

Wilkinson, I. and Graham-White, J. (1980). Psychogeriatric dependency rating scale. *Br. J. Psychiatry*, **137**, 558.

Woods, R. (1987). Psychological management of dementia. In: Pitt, B. (Ed.), *Dementia*, Churchill Livingstone, Edinburgh, pp. 281–294.

Zubenko, G. and Moossy, J. (1988). Major depression in primary dementia. *Arch. Neurol.*, **45**, 1182–1186.

Treatment and Care in Old Age Psychiatry
Edited by R. Levy, R. Howard and A. Burns
©1993 Wrightson Biomedical Publishing Ltd

6

Alternatives to Long-Stay Care

DAVID CHALLIS

Personal Social Services Research Unit, University of Kent, Canterbury, UK

In many developed countries it is possible to discern similar trends in the development of services for elderly people and for the provision of community care and long-term care more generally. The UK policy changes (Cm 849), in common with those in a number of other countries, can be seen as requiring a move from institutional care, an accompanying enhancement of home care and a focus upon co-ordination and case management as a means to these ends. These patterns of change are designed to produce, at least at the margin, a degree of downward substitution in the provision of care, moving away from institutional care, towards enhanced home-based care. Such changes are evident in policy changes in Sweden and the Netherlands (Kraan *et al.*, 1991; van den Heuvel and Gerritsen, 1991; Thorslund, 1991; Thorslund and Johansson, 1987), Israel (Morginstin and Shamai, 1988; Factor *et al.*, 1991), and are particularly close to recent developments in Australia (Department of Community Services, 1986; Ozanne, 1990).

In the UK, unlike many other countries, a significant part of long-stay care for elderly people has been provided in hospital settings, whereas elsewhere, as is increasingly the case here, the role of nursing and residential homes is relatively more important. Therefore, it is necessary to examine not just alternatives to hospital care but also other examples of 'downward substitution', of more intensive institutional environments by less intensive ones, nursing homes and residential homes by home-based care.

Both the scale of the elderly population receiving long-term care in institutional settings and the relative cost of such facilities are likely to determine the degree to which alternatives to institutional care can be and are pursued. Clearly the decision about the extent to which alternatives to hospital and other forms of institutional care can be pursued is, as noted earlier, dependent upon the expected balance of cost and advantage. There are likely to be different judgements depending on the relative price of institutional and community services in different parts of the same country and even more between countries. Jamieson (1991) notes that, whereas in the Netherlands receipt of more than 10 hours home care is broadly equivalent to the cost of institutional care, in Denmark receipt of up to 30 hours home care is equivalent to the cost of institutional care in some areas. Clearly this relative price effect will play an important part in the decision process.

A second element likely to influence the development of alternative patterns of provision to institutional care is the existing level of institutional provision in any society. Given the principle of diminishing returns, the higher the proportion of elderly people in institutional care the greater the possibility for consideration of alternatives. Thus for example in the Netherlands 12.6% of the population aged 65 and over were living in hospital, nursing homes or residential homes, in Sweden 8.7% and in England 4.9% (Kraan et al., 1991). The context for substitution is very different where there is such variation.

Whereas the move away from institutional care may arise from the coincidence of economic and social values, the enhancement of home care and improved co-ordination and case management are necessarily complementary to its achievement. The conclusion of a range of studies appears to be that services for vulnerable people in the community need to be more intensive in availability, more extensive in content and better planned and coordinated around the needs of each individual if adequate care is to be provided and unnecessary admission to institutional care prevented (Social Services Inspectorate, 1987; Sinclair et al., 1990; Goldberg and Connelly, 1982). The feasibility of downward substitution depends upon the proposition that there are some individuals who require lesser levels of care than that provided in the setting in which they are located and that it is therefore more cost effective for those people to receive care in a less dependent environment (Davies et al., 1990; Knapp, 1984). A considerable range of developments in the provision of services to older people have occurred in the last 15 years. It is helpful to consider three broad types of development: alternative homes, enhanced home care and case management developments.

ALTERNATIVE HOME SETTINGS

The development of different and more varied types of institutional care is one form of the attempt to achieve downward substitution from hospital care to nursing home care, and from residential care to community care, by providing more homely residential environments than hospitals. One important example is the evaluation of three specially developed NHS nursing homes. These were the subject of a randomized controlled trial of nursing home care compared with long-stay hospital care. The study found that special NHS nursing homes appeared to offer a higher quality of environment than hospital wards with no apparent loss to residents in terms of clinical indicators of survival or functional ability (Bond and Bond, 1990). There were important differences in favour of the NHS nursing homes in terms of the level and type of activities undertaken, degree of resident engagement and meal time interactions. Residents were more likely to express positive views about staff, have their own clothes and express positive views about their environment. Relatives also favoured nursing home care. A cost analysis (Donaldson and Bond, 1991) suggested that the NHS nursing home care was of no greater cost than its hospital counterpart although more costly than private sector nursing home accommodation. However it appeared that the NHS nursing homes catered for a less able population than private sector homes rendering comparison problematic. The authors also noted the crucial distinction between cost and funding identifying the perverse incentives of the funding of continuing care, depending upon whether it is located in the NHS or outside.

Another randomized controlled trial of NHS nursing home care found that, although residents in the nursing home environment tended to deteriorate more rapidly than hospital residents in mental and functional ability levels and experienced a higher accident rate, the earlier evidence that the quality of life offered in the nursing home was superior to that of the wards was confirmed (Bowling *et al.*, 1991). Cost information was not however collected in this study.

A specialized nursing home environment for patients with dementia, the Domus, was designed to improve quality of care by dealing with staff anxieties that lead to institutional regimes and poor resident quality of life. Higher levels of staff and training were provided. A specific focus was upon maintaining resident independence and residual skills in an environment with domestic rather than hospital standards. In a comparison with two psychogeriatric wards, the Domus was characterized by greater expectations for patient functioning, policy choice, resident control and availability of social and recreational activities with higher staffing levels. It was found that higher levels of activities and staff–resident interaction occurred in the Domus environment compared with hospital wards and the Domus staff expressed higher levels of job satisfaction (Lindesay *et al.*, 1991). Of course, environments such as the Domus that depend in part upon social security finance are markedly less costly to health authority budgets than NHS environments since much of the cost is accommodation and met from other budgets. Therefore, from the narrow agency point of view, such settings particularly meet the criteria of downward substitution. For example, only some 70% of the accommodation costs of the Domus are met by the District Health Authority yet overall the Domus costs appear to be higher than currently available hospital provision (Beecham *et al.*, 1991). Clearly the apparently greater costs require evaluation in the light of the greater resident benefits to formulate a judgement of cost effectiveness.

Studies have also been undertaken of group living schemes in ordinary housing for people with dementia (Wimo *et al.*, 1991) and boarding out in family care for frail elderly people (O'Shea and Costello, 1991) which appear to offer less costly alternatives although again careful evaluation of such schemes is required to ensure that realistic comparisons are made of like individuals in different care settings. More differentiated forms of environments providing accommodation and care can be expected to develop over the next few years.

ENHANCED HOME CARE

It has been argued, both in the UK and elsewhere, whether a greater level of provision of home care as currently organized is sufficient to offer a realistic substitute for institutional care (Davies *et al.*, 1990; Sinclair *et al.*, 1990; Social Services Inspectorate; 1987; Jamieson, 1991). Consequently there has been a considerable interest in attempts to develop innovations in home care (Ferlie *et al.*, 1989; Salvage, 1985; van den Heuvel and Schrijvers, 1986). These innovations have been undertaken to offer more extensive home-based long-term care and to free acute beds more speedily.

A small scale trial of intensive home nursing and augmented home care was undertaken as an alternative to hospital care, providing up to 21 hours per week of home help. There was little outcome data other than patient and relative satisfaction included. However this service appeared on average to be a less costly alternative to long-stay care for mentally intact but physically disabled elderly people although there was considerable variation in cost, largely due to accommodation costs. At least for those living with others, this was a less costly solution than hospital care. However the study group appeared less impaired than a hospital group, so caution is required in interpretation (Gibbins *et al.*, 1982). In the same part of the country a specialized unit designed to provide support for elderly mentally infirm old people and their carers, offering specialized respite, evening care and occasional residential care was compared with the effect of existing service provision (Donaldson and Gregson, 1989). Whereas the community care service costs of the special service were nearly three times those of the usual services there appeared to be a reduction in admissions to long-stay hospital beds. No data on outcome are available and it was assumed that the service was cost effective if life at home was preferable to elderly people and their carers. However the authors point out that even if the service may have been cost effective overall, from an individual agency perspective this may well not be the case since higher costs were incurred by the social services to reduce the provision of long-stay hospital beds.

A trial of augmented home care services to assist the discharge of elderly patients who experienced social problems from acute hospital beds proved largely unsuccessful, no evidence being found either of faster discharge from hospital or improvement in well-being, apparently because the relatively small additional elements of service were not sufficient for the wide range of needs identified (Victor and Vetter, 1988). An earlier pilot study had indicated the potential for rehabilitation of augmented home care for acute patients (Currie *et al.*, 1980). A second study which offered a more clearly targeted approach was concerned with support for patients over 75 discharged from hospital. Specially employed care assistants provided help for up to 12 hours per week for a two week period after discharge and under-took a range of tasks, personal and domestic, as well as providing encour-agement to increase activity. In this study the number of days spent in hospital by those receiving the service was reduced compared with the control population (Townsend *et al.*, 1988). An interesting difference between these two studies would seem to be the broadening of tasks in the second study although the total amount of care provided to elderly people was not large.

The Home Support Scheme for Dementia sufferers was designed to provide enhanced home support partly through the provision of additional paid carers to fill gaps in care not met by other agencies. It was hoped that the scheme would promote more individualized care, bridging gaps in care where existing provision was non-existent, collaborate with existing services to avoid overlap or competition and where necessary to co-ordinate services to ensure that a suitable package of care was provided. Thus neither case management nor even brokerage and co-ordination were seen as mainstream tasks but the main focus was 'gap-filling' and liaison with other services (Askham and Thompson, 1990, p. 41). The service was organized by devel-opment officers employed by Age Concern who were to recruit and organize the paid carers. Being in an external agency, lacking influence over decisions about mainstream resources and without a clear co-ordinatory remit, it is unsurprising that the development officers were reluctant to play the role of case manager, seeing this as the role of other agencies (Askham and Thompson, 1990, p. 45). There were problems experienced in the evaluation concerning sample size and adequacy which made the impact of the scheme difficult to discern. There were no evident overall effects upon institutional-ization although some elderly people living alone with no informal carer were supported who otherwise would probably have entered an institutional setting. There did not seem to be any evident gain for carers (Askham and Thompson, 1990).

A small-scale intensive domiciliary support scheme for dementia sufferers was developed in Liverpool (Crosby *et al.*, 1984) which provided care aides who effectively supplanted other social care services providing up to five hours per day, seven days a week. A comparison group appeared to spend more time in institutional care than those receiving the domiciliary care scheme (Crosby *et al.*, 1984).

From most countries it would seem that there is little evidence that expansion of home care services alone is sufficient to impact upon utilization of institutional care (Jamieson, 1991) although it has rarely been provided in sufficiently concentrated, extensive and integrated forms for this to be a realistic expectation. This latter task has been associated with case management.

CASE MANAGEMENT AND CO-ORDINATION

The fragmentation of services due to different sources of funding has been a problem for long-term care in many countries (Henrard *et al.*, 1991). Although the most obvious separation is that between health and social care in many countries (Webb and Wistow, 1986; Dieck and Garms-Homolova, 1991; Costanzi, 1991; Holstein *et al.*, 1991), even where these services are provided by a few organizations, such as the NHS and Social Services Departments in the UK, the range of separate assessors and providers can make the experience of the elderly person equally fragmented. At the level of services to the individual elderly person, case management, or care management as it has become known, is the third element in the shift in patterns of care. It can be defined most simply as a strategy for organizing and co-ordinating care services at the level of the individual client. Its objectives therefore involve mobilizing and co-ordinating a set of various agencies and services to achieve a clearly formulated goal, rather than each service or agency pursuing separate and diverse goals (Challis *et al.*, 1990). This concern with co-ordination is a matter of concern not only in the USA and Canada but also in the Netherlands (Pijl, 1991), France (Veysset-Puijalon and Bouquet, 1992), Israel (Brodsky *et al.*, 1988) and Australia (Abbey *et al.*, 1987; Sodaro, 1990).

Case management or care management can also be defined as the performance of the core tasks of long-term care: case-finding and screening, assessment, care-planning and implementation, and monitoring and review (Steinberg and Carter, 1983). Key elements in the definition of case management thus include a defined target population of people requiring long-term care (not all service recipients need case management), continuity of attention, systematic performance of core tasks, service co-ordination (Kane, 1990; Kane *et al.*, 1991) and a focus upon making improvements to the service system as well as meeting individual client needs (Steinberg and Carter, 1983). Case management usually is built upon comprehensive assessment and will, in more systematic applications, involve attempts to build from assessment to information systems that will permit better allocation of services (Kane, 1990).

Case management can be seen as occupying a pivotal position in the new care systems for very frail elderly people, attempting to balance more client centred approaches with more effective use of resources. Thus, on the one hand the focus is more upon client-centred rather than service-oriented modes of care, emphasizing flexibility and client choice based upon individualized care plans, which in aggregate may influence needs based planning. On the other hand, there is also a focus upon the concern of diverting elderly people from unnecessary admission to institutional care because of the perceived budgetary constraint of meeting the needs of ageing populations through commensurate expansion of institutional care facilities. In short, case management is the setting where the integration of social goals and economic constraints must occur at the level of service provision, where the balancing of needs and resources, scarcity and choice must take place (Challis, 1992).

Some of the earliest studies of case management in the UK were the Thanet, Gateshead and Darlington Schemes (Challis and Davies, 1986; Challis et al., 1988, 1989, 1990, 1991a,b, 1992; Davies and Challis, 1986). The first two of these studies focused on case management in social care. The later initiatives also involved joint health and social care case management interventions, both in primary care and geriatric care settings. Quasi-experimental designs were employed to compare the experience of matched cases, one group receiving this particular model of case management service, the other receiving existing services. The model of case management which was developed was designed to ensure that improved performance of the core tasks of case management could contribute towards more effective and efficient long-term care. The devolution of control of resources, within an overall cost framework, to individual social workers, acting as case managers, was designed to permit more flexible responses to needs and the integration of fragmented services into a more coherent package of care so as to provide a realistic alternative to institutional care.

The studies of case management in social care (Challis and Davies, 1985, 1986; Challis et al., 1988, 1990, 1992) indicated that social workers with greater budgetary flexibility, acting as case managers, were able to respond more effectively than is usually the case. The care provided was more individually varied and control of a budget meant that assessments became more wide ranging and problem focused. Consequently a number of problems often associated with the breakdown of community care, such as severe stress on carers, confusional states, and risk of falling, were more effectively managed at home than in the control groups. It was found that this approach reduced the need for institutional care of vulnerable elderly people significantly. Sixty-nine per cent of those receiving the case management scheme in Kent and 63% in Gateshead remained at home over one year compared with 34% and 36%, respectively, of the control groups receiving the usual services. For those individuals suffering from cognitive impairment, 50% remained at home over one year in the Kent scheme and 64% in Gateshead. This compares with 23% and 29%, respectively, for those receiving usual services. The schemes appeared to offer an alternative to long-stay care for a significant proportion of those liable to enter over one year. Overall there were marked improvements in the levels of satisfaction and well-being of elderly people and their carers and these were achieved at no greater cost to the social services, NHS or society as a whole than was expended upon the control group.

Within the case management service in Gateshead a pilot health and social care scheme was developed around primary care (Challis et al., 1990, 1992). A part-time doctor, a full-time nurse and a part-time physiotherapist were added to the existing team of social workers, with a flexible budget split equally between health and social services. This case management service was designed to focus upon the most frail of the previous target population on the margin of institutional care. It was based around a large group practice, all patients receiving the service being patients of this group of general practitioners. In this pilot study with a relatively small number of cases the only outcome data available was on destination for a small sample of 28 cases matched with a group receiving existing services. After 12 months 62% of those receiving the case management service remained at home compared with only 21% receiving the usual services, a similar result to the earlier findings. There was thus a marked reduction in the probability of admission to institutional care. As in the social care scheme, there was no significant difference in costs for the case management approach compared with the existing provision of services to similar cases.

A similar approach to case management was also tested in a multidisciplinary scheme based upon geriatric care for very frail elderly people in Darlington (Challis et al., 1989, 1991a,b). Here case managers employed by the social services department were members of a geriatric multidisciplinary team, most of the rest of whose members were health service employees. The case managers in this service not only deployed a flexible budget, but also were able to allocate the time of multipurpose care workers who combined the roles of home help, nursing aide and paramedical aide. Each case manager was responsible for between 15 and 20 elderly people and was also responsible for a team of approximately 18 home care assistants. Most of the budget was allocated to home care assistant time but resources were also spent on paying for additional services from members of the community to permit more flexible care as in the social care schemes. Although this service was located within a geriatric setting some 30% suffered marked cognitive impairment and over 80% appeared to experience a degree of anxiety and depression. Improvements in the well-being of elderly people and a lower level of carer stress were observed for those receiving this new service compared with patients in long-stay hospital care. These gains were achieved at a lower cost than was normally expended upon such patients (Challis *et al.*, 1989, 1991a,b) reflecting the higher cost of hospital care compared with other institutional settings.

Overall the findings of these UK case management studies suggest an increased efficiency in the provision of social care with improved outcomes at similar or slightly lower costs. This is not dissimilar to observations made in programmes in North America. In a review of Community Care Demonstrations for elderly people in the USA, nearly all of which included forms of case management, considerable variability was observed in the extent to which such expanded community care services appeared to substitute for nursing home care. Consequently it was concluded that on balance expanded community care was likely to increase costs through time. Nonetheless, this expansion of community care did produce evident benefits for recipients in terms of quality of life (Kemper *et al.*, 1987). A later review summarized the Channelling Programme, which was designed to provide carefully managed home care as a more appropriate and less costly substitute for nursing homes, and involved a randomized trial of models of case management in 10 States. The findings suggest that although a frail population was served, savings on nursing home placements did not offset the additional costs of home care services and case management, therefore there was a net increase in costs. Nonetheless elderly people and their families benefited from reduced needs, greater satisfaction with the care provided and higher morale (Kemper, 1988).

Case management and the support of people with dementia

Case management has been identified in a US Congress Report as one of the four components, along with public education, information and referral and outreach, of an effective system to link people with dementia to needed services (Office of Technology Assessment, 1990). The studies of case management cited have indicated that a particular case management approach can provide support at home for some cognitively impaired elderly people more effectively than existing services. Factors associated with that improved support appeared to be assessment focused upon both deficits and strengths providing an understanding of a person's daily routine, flexibility providing the capacity to commence intervention at a pace and in ways which were acceptable to the elderly person, involvement of and support for family members in care plans and careful risk minimization through anticipation and planning (Davies and Challis, 1986; Challis *et al.*, 1990). Also important, particularly for those living alone, was the creation of the role of a 'key carer' as one or more of the hands-on carers. Such a person can establish a relationship with the elderly person, may at times function as a 'cognitive surrogate', contribute to assessment and monitoring of well-being and act as a link for the provision of other care.

These factors have significance for the kind of case management role which has to be developed. In the US context there has emerged a debate about styles of case management often framed as between the virtues of clinical or administrative models of case management. Translated to the UK this would mean the extent to which the role of the case manager is primarily that of a broker with a focus upon service arrangement to the exclusion of more clinical concerns. Administrative models are likely not to be seen as the province of professional workers in contrast to the clinical approach. The latter would seem to be particularly relevant in the care of people suffering with dementia in view of the need for careful titration of support (Kanter, 1989), to provide for and balance the needs of carers and elderly people and to support and guide the activities of hands-on carers. As the US Congress report concluded: 'The kind of case management required ... to link people with dementia to services is the clinical process in which the case manager is a helper, problem solver, and client advocate' (Office of Technology Assessment, 1990, p. 24).

This latter point is relevant to how the separation of assessment and provision, or purchaser and provider roles, is effected. The needs of effective practice do not always lead to organizationally neat solutions. On occasions in work with people with dementia, part of the assessment function may be most effectively undertaken by a hands-on worker, because of their proximity to the elderly person over a considerable period of time, albeit closely supported by a case manager. Again in undertaking other core tasks such as monitoring well-being, routine, diet or medication intake such workers may be crucial especially for those living alone. Thus effective case management for these people would necessitate close links between those formally designated as providers and those formally designated as purchasers. The US Congress report comments: 'Agencies that provide services can provide comprehensive case management...case managers in agencies that provide services can be effectively insulated from financial pressures to refer clients to services of their own agencies rather than more appropriate service of other agencies (Office of Technology Assessment, 1990, p. 55).

SOME FURTHER IMPLICATIONS

Assessment

At the heart of the debate about misplacement of elderly people in institutional care, and therefore about alternative forms of care, is the quality of pre-entry assessment. More effective assessment has been identified as part of the changes in community care in Australia and the UK. In the UK concentration of responsibility for the public funding (save for hospital beds) of long-term care in the hands of the local authority will mean that assessment of need for this level of care will in future be undertaken prior to entry. However it will be the responsibility of each local authority to develop its own criteria and approach to assessment with the probability of considerable variability in the nature of the assessment undertaken and who is involved in the process. This is in interesting contrast to the Australian developments where multidisciplinary Geriatric Assessment Teams have been established to undertake this process of assessment (Department of Community Services, 1986; Cole, 1990; Gregory, 1991; Quartararo and O'Neill, 1990).

Particularly relevant to the topic of assessment is the question of the locus of case management services. This was not discussed in the US Congress report on dementia services (Office of Technology Assessment, 1990), but in the UK context there would seem to be a powerful argument for locating such services in health care settings (Lodge, 1991). In the support of people with dementia case management could be sited as part of the activity of a psychogeriatric service since this is a well developed area in the UK compared with many other countries.

Targeting

The theoretical argument for alternatives to hospital care has usually taken the form that certain patients requiring lower levels of care than the norm of institutional care can be more appropriately supported in other settings. The targeting problem has been to identify effectively the characteristics of these individuals.

The Kent, Gateshead and Darlington case management studies were carefully targeted services, focused on people with considerable needs and a high probability of entry to institutional care, and yet, although the results indicate that they achieved greater efficiency than existing services (greater improvements in welfare at similar cost), only the Darlington study shows significant cost savings, reflecting the high cost of long-stay hospital care. Hence it is probable that if a similar case management approach was applied to cases where the opportunity for substitution of institutional by community care was less, then rising average costs could occur. This is because individuals whose needs fall just below that of present criteria of entry to institutional care currently receive relatively low levels of provision, and it is likely that the case management approach, with its more detailed assessments of need, could well lead to increased expenditure beyond that currently incurred. While this might be justifiable in welfare terms it would not contribute to a policy of 'downward substitution'. Indeed, it is precisely the conflict between meeting broader welfare needs on the one hand and careful targeting on the other that would seem to account for the inability of some large-scale case management schemes elsewhere to achieve the desired downward substitution despite demonstrating welfare gains amongst those receiving the service (Kemper, 1988). This is a real policy concern over the expansion of home care, namely that there is no necessary reason that additional home care resources would lead to substitution but may rather lead to the meeting of more needs (Davies *et al.*, 1990; Jamieson, 1991).

The development of mechanisms for achieving effective case-finding and targeting is thus likely to be a continuing preoccupation of managers in providing alternatives to institutional care. Ideally, on the one hand such indicators need to permit discretion and thus avoid the rigidity of methods such as simple functional scores used in some areas (Morginstin et al., 1991; Liu and Cornelius, 1991; Luehrs and Ramthun, 1991) since such indicators of disability are relatively poor predictors of need for institutional care at the individual level. On the other hand it is seen as desirable that criteria are sufficiently standardized to be seen as equitable (Department of Health, 1991) and to permit effective monitoring of the characteristics of those receiving the service. Some US States address this problem by using identical approaches for screening applicants to nursing home care and for alternative home care programmes (McDowell *et al.*, 1990). An alternative targeting approach was adopted in the UK case management schemes described. Target guidelines were specified and agreed with potential referral sources but, recognizing the complexity of circumstances which lead to need for institutional care, no rigid threshold of dependency was specified. In short, accountability for targeting was held by local managers after a person had been accepted rather than at pre-entry using rigid criteria.

Perverse incentives and the funding of long-term care

Fragmented patterns of funding for long-term care have tended to distort the development of long-term care in the USA (Feder, 1991). Such fragmentation can produce perverse incentives in the ways in which alternative patterns of care may develop. In the UK the one sector of public long-term care provision which is funded separately from nursing and residential care homes is that of the long-stay beds in hospital. In the face of demands upon National Health Service resources by the acute sector, a reduction in the level of provision of long-stay hospital beds is almost inevitable. Equally, pressure on Social Services resources may lead that agency to define elderly people in hospital as of lower priority than those perceived to be requiring care in their own homes. Consequently the effects of the Community Care Policy upon the acute sector will need to be monitored carefully as was noted in the mid-term of the Australian Community Care Policy (Gregory, 1991). There is also room for fruitful local experimentation in the integration of long-term care budgets and the provision of joint health and social care services for elderly people with mental health problems.

REFERENCES

Abbey, R., Hall, J. and Rungie, M. (1987). Community options: a new approach in assessment and the delivery of services in the aged care field. *Aust. J. Ageing*, **6**, 10–14.

Askham, J. and Thompson, C. (1990). *Dementia and Home Care: A Research Report on a Home Support Scheme for Dementia Sufferers, Research Paper No. 4*, Age Concern Institute of Gerontology, Mitcham, Surrey.

Beecham, J., Cambridge, P., Hallam, A. and Knapp, M. (1991). *The Costs of Domus Care in Lewisham. Discussion Paper 774*, Personal Social Services Research Unit, University of Kent, Canterbury.

Bond, S. and Bond, J. (1990). Outcomes of care within a multiple case study in the evaluation of the experimental National Health Service nursing homes. *Age Ageing*, **19**, 11–18.

Bowling, A., Formby, J., Grant, K. and Ebrahim, S. (1991). A randomised controlled trial of nursing home and long-stay geriatric ward care for elderly people. *Age Ageing*, **20**, 316–324.

Brodsky, J., Cohen, M., Habib, J. and Heron, T. (1988). The organisation of long-term care services in Israel: An evaluation, *Social Security: J. Welfare Social Security Studies*, **30**, 167–195.

Challis, D. (1992). Community care of elderly people: bringing together scarcity and choice, needs and costs, *Financ. Accountabil. Manage.*, **8**, 77–95.

Challis, D., Darton, R., Johnson, L., Stone, M., Traske, K. and Wall, B. (1989). *Supporting Frail Elderly People at Home: The Darlington Community Care Project, PSSRU*, University of Kent, Canterbury.

Challis, D., Darton, R., Johnson, L., Stone, M. and Traske, K. (1991a). An evaluation of an alternative to long-stay hospital care for frail elderly patients: Part I The model of care. *Age Ageing*, **20**, 236–244.

Challis, D., Darton, R., Johnson, L., Stone, M. and Traske, K. (1991b). An evaluation of an alternative to long-stay hospital care for the frail elderly: Part II Costs and outcomes. *Age Ageing*, **20**, 245–254.

Challis, D. and Davies, B. (1985). Long term care for the elderly: the community care scheme. *B. J. Soc Work*, **15**, 563–579.

Challis, D. and Davies, B. (1986). *Case Management in Community Care*, Gower, Aldershot.

Challis, D., Chessum, R., Chesterman, J., Luckett, R. and Traske, K. (1992). Case management in health and social care. In: Lackzo, F. and Victor, C. (Eds), *Social Policy and Elderly People*, Gower, Aldershot, Avebury.

Challis, D., Chessum, R., Chesterman, J., Luckett, R. and Woods, B. (1988). Community care for the frail elderly: an urban experiment. *Br. J. Soc. Work*, **18** (Suppl.), 43–54.

Challis, D., Chessum, R., Chesterman, J., Luckett, R. and Traske, K. (1990). *Case Management in Social and Health Care*, Personal Social Services Research Unit. University of Kent, Canterbury.

Cm. 849 (1989). *Caring for People*, HMSO, London.

Cole, A. (1990). Assessment in the Community. In: Howe, A., Ozanne, E. and Selby Smith, C. (Eds), *Community Care Policy and Practice: New Directions in Australia*, Public Sector Management Institute, Monash University, Melbourne.

Costanzi, C. (1991). Home care services in Italy. In: Jamieson, A. (Ed.), *Home Care for Older People in Europe*, Oxford University Press, Oxford.

Crosby, C., Stevenson, R.C. and Copeland, J.R.M. (1984). The evaluation of intensive domiciliary care for the elderly mentally ill. In: Bromley, D.B. (Ed.), *Gerontology: Social and Behavioural Perspectives*, Croom Helm, Beckenham.

Currie, C.T., Burley, L.E., Doull, C., Ravetz, C., Smith, R.G. and Williamson, J. (1980). A scheme of augmented home care for acutely and sub-acutely ill elderly patients: report of a pilot study. *Age Aging*, **9**, 173–180.

Davies, B. and Challis, D. (1986). *Matching Resources to Needs in Community Care*, Gower, Aldershot.

Davies, B., Bebbington, A., Charnley, H., Ferlie, E., Hughes, M. and Twigg, J. (1990). *Resources, Needs and Outcomes in Community Care*. Gower, Aldershot, Avebury.

Department of Community Services (1986). *Nursing Homes and Hostels Review*, Australian Government Publishing Service, Canberra.

Department of Health (1991). *Care Management and Assessment: Managers Guide*, HMSO, London.

Dieck, M. and Garms-Homolova, V. (1991). Home care services in the Federal Republic of Germany. In: Jamieson, A. (Ed.), *Home Care for Older People in Europe*, Oxford University Press, Oxford.

Donaldson, C. and Bond, J. (1991). Cost of continuing care facilities in the evaluation of experimental National Health Service nursing homes. *Age Ageing*, **20**, 160–168.

Donaldson, C. and Gregson, B. (1989). Prolonging life at home: what is the cost? *Comm. Med.*, **11**, 200–209.

Factor, H., Morgenstin, B. and Naon, D. (1991). Home care services in Israel. In: Jamieson, A. (Ed.), *Home Care for Older People in Europe*, Oxford University Press, Oxford.

Feder, J. (1991). Paying for health care: the limits of current programs. In: Rowland, D. and Lyons, B. (Eds), *Financing Home Care: Improving Protection for Disabled Elderly People*, Johns Hopkins University Press, Baltimore.

Ferlie, E., Challis, D. and Davies, B. (1989). *Efficiency Improving Innovations in the Care of The Elderly*, Gower, Aldershot.

Gibbins, F.J., Lee, M., Davison, P., O'Sullivan, P., Hutchinson, M., Murphy, D. and Ugwu, C. (1982). Augmented home nursing as an alternative to hospital care for chronic elderly invalids. *Br. Med. J.*, **284**, 330–333.

Goldberg, E.M. and Connelly, N. (1982). *The Effectiveness of Social Care for the Elderly*, Heinemann, London.

Gregory, R. (1991). *Aged Care Reform Strategy: Mid-term Review 1990–91*, Australian Government Publishing Service, Canberra.

Henrard, J.C., Ankri, J. and Isnard, M.C. (1991). Home care services in France. In: Jamieson, A. (Ed.), *Home Care for Older People in Europe*, Oxford University Press, Oxford.

Holstein, B., Pernille, D., Almind, G. and Holst, E. (1991). The home help service in Denmark. In: Jamieson, A. (Ed.), *Home Care for Older People in Europe*, Oxford University Press, Oxford.

Jamieson, A. (1991). Trends in home care policies. In: Jamieson, A. (Ed.), *Home Care for Older People in Europe*, Oxford University Press, Oxford.

Kane, R. (1990). *What is Case Management Anyway?* Long Term Care Decisions Resource Center, University of Minnesota, Minneapolis.

Kane, R., Penrod, J., Davidson, G., Moscovice, I. and Rich, E. (1991). What cost case management in long term care? *Social Service Rev.*, **65**, 281–303.

Kanter, J. (1989). Clinical case management: definition, principles. *Hosp. Commun. Psychiatry*, **40**, 361–368.

Kemper, P., Applebaum, R. and Harrigan, M. (1987). Community care demonstrations: what have we learned? *Health Care Financing Rev.*, **8**, 87–100.

Kemper, P. (1988). The evaluation of the national long-term care demonstration: 10. Overview of findings. *Health Services Res.*, **23**, 161–174.

Knapp, M. (1984). *The Economics of Social Care*, Macmillan, London.

Kraan, R.J., Baldock, J., Davies, B., Evers, A., Johansson, L., Knapen, M., Thorslund, M. and Tunissen, C. (1991). *Care for the Elderly: Significant Innovations in Three European Countries*, Campus/Westview, Boulder, Colorado.

Lindesay, J., Briggs, K., Lawes, M., MacDonald, A. and Herzberg, J. (1991). The domus philosophy: A comparative evaluation of a new approach to residential care for the demented elderly. *Int. J. Ger. Psychiatry*, **6**, 727–736.

Liu, K. and Cornelius, E. (1991). Activities of daily living and eligibility for home care. In: Rowland, D. and Lyons, B. (Eds), *Financing Home Care: Improving Protection for Disabled Elderly People*, Johns Hopkins University Press, Baltimore.

Lodge, B. (1991). *Whither Now: Planning Services for Elderly People with Dementia*, British Association of Service to the Elderly, Stoke on Trent.

Luehrs, J. and Ramthun, R. (1991). State approaches to functional assessments for home care. In: Rowland, D. and Lyons, B. (Eds), *Financing Home Care: Improving Protection for Disabled Elderly People*, Johns Hopkins University Press, Baltimore.

McDowell, D., Barniskis, L. and Wright, S. (1990). The Wisconsin Community Options Programme: planning and packaging long-term support for individuals. In: Howe, A., Ozanne, E. and Selby Smith, C. (Eds), *Community Care Policy and Practice: New Directions in Australia*, Public Sector Management Institute, Monash University, Melbourne.

Morginstin, B. and Shamai, N. (1988). Issues in planning long-term care insurance in Israel's social security system, *Social Security: J. Welfare Social Security Studies*, **30**, 31–48.

Morginstin, B., Baich-Moray, S. and Zipkin, A. (1991). *The Long Term Care Insurance Law: Data from the First Two Years. Survey No. 85*, Research and Planning Administration, National Insurance Institute, Jerusalem.

O'Shea, E. and Costello, J. (1991). Boarding out as an option for the care of elderly people. *Age Ageing*, **20**, 95–99.

Office of Technology Assessment (1990). *Confused Minds, Burdened Families*, Office of Technology Assessment, Congress of the United States, Washington DC.

Ozanne, E. (1990). Development of Australian health and social policy in relation to the aged and the emergence of home care services. In: Howe, A., Ozanne, E. and Selby Smith, C. (Eds), *Community Care Policy and Practice: New Directions in Australia*. Public Sector Management Institute, Monash University, Melbourne.

Pijl. M. (1991). *Some Recent Developments in Care for The Elderly in The Netherlands*, Nederlands Instituut voor Maatschappelijk Werk Onderzoek, s'Gravenhage.

Quartararo, M. and O'Neill, T. (1990). Nursing home admissions: the effect of a Multidisciplinary Assessment Team on the frequency of admissions approvals. *Community Health Studies*, XIV, 47–53.

Salvage, A. (1985). *Domiciliary Care Schemes for the Elderly: Provision by Local Authority Social Services Departments*, Research Team for the Care of the Elderly, University of Wales College of Medicine.

Sinclair, I., Parker, R., Leat, D. and Williams, J. (1990). *The Kaleidoscope of Care: a Review of Research on Welfare Provision for Elderly People*, HMSO, London.

Sodaro, E. (1990). The New South Wales community options programme. In: Howe, A., Ozanne, E. and Selby Smith, C. (Eds), *Community Care Policy and Practice: New Directions in Australia*, Public Sector Management Institute, Monash University, Melbourne.

Social Services Inspectorate (1987). *From Home Help to Home Care: An Analysis of Policy, Resourcing and Service Management*, Department of Health and Social Security, London.

Steinberg, R.M. and Carter, G.W. (1983). *Case Management and the Elderly*, Heath, Lexington, Massachusetts.

Thorslund, M. and Johansson, L. (1987). The elderly in Sweden: current realities and future plans. *Ageing Soc.*, **7**, 345–355.

Thorslund, M. (1991). The increasing number of very old people will change the Swedish model of the Welfare State, *Soc. Sci. Med.*, **32**, 455–464.

Townsend, J., Piper, M., Frank, A., Dyer, S., North, W. and Meade, T. (1988). Reduction in hospital readmission stay of elderly patients by a community based hospital discharge scheme: a randomised controlled trial. *Br. Med. J.*, **297**, 544–547.

van den Heuvel, W. and Gerritsen, H. (1991). Home care services in the Netherlands. In: Jamieson, A. (Ed.), *Home Care for Older People in Europe*, Oxford University Press, Oxford.

van den Heuvel, W. and Schrijvers, G. (Eds) (1986). *Innovations in Care for the Elderly: European Experiences*, Uitgeversmaatschappij de Tidjstroom, Lochen-Gent.

Veysset-Puijalon, B. and Bouquet, B. (1992). Evolution de la coordination dans l'action sociale vieilleuse. In: Lallemand, D. (Ed.), *La Coordination Gerontologique*, Les Cahiers No. 5, Fondation de France, Paris.

Victor, C.R. and Vetter, N.J. (1988). Rearranging the deckchairs on the Titanic: failure of an augmented home help scheme after discharge to reduce the length of stay in hospital. *Arch. Geront. Geriatr.*, **7**, 83–91.

Webb, A. and Wistow, G. (1986). *Planning, Need and Scarcity*, Allen and Unwin, London.

Wimo, A., Wallin, J., Lundgren, K., Ronnback, E., Asplund, K., Mattson, B. and Krakau, I. (1991). Group living, an alternative for dementia patients, a cost analysis. *Int. J. Geriatr. Psychiatry*, **6**, 21–29.

Age-Associated Memory Impairment and Benign Senescent Forgetfulness

Treatment and Care in Old Age Psychiatry
Edited by R. Levy, R. Howard and A. Burns
©1993 Wrightson Biomedical Publishing Ltd

7

Age-Associated Memory Impairment: Real Entity or Statistical Artefact?

IAN HINDMARCH

University of Surrey, Milford Hospital, Guildford, UK

INTRODUCTION

Age-associated memory impairment (AAMI) has been introduced and defined as a clinical entity (Crook *et al.*, 1986). In any discussion on the identification of persons experiencing AAMI in the population and possible modes of treatment, there are three important topics that are worth a closer look. One concerns the validity of the statistical methods that are at present used to identify AAMI in the population. The question of validity applies to the basic statistical assumptions by which standard deviations of one age group are used as a baseline for performance in another group. Is this the correct way to proceed in the diagnostic sense? Another problem that requires thought relates to whether or not memory (if we decide what it is we are measuring) remains inviolate from the thousand-and-one other influences that could possibly change memory stores with respect to age. And the third factor concerns the role of psychopharmacological agents in the management of AAMI.

CAN WE DEFINE 'MEMORY'

A discussion of cognition and cognition-enhancing drugs may begin with the individual researcher's idea of the nature of memory. Up to 14 or 15 different CNS-mechanisms have been cited as having some place in such a system. Before we even begin to look at impairment, one of the big problems is how to define the complex subject memory — is it a discussion about input, or storage or another feature or a combination of these?

First, do we have an identifiable entity in our cognitive system called 'memory'? At present, there are clear distinctions between the roles of short-term and long-term memory processes, resulting from differential handling by the brain at the physiological level, although studies that involve 'neural network' models may modify this view in the future. Short-term or working memory processes enable information received through the sensory appara-tus to be interpreted against the frame of perceptual reference, through the operation of the differing components of the system. Long-term memory or 'learned memory' processing ensures that information received through sensory input is permanently stored by a physiological encoding system, to be retrieved at a later date. It is also interesting that research studies involv-ing subjects with impairments of short-term memory have shown that they are not necessarily impaired when it comes to learning new material (Vallar and Shallice, 1991).

Distinctions between the short- and long-term memory processing functions are demonstrated by patients with Alzheimer's disease. In these patients, the gradual extinction of the short-term memory function is accom-panied by a slower decrement in the long-term memory processes.

WHAT IS THE NORMAL ELDERLY POPULATION?

We start with one of the basic questions — what is normal in the elderly? Is a deficit in recognition of faces anything that is cause for clinical concern? It can happen even at an anecdotal level that one can have problems in retrieving names for faces. Is this a clinically definable abnormality or part of the normal ageing process? Is it equally demonstrated by the healthy, active elderly person living at home, and by those in the same age range who are for one reason or another, hospitalized or in social service accommoda-tion? Patients who are living by themselves or are married, living in residen-tial care or hospitalized because of a chronic long-term illness may show differences when undergoing memory tests that reflect in part at least, the effects of their environment (Table 1). There are studies that have looked at one or another group of elderly subjects and what has to be borne in mind

Table 1. Populations of elderly subjects investigated using psychometric tests.

1. Volunteer elderly
2. Elderly from a Senior Citizens Club
3. Elderly in retirement communities
4. Elderly in social service homes
5. Elderly hospital out-patients
6. Elderly hospital in-patients

when looking at their results, is that the subjects are using memory as an instrument in ways that reflect their needs in their individual surroundings.

Elderly in social services homes and hospital in-patients

Gilleard and Pattie (1977) reported the use of a modified version of the Stockton Geriatric Rating Scale (SGRS) in a variety of settings testing 400 patients over the age of 60 years, in the care of hospital and social services in North Yorkshire, UK. Monitoring individual change in an institutionalized framework is one of the uses of a rating scale in addition to its use as an objective method of assessment prior to placing the elderly within hospital and social services settings. The sample studied included 100 patients resident in the acute wards of a psychiatric hospital, 100 chronic psychiatric patients, 100 psychogeriatric patients and 100 patients resident in four different homes for the elderly (Part III accommodation), including 25 patients resident in a home for the elderly mentally infirm, the latter representing a more handicapped population than is found in most Part III homes. The authors produced a table of correlations between the modified (shorter) and full versions of the SGRS to validate the use of the shorter scale in a population of UK patients. They commented, 'The low correlations between age and scores suggest that with an elderly population age does not by itself account for much of the variance in behavioural competence.'.

Elderly in retirement communities

Pfeffer et al. (1982) addressed the perceived need for 'an objective and direct measure of social function in older adults in the community'. The rationale for their study was the understanding that instruments such as the IADL (Instrumental Activities of Daily Living) scale 'do not sample the more complex behaviours of older adults who live in the community'. They cited writing cheques, paying bills, assembling tax records, shopping alone, keeping track of current events, remembering appointments as useful indicators in a screening tool for social dysfunction in older adults in the community. Both the IADL scale and the instrument developed by the authors, the FAQ (Functional Activities Questionnaire), containing 'a hierarchy' of relevant skills were evaluated (Pfeffer et al., 1982). Accepted neurological, cognitive and affective assessments were used to validate the two measures of social function in community-based studies. The authors noted that tests of cognitive function are subject to a number of influences and may not be as useful as measures of performance in everyday life, as a test of social function. 'Measurement of social function is critical in identifying those organic and affective states that are sufficiently serious to require therapeutic intervention.'

Volunteer elderly, residential care

Holland and Rabbitt (1991) challenged the widely-held belief that ageing is associated with increased recall of early memories in the healthy elderly population, as well as the memory-impaired elderly. They commented that a problem in experimental analysis of old people's memory is often the failure to separate those subjects who do have severe memory impairments from those who do not. 'Without considering the current situation in which the individuals live, and so the use which they make of their memories, we cannot assume that differences between young and old individuals are a function of their chronological ages.' People may come to live in residential care homes because they are physically, rather than cognitively impaired (Morris and Kopelman, 1986). In addition, Morris and Kopelman (1986) report that 'overlearning' of remoter memories may result in their being favoured subjects for recall over recent events in memory tests, simply because they are better-learned and comparatively easy to recall.

These researchers found that they could show differences in scores on a variety of standardized psychometric batteries, in terms of the environment in which their population lived. This indicates the wisdom of a careful assessment before deciding that there is a disease entity or a psychological disturbance in a particular subject. Is this an abnormal state we are talking about or a state of normal existence, whatever normality might mean? As we age, we pass through a variety of life experiences that bring us into a number of different environments, from normal family environments, to states that are alien to our previous experience and these 'rites of passage' cannot help but affect us, so have to be taken into account.

THE STATISTICAL BASIS OF AAMI

Age-associated memory impairment, according to the definition accepted in the National Institute of Mental Health (NIMH) Diagnostic and Statistical Manual of Mental Disorders of the American Medical Association (DSM-IV) classification, affects 40% of those in their fifties and 75% of those over 75 years of age. The diagnosis of AAMI describes healthy persons over 50 years of age who have experienced age-related changes in memory and other cognitive abilities, but who are not demented (Crook et al., 1986). That this may be a normal age-related phenomenon is acknowledged, that it is often distressing to the otherwise healthy person is also true.

In order to consider these proposals in terms of some illustrative statistics, Fig. 1 represents what could be described as the distribution of the population

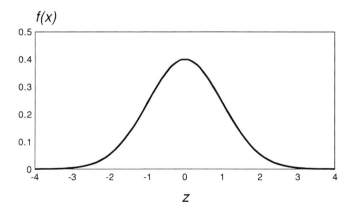

Figure 1. Distribution of total adult population related to memory test performance.

of all adults over 18 years, in terms of the distribution of their memory test performance. No particular test is cited here.

If a clinical criterion is adopted, this would indicate that anyone who has a memory impairment (in any age group) would probably fall somewhere between two standard deviations beneath the mean, as illustrated in Fig. 2(a). This clinical definition has been employed usefully in studies measuring intelligence, as one example Fig. 2(b) compares the clinical definition of memory impairment with the proposed AAMI definition in terms of their statistical distribution in the total adult population. Looking at the elderly population — those over the age of 60 years — we would expect that the distribution of memory functions in that population would be something lower than the mean, as shown in Fig. 3.

There are lengthy tails to these distributions and while they are not exact, they are a useful illustration of the point. Figure 4 shows the mean of the memory function scores for the younger, intelligent population. The proposal for a clinically-identifiable AAMI population uses a definition of one standard deviation below the mean of a young population (Fig. 5). The definition works within that particular sample of the population. However, there are far-reaching implications for the total population on which it is based, since the definition of one standard deviation from the mean of the normal young sample includes part of the overall population curve. Superimposing the curve for the elderly population and using this criterion, it then appears that the bulk of elderly people have AAMI (Fig. 6). The statistical foundation could be used to describe either a state of being or a psychological deficit, according to the interpretation placed upon it.

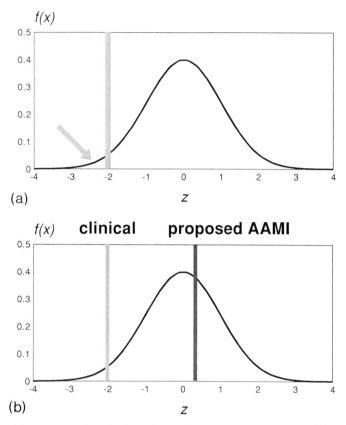

(a)

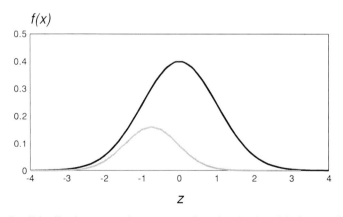

(b)

Figure 2. (a) A memory impaired section of the total adult population (b) Comparison of the clinical definition of impairment and proposed AAMI.

Figure 3. Distribution curve for memory function in the elderly population.

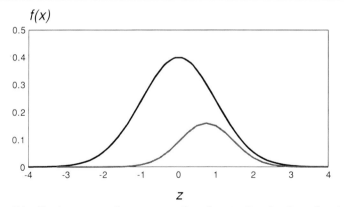

Figure 4. Distribution curve for memory function testing in the educated young population.

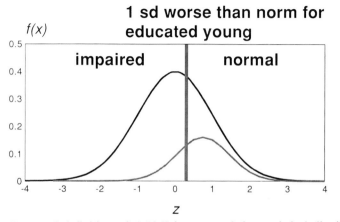

Figure 5. Proposed definition of AAMI in terms of the statistical distribution of memory test results in these populations.

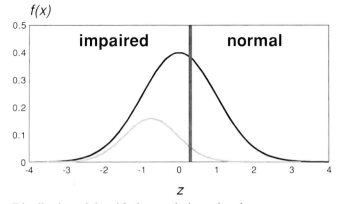

Figure 6. Distribution of the elderly population related to memory test performance

THE USE OF PERCENTILE SCORES

On the assumption that the distribution shown in Fig. 1 is true for 40 year olds, half that population will also fall into the category of AAMI (Fig. 7). In fact most adults have some age-associated memory impairment (Fig. 8).

This may be a simplistic argument but it does emphasize one very important point, concerning percentile scores and interpretation of statistical material. In the 1960s, people were very concerned about tests of intelligence. Hans Eysenck produced texts on intelligence testing and there was much debate on the subject and relevance of IQ (Intelligence Quotient) testing. Investigators and users of IQ data soon realised that the IQ score

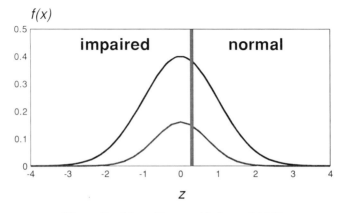

Figure 7.   Most 40 year olds have AAMI.

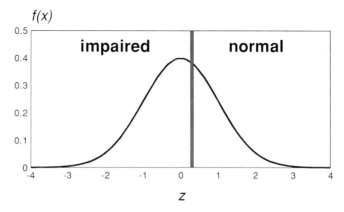

Figure 8.   Most adults have AAMI.

mattered less than the percentile in which it fell. An IQ of 129 of a university student aged 23 would be probably at the 80th percentile, representative of the intelligence of his or her population as a whole. The problem of going from a sample to an overall population distribution is that the tester may fail to take into account the performance of the peer group as a whole. For generations, psychologists have used percentile scores to ensure that the performance of the individual on the test is only given a baseline if it relates to the performance of other subjects from the same population. An IQ score of 129 in a person aged 92 might place that subject at the 99th percentile, giving information only in relation to the population to which he or she belongs.

Two approaches to the problem can be considered. One makes use of the definition of AAMI based on the scores of 26-year olds. Another clinical definition that can be employed refers back to the old percentile notions. Figure 3 could represent a population of 65 year old people anywhere in the UK. Each population would have its own environmental, social and educational history and character and these influences on behaviour and performance can be identified and described. There have been numerous studies that showed evidence for a deficiency of specific nutrients being correlated with psychiatric or cognitive status (Carney *et al.*, 1979; Goodwin *et al.*, 1983; Hancock *et al.*, 1985). It is an interesting reflection that many people within the same age cohort, who have been brought up, been educated and worked in similar conditions are different as regards their mental as well as their physical capacities. Some may be in hospital due to physical infirmities, a proportion may be in mental hospitals and others are able to remain in their own homes to the end of their lives. The reasons for such differences can only be found by looking at the population, and by isolating and defining the possible factors that represent identifiable, clinical, behavioural or social reasons for the differences. Such differences within the population are obviously not linked to ageing *per se*, nor to arbitrary values gleaned from the cognitive performance of modern-day young adults.

EFFECTS ON PERFORMANCE IN MEMORY TESTS

AAMI also presents a problem in regard to 'performance in memory tests', whatever is meant by the term. Is performance in memory tests stable in respect to age or not, or is it liable to be changed by education or other influences? If so, then it becomes a very variable measure and these influences have to be taken into account. Some of the possible influences on memory tests are listed in Table 2 and a number of these are discussed further in the sections which follow.

Table 2.   Possible influences on memory test
performance.

1. Age-related decline in sensory abilities
2. Physical health and disease
3. Sub-clinical psychological illness
4. Nutritional status and diet
5. Endogenous neuropeptides, endorphins and hormones
6. Educational and vocational experience
7. Cultural expectation
8. Social milieu
9. Frequency of testing
10. Overall intelligence and cognitive status
11. Cross-sectional or longitudinal study design
12. Sex differences
13. Expectations of the subject
14. Non-cognitive processes
15. Non-psychotropic drugs

Age, physical health and disease, sub-clinical psychological illness

Chronological age may also be a factor as in other investigative fields, or it
could be that we are too ready to imply a causal link in this case. It is essential to find a measure that is stable on a longitudinal basis in order to link
in performance at 26 years with performance at 50+ years of age. As we grow
older we suffer from a general debility and this will affect the sensory systems
on which memory processing depends. The memory receives information by
a sensory input and much essential memory rehearsal goes on using sensory
inputs, such as making lists, humming tunes, memorizing poetry. Is this what
we are talking about by 'memory'? Or is memory an executive function
which relates us to our real world? If so, then the gradual presbycusis that
we all suffer will affect that memory system.

   Physical health and disease may also have an influence on performance of
cognitive tests, and this is reasonably well established in the literature
(Siegfried *et al.*, 1984). A person's state of physical health may never have
received a full medical examination in their lives, so that the presence of
disease may go undetected. Many significant clinical disorders have a
profound influence on mental state, making it more difficult to isolate a
particular memory deficit. Wattis and Hindmarch (1988) list a number of
influences of psychoactive drugs on the elderly, who are the largest class of
patients for whom these medicines are prescribed. Side-effects of this class
of drugs may include effects on psychomotor performance and may also
influence information processing, memory and higher intellectual functions.
Subclinical psychological effects, where present, may also affect performance
in memory tests. Is it known when anxiety and depression reach such a level

as to start changing cognitive function in patients? Does the Hamilton score give this information? Patients may receive a psychological assessment and make a low score as regards cognitive ability, to be diagnosed afterwards as suffering from a depressive illness. Psychiatrists are well aware that masked depression is sometimes difficult to tease out, even in an experienced practitioner's hands. All these factors directly affect cognitive systems.

Nutritional factors, hormonal systems

Nutritional status of the subject may be a factor. Investigations into the base metal content of different water sources have been made in order to equate water regions with hospitalizations for mental disturbance. All the above factors can have an effect on memory states.

Hormonal systems may also affect memory. Major alterations in hormone status such as occur in the menopause should not be discounted. There is evidence that some memory systems are hormone-based. Reus and Miner (1985) proposed a role for the hormone cortisol in the regulation of selective attention processes. They studied the variation in hypothalamic –pituitary–adrenal (HPA) function in 17 hospitalized psychiatric patients with endogenous depression, compared with HPA function in 16 normal volunteers. The dexamethasone suppression test (DST) was used to produce an experimental dysfunction of the HPA axis and on the results of the test, the patients were divided into groups of nine 'suppressors' and eight 'non-suppressors' of cortisol production. Based on the understanding that the hypothalamus plays an integral role in the regulation of emotion and autonomic nervous system function, disturbances in the electrophysiological response (skin conductance response, SCR) were used to indicate whether or not hormonal changes were consistent with hypothalamic dysregulation. They found that depressed patients who did not suppress plasma cortisol levels following dexamethasone showed essentially no physiological response to the presentation of a novel stimulus. Commenting on the clinical application of their findings, they noted, 'Clinically, such an impairment may be relevant to a behavioural understanding of depressive phenomenology, specifically, a common inability to perceive or respond to circumstances of environmental change' (Reus and Miner, 1985).

Education, vocation, social milieu

In addition, educational and vocational experience of people may be a factor to take into account when examining an individual's performance in memory tests. A population of well American college students with a history of good nutrition and education may perform on a different level to a population of American 50-year-olds with a different nutritional history in their youth, and a different level of educational experience. These variables may make meaningful comparisons of test scores difficult. Cultural expectation also affects test performance. Elderly people in our culture are expected to be a little bit doddery, a little bit eccentric, a little bit forgetful although this may be an important defence structure. It might be that the people who are being asked to perform the test may have a completely different view of the test than the psychologist who is administering it.

Frequency of testing

The frequency of testing can show the effects of learning and practice. Learning effects should not be discounted, making it a moot point when a test score has been made. The uses of the Mental Status Questionnaire (MSQ) as an aid in the diagnosis and initial assessment of intellectual deterioration in the elderly were described by Stonier (1974). He looked at memory scores for people who had been tested once compared for memory scores for those who had been tested several times, showing a significant difference between the two groups. MSQs are used not only in the primary assessment of the patient to recognize early signs of dementia, but also in trials of psychotropic agents claimed to retard the progress of early dementia. When administered only once each to mentally normal and demented hospitalized female patients, the MSQ failed to take into account the learning process. On the basis of one test, some patients were classified by the MSQ as mildly demented. Re-testing those patient groups took account of the various phenomena that affect performance in the MSQ, such as increased motivation, concentration and co-operation as well as actual learning and their performance and subsequent classification improved as a result (Stonier, 1974).

IQ and overall intelligence

The same question arose over IQ testing as to whether or not the same test should be administered twice to the same person and for this reason, parallel forms of the test were developed. These developments in psychometrics were necessary to answer the need for a reliable baseline score. An individual's cognitive status cannot be separated from their overall intelligence quotient so that the tests used to assess memory are based on tests such as the Wechsler Adult Intelligence Scale (WAIS). Commenting on the results of Jarvik and colleagues' (1962) eight year follow-up in a study of the longitudinal IQ changes in elderly twins, Eisdorfer (1963) suggested, 'These results raise the suspicion that normative data for intelligence, collected by cross-sectional sampling, may exaggerate the pattern of decline of old persons, at least for relatively short periods'. Eisdorfer (1963) tested a sample of 165 aged volunteers who had been enrolled in the Duke University (US) Geriatrics Project, using the WAIS as the test instrument. The mean interval of follow-up was three years after the completion of the Duke Geriatrics Project. No evidence of a clear progressive intellectual decline over the three year period could be inferred from the subjects' performance in the WAIS test (Eisdorfer, 1963).

We do know that people differ significantly in their ability to handle different types of material, as we have different mnestic abilities. These are only aspects of what we know as memory. Again, unless these are taken account of, and unless we can be assured that the sort of memory that we are talking about when we refer to AAMI remains relatively untouched, we have a problem.

Cross-sectional or longitudinal study design

One of the biggest hurdles for the investigator is that the bulk of the data on the ageing process is cross-sectional. This raises problems of interpretation of cross-sectional study results with regard to AAMI. The clinical literature contains very few cross-sectional studies of any magnitude and length that address the changes in memory between the ages of 26 and death. Longitudinal studies are needed to reveal the cause of the changes in these psychological functions in order to produce a reliable criterion for deciding when a person is impaired.

Rubin and colleagues (Rubin and Kinscherf, 1989; Rubin et al., 1989) commented, 'The term age-associated memory impairment has been introduced and defined, yet its separation from very mild SDAT (senile dementia of the Alzheimer type) has yet to be clarified'. Emphasizing that accurate recognition of the very mild stages of SDAT is important for research and clinical practice, they continued, 'Defining the symptoms of very mild SDAT depends on longitudinal evaluation to demonstrate clinical progression'. They investigated 16 otherwise healthy US subjects with a diagnosis of 'questionable' dementia according to the Clinical Dementia Rating (CDR) together with 58 control subjects and 44 subjects with mild SDAT again otherwise healthy, recruited from 1979 to 1981, into a longitudinal study with an 84 month follow-up period. The mean age of the groups was 71 years. They examined the psychometric performance of the three subject groups at entry and compared these 'baseline' results with those gained from testing every 12 to 15 months thereafter. Over this period, the investigators found that the 16 subjects with 'questionable' SDAT could be differentiated as a group from the control and SDAT populations, on the basis of psychometric testing involving the Dementia Scale (DS), Short Portable Mental Status Questionnaire (SPMSQ) and Information Memory Concentration (IMC) test. At the end of the seven year follow-up period, 10 of the 16 had clinically progressed to definite dementia and one further subject had Alzheimer's disease confirmed at autopsy. The authors concluded that 'questionable' cognitive impairment as defined on the CDR scale, actually represents very mild SDAT in the large majority of the cases studied, and that this group differed from both the control and SDAT populations in their performance in psychometric tests. Subjects' performance on standard clinical batteries did not allow differentiation of those who progressed from those who did not, leading the authors to recommend that continued longitudinal studies be performed until tests are validated that allow accurate predictions of those who will progress to the full clinical syndrome (Rubin and Kinscherf, 1989; Rubin et al., 1989).

A limited, five year longitudinal study failed to find any age-related factor, using a series of objective, psychological, performance-related measures (Kilminster, 1991). Nakano et al. (1992) examined EEG changes and their association with deterioration in mental function in the healthy aged in a quantitative, nine year, longitudinal follow-up study. Computer analysed EEG data was compared with the results of psychometric tests in a healthy aged population (28 survivors and 20 non-survivors). The electroencephalogram of the aged has some characteristics that differ from those found in the EEG of young adults, and the investigators noted the lack of quantitative follow-up studies performed with normal, elderly adults that would help to chart the longitudinal changes of EEG with senescence in this population. Previous studies of EEG changes had been qualitative assessments using visual recognition and manual measurement techniques. Computerized analysis of the longitudinal data indicated that a decrease in fast waves occurred in this population from early senescence onwards. An increase in theta waves, slowing of EEG and decreasing alpha frequency was obvious in late senescence, after the late 70s or beyond the age of 80 years. A gradual decline in mental functions, demonstrated by psychometric testing during the length of the study, correlated with the slowing of the EEG in late senescence and this also correlated with longevity in this study.

There is a clear need for more major longitudinal studies where cohorts are followed through. Large cohort studies set up 10 years ago are looking at ageing in other functional processes, so unfortunately there is very little information on the age-related effects on psychological or psychiatric measures.

Sex differences, expectations of the subject, non-psychotropic drug use

Sex-related differences have been identified. Elias and Kinsbourne (1974) studied groups of intellectually active, socially advantaged male and female elderly patients (63–77 years) and young subjects (23–33 years), with the objective of exploring age–cohort differences in the processing of verbal and non-verbal stimuli. Within each age group, men performed well on both tasks set, but young women were less proficient non-verbally than verbally and the same result obtained, with a lower level of performance in the group of older women. The authors emphasized that the results of their study should only be applied to a similar cohort of the population. Other investigators have found similar sex-related differences in verbal and non-verbal processing and this should be taken into account.

It is probably the case that some subjects will be more aware of their gradual memory deficit; some will act on this perception and some will not. Personal awareness of a subject of their own performance in memory tests using these long-term stores, is described by Rabbitt and Abson (1991) as 'metamemory'. They have investigated whether 'metamemory' is independent of age-related decline in the short-term and long-term memory processes. 'These results suggest that the accuracy of individuals' assessments of their own abilities does alter with age-related changes in fluid IQ, but probably more radically by age-related changes in self-regard and in life-style' (Rabbitt and Abson, 1991). Two further questions with regard to the operation and efficiency of memory were revealed through examination of data from longitudinal studies on two groups of 3000 individuals in age group 50–96 years (see Rabbitt, Chapter 2). Is loss of memory efficiency independent of or linked to other parameters of human performance such as rate of information acquisition and rate of forgetting, and is the pattern of age-related cognitive change identical across all healthy older people?

Non-cognitive processes such as mood, arousal, activation and existing sub-clinical psychological states will all alter memory and learning and acquisition recall processes. Non-psychotropic drugs are commonly used in elderly people and evidence in the literature suggests that these drugs also produce cognitive changes. Polypharmacy is often a feature of the clinical management of the elderly hospitalized patient. A survey in general practice by Hamdy and Zakaria (1977) revealed that even the fit elderly person able to live at home had on average one illness for which medication was taken on a regular basis. They emphasized that the vast majority of people are able to lead independent lives, free from serious illness. Only 5% of the group aged 65–69 years are unable to go out of doors on their own. The prevalence of disability does increase with age but even so, half of the population aged 85 years and above are able to go out and about without any assistance and over 90% can lead independent lives within their homes.

THE DECISION TO TREAT

Elderly patients are the highest users of prescribed medications of any age group (those over 60 years). They are also generally considered to make frequent purchases of over-the-counter medicines (Petrie, 1983). The complex of benign problems, of their difficulties in remembering some people's names, of recalling only a part of a poem they learned in school, of becoming a little bit disoriented at times, will not necessarily vanish if they are given a diagnosis of AAMI and treated with a pharmacotherapeutic agent designed for such a 'disorder'. Most aspects of growing old can be seen as an age-related disorder if reference is made to young adult performance criteria. The origins of benign senescence are multivariate and not understood. To suggest a 'cure-all' remedy for instant youthfulness of thought processes will not, in the majority of patients, be ever fulfilled. It is even difficult to demonstrate that AAMI as a clinical disorder exists. The clinical problem for elderly patients with profound disturbances of memory remains dementia — and particularly Alzheimer's dementia. To help these patients, the prime focus for clinical and psychotherapeutic research should be to identify the early diagnostic markers and develop successful therapies. Until controlled longitudinal studies have demonstrated an identifiable dysfunction corresponding to AAMI, such impairments as are now reported must be regarded as epiphenomena of the statistical basis for application of AAMI diagnostic criteria.

REFERENCES

Carney, M.W.P., Williams, D.G. and Sheffield, B.F. (1979). Thiamine and pyridoxine lack in newly admitted psychiatric patients. *Br. J. Psychiatry*, **135**, 249–254.

Crook, T., Bartus, R.T., Ferris, S.H., Whitehouse, P., Cohen, G.D. and Gershon, S. (1986). Age-associated memory impairment: proposed diagnostic criteria and measures of clinical change: report of a National Institute of Mental Health work group. *Dev. Neuropsychol.*, **2**, 261–276.

Eisdorfer, C. (1963). The WAIS performance of the aged: a retest evaluation. *J. Gerontol.*, **18**, 169–172.

Elias, M.F. and Kinsbourne, M. (1974). Age and sex differences in the processing of verbal and non-verbal stimuli. *J. Gerontol.*, **29**, 162–171.

Gilleard, C.J. and Pattie, A.H. (1977). The Stockton Geriatric Rating Scale: a shortened version with British normative data, *Br. J. Psychiatry*, **131**, 90–94.

Goodwin, J.S., Goodwin, J.M. and Garry, P.J. (1983). Association between nutritional status and cognitive functioning in a healthy population. *J. Am. Med. Assoc.*, **249**, 2917–2921.

Hamdy, R. and Zakaria, G. (1977). A special clinic for the over 65s in a general practice surgery. *Practitioner*, **219**, 365–375.

Hancock, M.R., Hullin, R.P., Aylard, P.R., King, J.R. and Morgan, D.B. (1985). Nutritional state of elderly women on admission to mental hospital. *Br. J. Psychiatry*, **147**, 404–407.

Holland, C.A. and Rabbitt, P.M. (1991). Ageing memory: use versus impairment. *Br. J. Psychol.*, **82**, 29–38.

Jarvik, L.F., Kallman, F.J. and Falek, A. (1962). Intellectual changes in aged twins. *J. Gerontol.*, **17**, 289–294.

Kilminster, S.G. (1991). Longitudinal data showing no significant age-related trends. In: Hindmarch, I., Hippius, H. and Wilcock, G. (Eds), *Dementia, Molecules, Methods and Measures*, Wiley, New York.

Morris, R.G. and Kopelman, M.D. (1986). The memory deficits in Alzheimer-type dementia: A review. *Q. J. Exp. Psychol.*, **38**, 575–602.

Nakano, T., Miyasaka, M., Ohtaka, T. and Ohmori, K. (1992). Longitudinal changes in computerised EEG and mental function of the aged: A nine-year follow-up study. *Int. Psychogeriatr.*, **4**, 9.

Petrie, W.M. (1983). Drug treatment of anxiety and agitation in the aged. *Psychopharmacol. Bull.*, **19**, 238–246.

Pfeffer, R.I. Kurosaki, T.T., Harrah, C.J.H., Chance, J.M. and Filos, S. (1982). Measurement of functional activities in older adults in the community. *J. Gerontol.*, **37**, 323–329.

Rabbitt, P. and Abson, V. (1991). Do older people know how good they are? *Br. J. Psychol.*, **82**, 137–151.

Reus, V.I. and Miner, C. (1985). Evidence for the physiologic effects of hypercortisolaemia in psychiatric patients. *Psychiatr. Res.*, **14**, 47–56.

Rubin, E.H. and Kinscherf, D.A. (1989). Psychopathology of very mild dementia of the Alzheimer type. *Am. J. Psychiatry*, **146**, 1017–1021.

Rubin, E.H., Morris, J.C., Grant, E.A. and Vendegna, T. (1989). Very mild senile dementia of the Alzheimer type. I. Clinical Assessment. *Arch. Neurol.*, **46**, 379–383.

Siefried, K., Jansen, W. and Pahnke, K. (1984). Cognitive dysfunction in depression. *Drug Dev. Res.*, **4**, 533–553.

Stonier, P.D. (1974). Score changes following repeated administration of mental status questionnaires. *Age Ageing*, **3**, 91–96.

Vallar, G. and Shallice, T. (Eds) (1991). *Neuropsychological Impairments of Short-term Memory*, Cambridge University Press, Cambridge.

Wattis, J.P. and Hindmarch, I. (1988). Measuring effects of psychotropic drugs. In: Wattis, J.P. and Hindmarch, I. (Eds). *Psychological Assessment of the Elderly*. Churchill Livingstone, Edinburgh.

Treatment and Care in Old Age Psychiatry
Edited by R. Levy, R. Howard and A. Burns
©1993 Wrightson Biomedical Publishing Ltd

8

Diagnosis and Treatment of Memory Loss in Older Patients Who Are Not Demented

THOMAS H. CROOK III

Memory Assessment Clinics, Inc., Bethesda, Maryland, USA

In considering the diagnosis of memory impairment in later life, it is helpful to draw parallels with other physiologically based aspects of human performance that may decline with advancing age. For example, in the case of vision it is normal for age-related declines to occur in the amplitude of accommodation with a recession or the nearpoint of focus (i.e. presbyopia) (Kleinstein, 1987). If these changes are not corrected they may seriously affect the ability of the older individual to read and, thus, carry out important tasks of everyday life. When older adults appear for treatment with complaints of difficulty reading it would scarcely occur to the clinician to inform them that their problems are no worse than those of other persons of the same age and, therefore, that they do not merit treatment. Neither is it likely that arguments would be advanced in the academic community that such visual problems are not entirely disabling and, for that reason, do not merit attention and treatment. Of course, a consequence of such arguments would be that only blindness would be treated and, in most cases, treatment would fail.

Arguments against the treatment of normal age-related changes in vision, blood pressure, or bone composition might appear difficult to accept, yet such arguments are readily and strongly advanced in some quarters in the case of memory and related cognitive functions. In general, two principal arguments are advanced against the diagnosis and treatment of normal age-related memory impairment. First, it is argued that such loss should not be treated because it is *too prevalent*, and second, that the functional consequences of normal memory loss are not serious enough to merit attention and treatment. In the following paragraphs, a set of criteria will be outlined

Table 1. Age-Associated Memory Impairment: diagnostic criteria.

(1) Inclusion criteria
   (a) Males and females at least 50 years of age

   (b) Complaints of memory loss reflected in such everyday problems as difficulty remembering names of persons after being introduced, misplacing objects, difficulty remembering multiple items to be purchased or multiple tasks to be performed, problems remembering telephone numbers or mailing codes, and difficulty recalling information quickly or following a distraction. Onset of memory loss must be described as gradual, without sudden worsening in recent months.

   (c) Memory test performance that is at least 1 standard deviation below the mean established for young adults on a standardized test of secondary memory (recent memory) with adequate normative data. Examples of specific tests and appropriate cut-off scores follow, although other measures with adequate normative data are equally appropriate:

   Benton Visual Retention Test (Benton, 1963) (number correct, Administration A)
                                                                              7 or less
   Logical Memory subtest of the Wechsler Memory Scale (WMS) (Wechsler and Stone, 1983)   6 or less
   Associate Learning subtest of the WMS (score on 'hard' associates)   6 or less

   (d) Evidence of adequate intellectual function as determined by a scaled score of at least 9 (raw score of at least 32) on the Vocabulary Subtest of the Wechsler Adult Intelligence Scale (Wechsler, 1955).

   (e) Absence of dementia as determined by a score of 24 or higher on the Mini-Mental State Examination (Folstein *et al.*, 1975). Many investigators have chosen a score of 27 rather than 24 to exclude questionable cases of dementia.

(2) Exclusion criteria
   (a) Evidence of delirium, confusion, or other disturbances of consciousness.

   (b) Any neurologic disorder that could produce cognitive deterioration as determined by history, clinical neurologic examination, and, if indicated, neuroradiologic examination. Such disorders include AD, Parkinson's disease, stroke, intracranial haemorrhage, local brain lesions, including tumors, and normal pressure hydrocephalus.

   (c) History of any infective or inflammatory brain disease, including viral, fungal, and syphilitic.

   (d) Evidence of significant cerebral vascular disease as determined by a Hachinski Ischaemia Score (modified version; Rosen *et al.*, 1980) of 4 or more or by neuroradiologic examination.

   (e) History of repeated minor head injury (as in boxing) or single injury resulting in a period of unconsciousness for 1 hour or more.

   (f) Current psychiatric diagnosis according to DSM-IIIR (American Psychological Association, 1980) criteria of depression, mania, or any major psychiatric disorder.

   (g) Current diagnosis or history of alcoholism or drug dependence.

   (h) Evidence of depression as determined by a Hamilton Depression Rating Scale (Hamilton, 1967) score of 13 or more.

   (i) Any medical disorder that could produce cognitive deterioration, including renal, respiratory, cardiac, and hepatic disease; diabetes mellitus unless well controlled by diet or oral hypoglycaemic agents; endocrine, metabolic, or haematologic disturbances; and malignancy not in remission for more than 2 years. Determination should be based on complete medical history, clinical examination (including electrocardiogram), and appropriate laboratory tests.

   (j) Use of any psychotropic drug or any other drug that may significantly affect cognitive function during the month before psychometric testing.

for operationalizing memory impairment in older persons who are not demented and, then, the dual issues of prevalence and degree of impairment will be considered. Strategies for treating age-related memory impairment will then be reviewed and, finally, consideration will be given to the clinical significance of diagnosing memory impairment in the non-demented elderly patient.

DIAGNOSTIC CRITERIA FOR AGE-ASSOCIATED MEMORY IMPAIRMENT (AAMI)

In 1985, the National Institute of Mental Health (NIMH) in the United States convened a workgroup of experts to develop criteria for operationalizing age-related memory loss that falls within the broad boundaries of normality. The group met on several occasions, adopted the term Age-Associated Memory Impairment (AAMI), and specified a set of operational criteria for the condition (Crook et al., 1986). These criteria are provided in Table 1.

Examination of the table reveals that the inclusion criteria are intended to select persons over 50 who are not demented, who have adequate intellectual function, who complain of gradual memory loss since early adulthood that interferes with important tasks of daily life, and who show objective evidence on performance tests that such loss has occurred. The exclusion criteria are intended to eliminate persons with any condition that might be of aetiologic significance in adult-onset memory impairment. The exclusion criteria are very similar to those employed in the diagnosis of Alzheimer's disease (AD) (e.g. McKhann et al., 1984).

Criticism of the AAMI criteria has ranged from conceptual challenges (Smith et al., 1991), to methodologic criticism of secondary conceptual significance (Blackford and LaRue, 1989), to confused and generally irrelevant commentary (Rosen, 1990). The principal criticism of conceptual significance relates to the inclusion criteria requiring subjects to score at least one standard deviation below the mean established for *young adults* on standardized memory tests. Of course, in attempting to select subjects with objective evidence of memory loss since early adult life, this is an imperfect criterion. The ideal would be to have tested each older individual when he or she was a young adult, so that test performance at that time could be compared with present performance. Obviously, however, test results from early adulthood are almost never available.

Under the AAMI criteria it is assumed that the individual fell within the normal range of performance when he or she was a young adult. Obviously, 16% of persons fell beneath the normal range and 16% above the normal range as young adults. Thus, an individual with superior performance as a young adult might experience significant loss and fail to qualify, while persons with poor performance as young adults may experience no loss and still qualify. This second case may be rare for several reasons, including the following: (1) memory loss occurs in the great majority of persons over the life span and persons with poor initial performance are *more* rather than less likely to experience such loss (Botwinick, 1973); (2) a high percentage of persons with poor initial performance may experience a more generalized intellectual deficit and would, thus, be excluded under criteria requiring adequate intellectual function; (3) an aetiologic factor (e.g. head injury) will be identified in the history of some patients with low initial performance and lead to their exclusion; and (4) poor objective performance alone is not sufficient to qualify for the AAMI diagnosis, the individual must also report significant loss over the life span. Regarding this last point, critics have cited numerous studies (e.g. Kahn *et al.*, 1975) reporting low correlations between memory test performance and ratings of memory abilities. However, in these studies subjects are asked to rate their memory abilities relative to the abilities of others, whereas in the diagnosis of AAMI the individual is asked to judge changes in his or her *own* abilities since early adulthood.

One of the more amusing solutions to the problem of establishing that memory loss has occurred is that each person be tested longitudinally (Rosen, 1990). Such solutions are obviously not provided by clinicians faced with patients who may not wish to endure a diagnostic process requiring several decades. Others have proposed that the criteria simply be tightened by requiring deviation of two rather than one standard deviation from the mean performance of young adults (Blackford and LaRue, 1989). This modification must be considered together with the sensitivity of tests employed in diagnosis to the effects of normal ageing. Traditional memory tests may, in some cases, be so crude that a two standard deviation criteria will select only demented patients. In the case of more sensitive computerized tests of everyday memory abilities (e.g. Crook and West, 1990; Youngjohn *et al.*, 1991) a cut-off score of two standard deviations will select patients who are quite clearly not demented. Indeed, in the original NIMH workgroup considerable discussion took place concerning a one versus two standard deviation criterion. The former cut-off was adopted by the group in order to select a broad group of subjects in whom studies of sub-groups could be undertaken and diverse questions related to age-related memory impairment could be examined empirically. In the past several years, cluster analysis techniques have been employed to identify clinically distinct subgroups of subjects within the AAMI continuum (Larrabee and Crook, 1989a) and these sub-groups have been shown to be differentially responsive to treatment (Crook *et al.*, 1991).

The proposed methodologic modifications discussed above are generally compatible with the AAMI construct. However, another modification proposed by Smith and his colleagues (Smith *et al.*, 1991) would fundamentally alter the construct. This proposal calls for a diagnostic entity similar to that proposed by Kral three decades ago (Benign Senescent Forgetfulness; Kral, 1962, 1966) in which the reference group with whom the older individual is compared is composed of *other older persons*. Thus, the construct does not describe normal, age-related memory impairment and, indeed, specifically excludes persons who do not show memory loss beyond that expected in the course of normal ageing. By contrast, AAMI criteria describe the full range of persons who have experienced memory loss that lies within the boundaries of normality, including those who deviate from age-adjusted norms and may be on the borderline of dementia. To return to the vision analogy, the critical issue is functional problems in everyday life that arise, not as a result of deviation from age-adjusted norms, but as a result of deviation from the range of optimal performance.

PREVALENCE OF AAMI AND THE INTERESTING ARGUMENT THAT HIGH PREVALENCE ARGUES AGAINST RECOGNITION AND TREATMENT OF A PHENOMENON

Elsewhere in this volume Hindmarch (Chapter 7) advances the argument that AAMI merits neither attention nor treatment because it is *too* prevalent. The logic behind this curious argument is not provided, but an inevitable consequence is that many disorders of later life should be neither acknowledged nor treated. For example, Fig. 1 illustrates the relationship between age and the distance at which printed letters can be seen clearly without corrective lenses (Cline *et al.*, 1980). The clinical significance of this relationship is that presbyopia is a nearly universal condition after age 50 (Kleinstein, 1987), nevertheless, it is certainly accepted as a condition that merits treatment.

Similarly, as seen in Fig. 2, the relationship between age and performance on selected tests of memory and other cognitive functions yields a relationship that is generally similar to that seen with vision (Wechsler, 1955). Again, one must ask how this relationship argues against treatment of age-related cognitive disorders.

The prevalence of AAMI may be considered independent of the issue of treatment and, fortunately, empirical data have been published on the issue. Reported prevalence rates for AAMI have varied considerably and this may be due to investigators applying only partial criteria, for example omitting subjective reports and all exclusion criteria, and to calculation of rates within cohorts of widely varying age distributions. In two published studies, complete diagnostic criteria were applied to random samples of community dwelling elderly persons. Lane and Snowdon (1989) examined a random

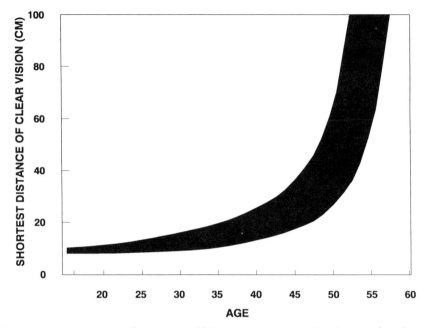

Figure 1. The shortest distance at which targets are seen clearly, as a function of observer's age.

sample of 146 elderly Australian subjects with a mean age of 73.6 years and reported the AAMI prevalence rate as 34.9%. In the second study, Reinikainen and his colleagues (1990) examined a random sample of 387 elderly Finnish subjects with a mean age of 71.3 years and reported a prevalence rate of 55.8%.

The upper limits of AAMI prevalence based on the use of traditional memory tests have been examined by Larrabee and Crook (1993). Normative data were examined from a broad range of memory tests, including standard measures such as the Wechsler Memory Scale (Wechsler and Stone, 1983) and Benton Visual Retention Test (Benton, 1963), and newer clinical measures shown to be highly sensitive to the effects of age, e.g. Verbal Selective Reminding (Larrabee *et al.*, 1988), and The Rey Auditory Verbal Learning Test (Ivnik *et al.*, 1990). Raw scores were calculated for each test corresponding to one standard deviation below the mean obtained by 17–29 year old subjects, z scores corresponding to the raw score were calculated for each successive age cohort, and the average z score for each age cohort was pooled across tests. Results are shown graphically in Fig. 3. Figures corresponding to the graph are 45% for persons 50–59 years, 55% for persons 60–69 years, 71% for persons 70–79 years, and 86% for persons over

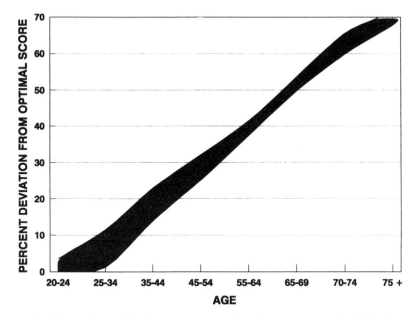

Figure 2. The relationship between age and performance on the Digit Symbol Substitution subtest of the Wechsler Adult Intelligence Scale.

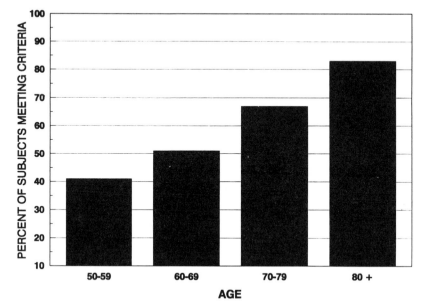

Figure 3. Upper limits of AAMI prevalence — percentage of older subjects at different decades meeting AAMI performance criteria only — no other inclusion or exclusion criterion are applied.

80 years of age. These figures point out the expected clear gain in prevalence with age. Of course AAMI prevalence would be expected to fall substantially below these figures when subjective report is considered, demented and intellectually compromized patients are excluded, and all medical and psychiatric exclusion criteria are applied.

Thus, memory loss, like presbyopia, influences a large portion of the older adult population and the prevalence increases markedly decade by decade.

IS THE MAGNITUDE OF THE MEMORY DEFICIT IN AAMI SUFFICIENT TO MERIT ATTENTION AND TREATMENT?

Data shown in Figure 2 illustrate the magnitude of the cognitive deficit seen with advancing age. The test used in that case is somewhat artificial in that stimuli are abstract and rapid psychomotor response is required. Results from tests that are closely related to memory tasks of everyday life show similar patterns, however, and suggest the ability to learn and remember new information may decline by 50% or more between the ages of 25 and 75 years among healthy persons without neurologic impairment (Crook and West, 1990). Figure 4 illustrates changes with age in the ability to remember the names of persons to whom one is introduced. In this case the sample is composed of 2549 persons of superior education and intellectual function selected primarily from university communities in the United States (Crook and West, 1990). Among these subjects West and her colleagues (West *et al.*, 1992) have examined individual difference variables and shown that age is consistently the most significant predictor or memory performance across many diverse measures of everyday memory performance in addition to name-face recall. Figure 5 represents data from the same test administered in a random sample of the normal population of the Republic of San Marino (Crook *et al.*, 1993). In the latter case the magnitude of the deficit seen in normal ageing is significantly greater than that seen in the select population studied in the United States. Similar results have been reported using the same test in other cultures as well (Crook *et al.*, 1992d).

It is clear that the ability to deal with critical memory tasks in daily life changes differentially with age, depending upon the nature of the task, but across a wide variety of important everyday memory tests, striking declines are seen with advancing age (Youngjohn *et al.*, 1991; West and Crook, 1990; Crook *et al.*, 1990). These changes can be clearly distinguished from those associated with AD (Youngjohn *et al.*, 1992), but they are nevertheless striking in their magnitude and highly troublesome to many older persons.

The critical questions related to the magnitude of the deficit seen in AAMI are as follows: 'If a cognitive deficit of 50% or more were seen in a young adult, would it merit attention and treatment?' and, if so, 'Why would a

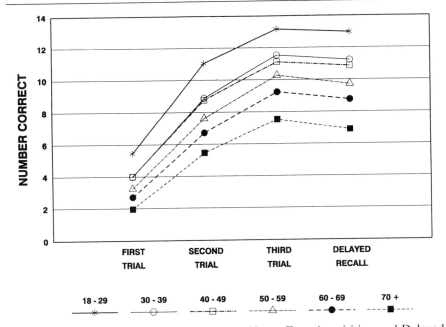

Figure 4. Differences among age groups on Name–Face Acquisition and Delayed Recall — high education US sample.

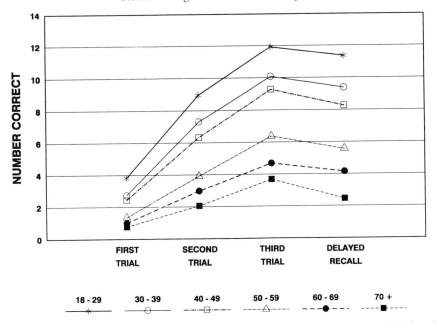

Figure 5. Differences among age groups on Name–Face Acquisition and Delayed Recall — random sample of the Republic of San Marino.

deficit of the same magnitude not merit attention and treatment in an older adult?'. These are questions that persons who argue against the treatment of normal age-related memory loss may wish to address.

CAN AAMI BE TREATED?

The process of specifying criteria for age-related memory loss would amount to little more than an exercise in labelling victims of an inexorable process if treatment were not possible. Of course the analogy between visual and cognitive changes with age has been employed, in part, because corrective lenses are available for 'treating' most age-related deficits. The question regarding memory is whether effective means can be found to mitigate or reverse the loss. In addressing the question, both pharmacological and non-somatic treatments will be considered.

Although a number of drugs have been tested in AAMI, AD, and other late-life cognitive disorders (Crook, 1989), at the present time none of these drugs has been demonstrated to be effective (McEntee and Crook, 1989). Neurochemical deficits underlying AAMI have been identified (McEntee and Crook, 1990, 1991, 1992) and, in general, these are the same deficits that underlie AD (Gottfries, 1985). Thus, drugs found effective for treating AAMI may also be effective in altering the onset or early course of AD. Of course, they may not be effective after the disease has progressed and substantial neuronal damage has occurred.

In considering the treatment of AAMI, it is of major significance that compounds affecting one or more of the neurochemical deficits associated with AAMI have repeatedly been shown to reverse or mitigate age-related memory deficits in healthy aged animals (Bartus et al., 1987). However, despite the sound theoretical basis for treatment and encouraging results from animal studies, results of a number of early clinical trials were negative. For example, noradrenergic function appears to be compromised in AAMI (McEntee and Crook, 1990) and studies of α_2-agonists such as clonidine and guanfacine have been shown to mitigate or reverse age-related memory deficits in non-human primates (Arnsten and Goldman-Rakic, 1985; Arnsten et al., 1988). Nevertheless, results of carefully controlled trials of guanfacine in both AAMI (McEntee et al., 1991) and early AD (Crook et al., 1992c) were unequivocally negative. Similarly negative effects have been reported in AAMI with a number of compounds, ranging from angiotensin-converting enzyme (ACE) inhibitors to widely used nootropic agents (e.g. Sudilovsky et al., 1988).

Against this background of disappointing clinical findings in AAMI (and in AD), are positive findings from two recent studies. The first (Crook et al., 1991) reported positive effects of a formulation of phosphatidylserine (PS)

Table 2. Significant differences between phosphatidylserine (PS) and placebo in relatively impaired AAMI subjects.

Variable	Week	PS	Placebo	F	Significance	Favours	Treatment by clinic interaction
Name–Face	3	8.36	6.41	8.14	0.01	PS	No
acquisition	6	8.51	6.98	4.47	0.04	PS	No
	9	9.69	7.87	7.75	0.01	PS	No
Name–Face	3	7.17	5.89	3.91	0.05	PS	No
delayed recall	12	8.84	7.58	4.59	0.04	PS	No
Facial	3	12.37	9.32	5.22	0.03	PS	No
recognition	6	12.20	9.38	5.50	0.02	PS	No
	12	13.06	9.68	5.43	0.02	PS	No
	16	13.29	9.60	7.38	0.01	PS	No
Telephone	12	4.23	3.48	3.38	0.07	PS	No
number recall	16	4.54	3.44	8.92	0.00	PS	No
Misplaced	6	14.60	12.53	9.29	0.00	PS	No
objects recall	16	15.38	13.45	5.30	0.03	PS	No

in 149 AAMI patients and, particularly, in a sub-group of relatively impaired AAMI patients. These relatively impaired patients were subjects who would meet the two standard deviation from the memory performance mean of young subjects. Table 2 illustrates the effects of PS among such patients on a computerized battery of everyday memory tests (Crook *et al.*, 1990a; Larrabee and Crook, 1991). Effects were also seen among these patients on a standard neuropsychological memory test and on global clinical improvement ratings. It is of interest that in a second study, positive effects of the compound were also reported among patients in the early stages of AD (Crook *et al.*, 1992b).

A positive study with another compound was undertaken to test the hypothesis that serotonin is implicated in AAMI (and AD) and that $5HT_3$ antagonists may be of therapeutic value in the condition (McEntee and Crook, 1991). In testing this approach the compound ondansetron was administered to 232 patients who met the criteria for AAMI (Crook and Lakin, 1991). Patients were randomly assigned to three doses of the drug or to placebo and treated double-blind for 12 weeks. The same computerized test battery used to assess efficacy with PS was employed. Results

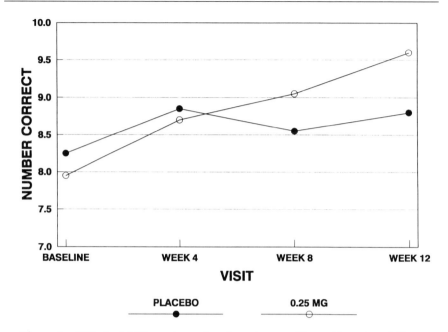

Figure 6. Effect of 0.25 mg dose of ondansetron on Name–Face Acquisition.

of the study indicated that ondansetron may improve cognitive performance in AAMI and that drug effects appear to be dose-related. Effects
of a 0.25 mg dose of ondansetron on name-face acquisition (Crook and
West, 1990) are illustrated in Fig. 6. The test is the same in which data
related to changes in performance with age are provided in Figs 4 and 5.
In general, then, at least limited and preliminary clinical evidence exists
to suggest that the symptoms of AAMI may be responsive to pharmacological treatment.

Evidence that non-somatic techniques may improve function in AAMI is
better developed than is that related to pharmacological treatment. Yesavage
(1985) and West and her colleagues (West, 1989; West and Crook, 1991) have
demonstrated that performance in such everyday memory tasks as name-face
association and narrative recall can be improved significantly through
mnemonic training.

If effective drugs are eventually developed for AAMI, clinicians and
patients may have options now available in other central nervous system
disorders such as anxiety and depression. That is, for some patients non-
somatic therapies may be the treatment of choice and in other cases pharmacotherapy may be indicated.

THE DIAGNOSIS OF AAMI FROM THE PATIENT'S PERSPECTIVE: THE BAD AND GOOD NEWS

The bad news communicated to a patient in his sixties or seventies by a diagnosis of AAMI is that he, like most other persons his age, has experienced changes in the ability to learn and remember certain types of information. He will not be as able as when he was 25 to learn and remember large amounts of new information and this will be particularly apparent under conditions where the task is complex, there is limited time for learning and recall, and multiple tasks must be performed simultaneously (Larrabee and Crook, 1989b). This bad news comes as little surprise to most older adults (Crook *et al.*, 1992a).

The good news consists of at least three components. First, many patients seen for memory evaluation come with the fear, expressed or not, of Alzheimer's disease (Larrabee *et al.*, 1990). It is not unusual, particularly in the United States, to see patients who have been exposed to the myth that learning and memory do not decline with age and, at the same time, know that Alzheimer's disease is a dehumanizing, tragic disorder marked by forgetfulness that may at first appear benign. Having heard these two messages and recognized that his memory is not what it once was, it is not a great logical leap for the patient to conclude that he may have Alzheimer's disease.

Such patients may be reassured that, although AD is a tragic disorder, it is a rare disorder, until quite late in life. For example, the prevalence of AD between age 65 and 75 is probably in the order of 1–2% (Rocca *et al.*, 1986). By contrast, as shown previously, most persons in this age group will meet the psychometric criteria for AAMI. Thus, a critical message is that difficulty in remembering names, remembering what one just read, or misplacing one's eyeglasses are quite unlikely to be the first signs of a dementing disorder that will lead in the course of a few months or years to total disability. Rather, AAMI is a stable condition in which gradual changes occur over years and decades and these changes are not comparable in magnitude to those seen in AD (Youngjohn *et al.*, 1992; Youngjohn and Crook, 1993).

The second component of the good news is that, although aspects of learning and memory do decline with advancing age, many of the most important intellectual abilities do not (Botwinick, 1973). Indeed, verbal intellectual abilities and analytical abilities which may be grouped under the construct of 'wisdom' often continue to improve until quite late in life (Botwinick, 1973).

Finally, as discussed previously, many of the symptoms of AAMI are responsive to non-somatic treatments. Although the older individual may have to exert greater effort and learn specific techniques, there is no reason why a 75 year old man cannot function as well as a 25 year old man in such important everyday memory tasks as remembering names.

Obviously, age-related deficits in the most demanding and complex learning and memory tasks may not be offset by such efforts, but in the case of most everyday memory tasks mnemonic training techniques may work quite well. Beyond these non-somatic approaches to the treatment of AAMI may lie pharmacological treatments, the first generation of which is now under evaluation.

SUMMARY

The later decades of adult life were once a time when loss of physical and mental capacities was simply accepted as inevitable. Increasingly, however, loss of function is recognized and treated as vigorously in the aged as in young adults. 'Normal' age-related visual cardiovascular, musculoskeletal, or other deficits are now treated as a matter of routine and the development of effective pharmacological treatments will allow physicians to treat age-related cognitive deficits in the same manner. O'Brien and Levy (1992) have argued that the time has not yet arrived to undertake the search for pharmacological treatments for AAMI, while others (Crook and Ferris, 1992) have taken a more positive stance. This is an honest debate undertaken from different philosophical perspectives, but whatever the outcome of this debate, problems posed by memory loss in non-demented elderly persons will not be solved by denying they exist and effective treatments will not be found if they are not sought.

REFERENCES

American Psychiatric Association (1980). *Diagnostic and Statistical Manual of Mental Disorders, 3rd edn*, American Psychiatric Association, Washington, DC.
Arnsten, A.F.T. and Goldman-Rakic, P.S. (1985). Alpha-2 adrenergic mechanisms in prefrontal cortex associated with cognitive decline in aged nonhuman primates. *Science*, **230**, 1273–1276.
Arnsten, A.F.T., Cai, J.X. and Goldman-Rakic, P.S. (1988). The alpha-2 adrenergic agonist guanfacine improves memory in aged monkeys without sedative or hypotensive side effects: Evidence for alpha-2 subtypes. *J. Neurosci.*, **8**, 4287–4298.
Bartus, R.T., Crook, T.H. and Dean, R.L. (1987). Current progress in treating age-related memory problems: A perspective from animal preclinical and human clinical research. In: Wood, W.G. (Ed.), *Geriatric Clinical Pharmacology and the Aging Individual*, Raven Press, New York.
Benton, A.L. (1963). *The Revised Visual Retention Test: Clinical and Experimental Applications*, Psychological Corporation, New York.
Blackford, R.C. and LaRue, A. (1989). Criteria for diagnosing Age-Associated Memory Impairment: Proposed improvements from the field. *Dev. Neuropsychol.*, **5**, 295–306.
Botwinick, J. (Ed.) (1973). *Aging and Behavior*, Springer, New York, p. 192.

Cline, D., Hoffstetter, H.W. and Griffin, J.R. (1980). *Dictionary of Visual Science (3rd edn)*, Chilton, Radnor, Pennsylvania.

Crook, T.H. (1989). Diagnosis and treatment of normal and pathologic memory impairment in later life. *Semin. Neurol.*, **9**, 20–30.

Crook, T.H. and Ferris, S.H. (1992). Age-Associated Memory Impairment. *Br. Med. J.*, **304**, 714.

Crook, T.H. and Lakin, M. (1991). Effects of ondansetron in Age-Associated Memory Impairment. In: Racagni, G. *et al.* (Eds), *Biological Psychiatry, Vol. 2.* Elsevier Science Publishers, Amsterdam, pp. 888–890.

Crook, T.H. and West, R.L. (1990). Name recall performance across the adult life span. *Br. J. Psychol.*, **81**, 335–349.

Crook, T.H., Bartus, R.T., Ferris, S.H., Whitehouse, P., Cohen, G.D. and Gershon, S. (1986). Age-Associated Memory Impairment: Proposed diagnostic criteria and measures of clinical change — Report of a National Institute of Mental Health Work Group. *Dev. Neuropsychol.*, **2**, 261–276.

Crook, T.H., Johnson, B.A. and Larrabee, G.J. (1990a). Evaluation of drugs in Alzheimer's disease and Age-Associated Memory Impairment. In: Benkert, O., Maier, W. and Rickels, K. (Eds), *Methodology of the Evaluation of Psychotropic Drugs.* Springer-Verlag, Berlin-Heidelberg, pp. 37–55.

Crook, T.H., Youngjohn, J.R. and Larrabee, G.J. (1990b). Misplaced Objects Test: A measure of everyday visual memory. *J. Clin. Exp. Neuropsychol.*, **12**, 808–822.

Crook, T.H., Tinklenberg, J., Yesavage, J., Petrie, W., Nunzi, M.G. and Massari, D. (1991). Effects of phosphatidylserine in Age-Associated Memory Impairment. *Neurology*, **41**, 644–649.

Crook, T.H., Feher, E.P. and Larrabee, G.J. (1992a). Assessment of memory complaint in Age-Associated Memory Impairment: The MAC-Q. *Int. Psychogeriatr.*, **4**.

Crook, T.H., Petrie, W., Wells, C. and Massari, D.C. (1992b). Effects of phosphatidylserine in Alzheimer's disease. *Psychopharmacol. Bull.*, **28**, 61–66.

Crook, T.H., Wilner, E., Rothwell, A., Winterling, D. and McEntee, W. (1992c). Noradrenergic intervention in Alzheimer's disease. *Psychopharmacol. Bull.*, **28**, 76–80.

Crook, T.H., Youngjohn, J.R., Larrabee, G.J. and Salama, M. (1992d). Aging and everyday memory: A cross-cultural study. *Neuropsychology* **6**, 123–136.

Crook, T.H., Zappala, G., Cavarzeran, F., Measso, G., Pirozzolo, F. and Massari, D. (1993). Recalling Names after Introduction: Changes across the adult life-span in two cultures. *Dev. Neuropsychol.*, in press.

Folstein, M.D., Folstein, S.E. and McHugh, P.R. (1975). 'Mini-Mental State': A practical method for grading the cognitive state of patients for the clinician. *J. Psychiatr. Res.*, **12**, 189–198.

Gottfries, C.G. (1985). Alzheimer's disease and senile dementia: Biochemical characteristics and aspects of treatment. *Psychopharmacology*, **86**, 245–252.

Hamilton, M. (1967). Development of a rating scale for primary depressive illness. *Br. J. Soc. Clin. Psychol.*, **6**, 278–296.

Ivnik, R.J., Malec, J.F., Tangalos, E.G., Petersen, R.C., Kokmen, E. and Kurland, L.T. (1990). The Auditory Verbal Learning Test (AVLT): Norms for age 55 and above. *Psychol. Assess. J. Consult. Clin. Psychol.*, **2**, 304–312.

Kahn, R.L., Zarit, S.H., Hilbert, N.M. and Niederehe, G. (1975). Memory complaint and impairment in the aged: The effect of depression and altered brain function. *Arch. Gen. Psychiatry*, **32**, 1569–1573.

Kleinstein, R.N. (1987). Epidemiology of presbyopia. In: Stark, L. and Obrecht, G.

(Eds), *Presbyopia: Recent Research and Reviews from the Third International Symposium*, Fairchild Publications, New York, pp. 12–18.

Kral, V.A. (1962). Senescent forgetfulness: Benign and malignant. *J. Can. Med. Assoc.*, **86**, 257–260.

Kral, V.A. (1966). Memory loss in the aged. *Dis. Nerv. Syst.*, **27** (Suppl. 1), 51–54.

Lane, F. and Snowdon, J. (1989). Memory and dementia: A longitudinal survey of suburban elderly. In: Lovibond, P. and Wilson, P. (Eds), *Clinical and Abnormal Psychology*, Elsevier, Amsterdam, pp. 365–376.

Larrabee, G.J. and Crook, T.H. (1989a). Performance subtypes of everyday memory function. *Dev. Neuropsychol.*, **5**, 267–283.

Larrabee, G.J. and Crook, T.H. (1989b). Dimensions of everyday memory in Age-Associated Memory Impairment. *Psychol. Assess.*, **4**, 54–59.

Larrabee, G.J. and Crook, T.H. (1991). Computerized memory testing in clinical trials. In: Mohr, E. and Brouwers, P. (Eds), *Handbook of Clinical Trials: Neurobehavioral Approach*, Swets & Zeitlinger, Amsterdam, pp. 293–306.

Larrabee, G.J. and Crook, T.H. (1993). Estimated prevalence of Age-Associated Memory Impairment (AAMI) derived from standardized test of memory function. *Psychol. Aging*, in press.

Larrabee, G.J., Trahan, D.E., Curtiss, G. and Levin, H.S. (1988). Normative data for the Verbal Selective Reminding Test. *Neuropsychology*, **2**, 173–182.

Larrabee, G.J., Pathy, M.S.J., Bayer, A.J. and Crook, T.H. (1990). Memory assessment clinics: State of development and future prospects. In: Bergener, M. and Finkel, S.I. (Eds), *Clinical and Scientific Psychogeriatrics, Vol. 2: The Interface of Psychiatry and Neurology*, Springer, New York, pp. 83–97.

McEntee, W.J. and Crook, T.H. (1989). Pharmacological treatments of age-related cognitive loss. *Curr. Opin. Psychiatry*, **2**, 543–547.

McEntee, W.J. and Crook, T.H. (1990). Age-Associated Memory Impairment: A role for catecholamines. *Neurology*, **40**, 526–530.

McEntee, W.J. and Crook, T.H. (1991). Serotonin, memory, and the aging brain. *Psychopharmacology*, **103**, 143–149.

McEntee, W.J. and Crook, T.H. (1992). Cholinergic function in the aged brain: Implications for treatment of memory impairments associated with aging. *Behav. Pharmacol.*, **3**, 327–336.

McEntee, W.J., Crook, T.H., Jenkyn, L.R., Petrie, W., Larrabee, G.J. and Coffey, D.J. (1991). Treatment of Age-Associated Memory Impairment with guanfacine. *Psychopharmacol. Bull.*, **27**, 41–46.

McKhann, G., Drachman, D., Folstein, M., Katzman, R., Price, D. and Stadlan, E.M. (1984). Clinical diagnosis of Alzheimer's disease: Report of the NINCDS-ADRDA work group under the auspices of Department of Health and Human Services Task Force on Alzheimer's Disease. *Neurology*, **34**, 939–944.

O'Brien, J.T. and Levy, R. (1992). Age-Associated Memory Impairment. Editorial, January 4. *Br. Med. J.*, **304**, 5–6.

Reinikainen, K.J., Koivisto, K., Mykkanen, L., Hanninen, T., Laakso, M., Pyorala, K. and Riekkinen, P. (1990). Age-Associated Memory Impairment in aged population: An epidemiologic study. *Neurology*, **40** (Suppl. 1), 177.

Rocca, W.A., Amaducci, L.A. and Schoenberg, B.S. (1986). Epidemiology of clinically diagnosed Alzheimer's disease. *Ann. Neurol.*, **19**, 415–424.

Rosen, T.J. (1990). Age-Associated Memory Impairment: A critique. *Eur. J. Cog. Neuropsychol.*, **2**, 275–287.

Rosen, W.G., Terry, R.D., Fuld, P.A., Katzman, R. and Peck, A. (1980). Pathological verification of ischemic score in differentiation of dementias. *Ann. Neurol.*, **7**, 486–488.

Smith, G., Ivnik, R.J., Petersen, R.C., Malec, J.F., Kokmen, E. and Tangalos, E. (1991). Age-Associated Memory Impairment Diagnoses: Problems of reliability, concerns for terminology. *Psychol. Aging*, **6**, 551–558.

Sudilovsky, A., Turnbull, B., Croog, S.H. and Crook, T.H. (1988). Angiotensin converting enzyme and memory: Preclinical and clinical data. *Int. J. Neurol.*, **22**, 145–162.

Wechsler, D. (1955). *Manual: Wechsler Adult Intelligence Scale*. Psychological Corporation, New York.

Wechsler, D. and Stone, C.P. (1983). *Manual: Wechsler Memory Scale*. Psychological Corporation, New York.

West, R.L. (1989). Planning practical memory training for the aged. In: Poon, L.W., Rubin, D.C. and Wilson, B.C. (Eds), *Everyday Cognition in Adulthood and Late Life*. Cambridge University Press, Cambridge, pp. 573–597.

West, R.L. and Crook, T.H. (1990). Age differences in everyday memory: Laboratory analogues of telephone number recall. *Psychol. Aging*, **5**, 520–529.

West, R.L. and Crook, T.H. (1991). Video training of imagery for mature adults. *Appl. Cogn. Psychol.*, **6**, 307–320.

West, R.L., Crook, T.H. and Barron, K.L. (1992). Everyday memory performance across the life span: The effects of age and noncognitive individual differences. *Psychol. Aging*, **7**, 72–82.

Yesavage, J.A. (1985). Nonpharmacologic treatment for memory losses with normal aging. *Am. J. Psychiatry*, **142**, 600–605.

Youngjohn, J.R. and Crook, T.H. (1993). The Stability of everyday memory in Age-Associated Memory Impairment: A longitudinal study. *Neuropsychology*, in press.

Youngjohn, J.R., Larrabee, G.J. and Crook, T.H. (1991). First-last names and the grocery list selective reminding tests: Two computerized measures of everyday verbal learning. *Arch. Clin. Neuropsychol.*, **6**, 287–300.

Youngjohn, J.R., Larrabee, G.J. and Crook, T.H. (1992). Discriminating Age-Associated Memory Impairment from Alzheimer's disease. *Psychol. Assess.*, **4**, 54–59.

Treatment and Care in Old Age Psychiatry
Edited by R. Levy, R. Howard and A. Burns
©1993 Wrightson Biomedical Publishing Ltd

9

Ability of the 5HT$_3$ Receptor Antagonists to Improve Memory Impairments

B. COSTALL, A.M. DOMENEY, M.E. KELLY and R.J. NAYLOR

Postgraduate Studies in Pharmacology, University of Bradford, UK

INTRODUCTION

The cholinergic hypothesis underpinning past and present concepts of the underlying mechanisms involved with memory impairments is a major stimulus to the development of new preclinical tests and chemicals to detect agents which may ameliorate the symptoms of dementia (Bartus *et al.*, 1982; Candy *et al.*, 1986; Kensner *et al.*, 1987; Sahakian, 1988). Whilst it is logical in a situation of cholinergic deficit to develop cholinomimetic drugs, this approach has proven to be disappointing since it has been difficult or impossible to separate out the central and peripheral actions of such compounds. This does not mean that cholinergic agonists do not have any efficacy in the dementias, indeed, there is evidence that they do (Bartus *et al.*, 1982; Heise, 1987), and such compounds are certainly effective in animal tests based on the production of memory deficits by cholinergic disruption: the problem in all situations is the unacceptable level of peripheral autonomic side effects (Bartus *et al.*, 1982; Heise, 1987) which particularly afflict the elderly who are noted for their increased sensitivity to a wide variety of centrally-acting compounds. It is particularly pertinent to the present chapter that a cholinomimetic such as arecoline can be used to ameliorate the memory impairment in animal tests which relate to cholinergic deficits, for example as induced by use of scopolamine or as a consequence of lesioning of the cell body area of the mesocortical/cortical acetylcholine system at the level of the nucleus basalis magnocellularis (Salamone *et al.*, 1987). The technique which has been employed in animals to avoid the side effects of bolus drug injections has been slow and persistent delivery of drug, 24 hours per day by a systemic route. This approach minimizes the side effects of a cholinomimetic and has shown their efficacy in mouse, rat and primate tests of memory impairment, in particular, in an habituation test, a T-maze task and by use of a Morris water maze (e.g. see Costall *et al.*, 1989c).

It is relevant to consideration of the cholinergic basis for the dementias or memory impairments that these can, in several of the test situations, be linked with a loss of choline acetyltransferase (ChAT) in the key cortical areas. Such losses also occur in aged animals which perform as poorly in the battery of test procedures used to indicate memory impairments as animals subject say, to lesions of the nucleus basalis. The aged animals are equally responsive to treatment with cholinomimetic agents, but their side effect propensity is exaggerated and the use of such compounds is difficult in the extreme.

Whilst a range of mouse, rat and primate tests, which will be described subsequently, have shown a sensitivity to cholinomimetic agents, which helped to validate their status as predictive models for man, they have consistently failed to show any efficacy for the so-called nootropic agents which include the calcium antagonists, dilantin, vasodilators, piracetam-type drugs and hydergine. It is difficult to find any evidence that such nootropic compounds are of any value in memory disorders in man, and it would be difficult to explain any efficacy for these compounds in the animal tests if they are indeed based on parameters which extrapolate to the human dementias.

Against this background of failure to advance adequate treatments for memory disorders, attention has turned in recent years to ways of influencing deficit cholinergic systems more indirectly, in particular, to facilitate the function of cholinergic neurones which have a reduced or minimized activity. The concept has been one of neuromodulation, and the search has been for compounds which will enhance a reduced cholinergic function via neurotransmitter mechanisms which may be thought to interact with acetylcholine. Whilst several neurotransmitters have a close functional relationship with acetylcholine in several brain areas, the one which has been repeatedly identified for its important role in the control of cognitive function is 5-hydroxytryptamine (5HT). There is considerable evidence that acetylcholine release is under an inhibitory 5HT tone: systemically administered 5HT agonists increase striatal acetylcholine levels and reduce acetylcholine release, and acetylcholine release is enhanced in the striatum, cortex and hippocampus by 5HT cell destruction or synthesis inhibition (Euvrard *et al.*, 1978; Gillett *et al.*, 1985; Jackson *et al.*, 1988; Robinson, 1983; Vizi *et al.*, 1981). Fibiger *et al.* (1978) concluded that the inhibitory effect of a 5HT input on hippocampal cholinergic activity may be relevant to memory.

The links between acetylcholine and 5HT have, therefore, existed for many years, but it was only with the advent of drugs which selectively influenced

5HT receptor subtypes that advances in the treatment of memory impairments have occurred. Agents are now available which selectively influence the $5HT_{1A}$, $5HT_2$ and $5HT_3$ sites (more recently, selective agents for a $5HT_4$ recognition site have been profiled). Generally the $5HT_{1A}$ and $5HT_2$ ligands are without effect on memory, although a new series of compounds which influence the $5HT_{1A}$ site, prototyped by lesopitron (Costall *et al.*, 1992), appear to be efficacious. Nevertheless, emphasis has been placed on the action of antagonists at the $5HT_3$ receptor, and agents such as ondansetron, zacopride, tropisetron and granisetron have been fully analysed for their potential to inhibit memory impairments. Indeed, as will be discussed, the preclinical efficacy of agents such as ondansetron has led to testing in man, both in age-related disorders and in the dementias. It would be naïve to dismiss, at this stage, any action for the $5HT_4$ receptor ligands on cognition since the emergence of selective compounds is relatively recent (Bockaert *et al.*, 1991; Craig and Clarke, 1990) and the complexity of actions of agonist, partial agonist and antagonist drugs are still being investigated, in cognition as well as in other psychological states. The intention of this chapter, therefore, is to collate the evidence that $5HT_3$ receptor antagonists may have a valuable role to play in the inhibition of memory impairments, including those associated with old age.

USE OF THE MOUSE HABITUATION TEST

Many complex procedures have been used to measure the memory capacity of the mouse, and the consequences of interventions to cause impairment. In our laboratories we developed a simple test using a two-compartment black and white box (see Barnes *et al.*, 1990a) in which the mouse is initially placed in the white compartment which is brightly-lit and aversive. In this compartment mice are open to predatory attack and normal behaviours in such an arena are suppressed. The normal behaviour of a mouse is to move around the perimeter of the white compartment until it locates a door interconnecting with the black compartment. After a few head movements in and out of the black compartment from the doorway, a mouse makes a decision to move into the less aversive black compartment where it then expresses a normal behaviour repertoire, rearing and moving about all parts of the floor area. On the first day of test a mouse will normally be delayed in its movement from the white to the black compartment by some 10–14 s. On repeated exposure, the mouse 'learns' to locate the opening from the white to the black compartment and will traverse the central area of the white compartment to pass most rapidly into the black area. The latency of this initial move can be reduced to 1 s or less by the fourth day of testing. The procedure is extremely robust and reproducible and can be used to show the deficits associated with old-age, scopolamine treatment or lesioning of the nucleus basalis magnocellularis.

The experimental procedure is to use male albino BKW mice which are young adult (6–8 weeks old and weighing 25–35 g) or aged (8–10 months and weighing 35–42 g). The mice are normally housed in groups of 10 with free access to food and water, on a 12 hour light/dark cycle with lights off at 07.00 h.

The studies have investigated three types of impairment in habituation behaviour. First, that associated with old age. Secondly, that induced in young adult mice using scopolamine (0.25 mg/kg s.c. b.d., a dose carefully selected as the maximum to impair memory without overt effect on the autonomic nervous system, in particular, no effect on pupil diameter and hence vision to perform the test) and, thirdly, that induced by lesion of the nucleus basalis magnocellularis of young adult mice. In order to induce such lesions mice were anaesthetized with chloral hydrate (150 mg/kg i.p.) and placed in a Kopf stereotaxic frame. Electrolesions of the nucleus basalis magnocellularis were induced at Ant. 2.3 mm (relative to the zero of the Kopf frame), Vert. 4.5 mm (below the skull surface) and Lat. ±2.1 mm from the midline. The electrode employed was constructed from 0.3 mm external diameter stainless steel tubing which was insulated except at the tip to which a current of 1 mA was delivered for a 10 s period. On completion of the experiments the correct location of the lesion was confirmed both histologically and biochemically. The biochemical tests showed that the lesions reduced levels of ChAT selectively in the frontal cortex by 34–57%. Other experiments have utilized ibotenic acid lesions of the nucleus basalis: these lesions have been equally accurate in location and effect. Indeed, the behavioural consequences of electrolesions and ibotenic acid lesions of the nucleus basalis, as regards cognitive performance, differ so little that data are only presented for the electrolesions. It is emphasized that the data presented are representative of a vast amount of data all confirming the consequence of nucleus basalis lesions to impair memory in the mouse habituation test.

The habituation test was carried out daily between 08.30 and 12.30 h. Mice were taken from a dark home environment in a dark container to the experimental room which was maintained in low red lighting. For test, mice were placed individually at the centre of the white section of a white and black test box (45 × 27 × 27 cm high, with 40% of the area painted black and illuminated under a red light, 1 × 60 W, 0 Lux, and the other painted white and brightly illuminated with a white light, 1 × 60 W, 400 Lux, located 17 cm above the box). Access between the two areas was enabled by a 7.5 × 7.5 cm opening located at the floor level of the central partition. Behaviour was assessed via remote video-recording and the latency of the initial move from the white to the black section was measured.

The consistent ability of the young adult mice to 'learn' to locate the opening in the central compartment within four days of repeated exposure is remarkably absent in aged animals. Indeed, whilst the aged animals will move to the location of the door into the less aversive black and darkened compartment, and often place their nose into the opening, they appear never to associate the movement through the doorway with passage into a less aversive environment. This does not appear to reflect a situation in which the old mice are less anxious and therefore less concerned about the environment of the white compartment since they remain hesitant in their movements in the white, mostly utilizing the edges of the compartment and rarely traversing to the centre of the arena. This is consistent with recent findings in our laboratories that aged animals do have enhanced levels of anxiety. In a state of enhanced anxiety, therefore, it would be more logical for the aged mice to more rapidly seek the safer environment of the black compartment of the black:white box. The aged mice are clearly unable to 'learn' this and persist in delaying their move into the black. Whilst data in Fig. 1 only show the behaviour over the six day habituation period, it should be noted that experiments have been extended and, even after two–three weeks of exposure to the test box, it has been found that the aged animals do not learn to move more speedily into the black.

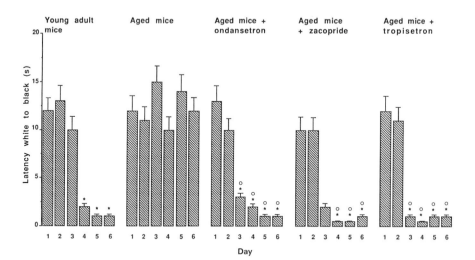

Figure 1. Influence of ondansetron, zacopride or tropisetron (10 ng/kg i.p. b.d.) on the habituation performance of aged mice over a six day period using a black:white box. $n = 5$, * = $p<0.001$ (for improvement in performance compared with day 1), $\bigcirc$ = $p<0.001$ (for inhibition of impaired performance). See Barnes *et al.* (1990a) for experimental details.

It is against this background of lack of ability to locate the black compartment that the influence of the 5HT$_3$ receptor antagonists can be seen. Each
of the compounds shown here, ondansetron, zacopride and tropisetron, were
given daily throughout the test period at a dose of 10 ng/kg i.p. b.d. It can
be seen that under the influence of the 5HT$_3$ receptor antagonists habituation problems of the aged mice are reinstated such that they perform equally
well or even better than the young adult mice. Thus, whilst the latency of
move from the white to the black of young adult mice changes from 10–12
s to 1–2 s over a four day period, the latency of the aged animals is changed
from 10–13 to 0.5–3 s over a three day period when treatment with
ondansetron, zacopride or tropisetron is pursued (Fig. 1). At this stage it is
important to emphasize that the 5HT$_3$ receptor antagonists reinstate only the
loss of a learning facility, i.e. to habituate to a test box, since any ability to
enhance performance above and beyond normal is not upheld in other test
paradigms. It is possible that the aged mice are particularly sensitive to the
actions of the 5HT$_3$ receptor antagonists since we have recently shown that
aged rats have increased sensitivity to a number of psychoactive agents,
including diazepam and the anxiolytic properties of the 5HT$_3$ receptor antagonists. Similarly, animals with impaired cerebral function may have enhanced
responsiveness to the actions of certain psychotherapeutic agents, and this
should influence too tight an interpretation of data shown in Figs 2 and 3.

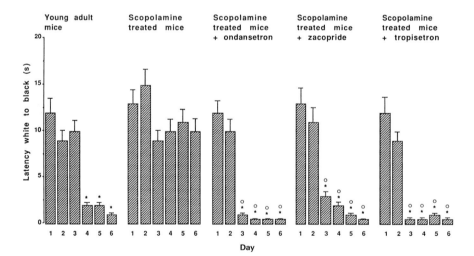

Figure 2. Influence of ondansetron, zacopride or tropisetron (10 ng/kg i.p. b.d.) on
the habituation performance of mice treated with scopolamine (0.25 ng/kg i.p.) over
a six day period using a black:white box. $n = 5$. * = $p<0.001$ (for improvement in
performance compared with day 1), $\bigcirc$ = $p<0.001$ (for inhibition of impaired performance). See Barnes *et al.* (1990a) for experimental details.

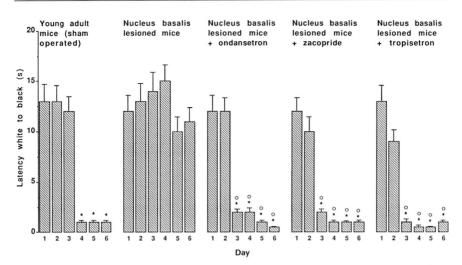

Figure 3. Influence of ondansetron, zacopride or tropisetron (10 ng/kg i.p. b.d.) on the habituation performance of mice subject to lesions of the nucleus basalis magnocellularis and tested over a six day period in a black:white box. Control animals were sham lesioned. * = $p<0.001$ (for improvement in performance compared with day 1), $\bigcirc$ = $p<0.001$ (for inhibition of impaired performance). See Barnes *et al.* (1990a) for experimental details.

Here, again, it can be shown that habituation patterns of young adult mice can be impaired such that normal habituation patterns are abolished. Thus, over a six day test period (and even over an extended 14 day test period) mice given twice daily scopolamine administrations or which have been subject to lesions of the nucleus basalis magnocellularis fail to habituate. Both groups of animals showing persistent memory impairments respond to challenge with the 5HT$_3$ receptor antagonists, for example, ondansetron, zacopride or tropisetron, again at the low 10 ng/kg dose, with a reinstatement of habituation performance (Figs 2 and 3).

USE OF A RAT FOOD-REINFORCED T-MAZE ALTERNATION TASK

In this test rats which have been food-deprived to 85% of body weight are required to learn a task in which they traverse down a runaway and turn either left or right down an arm of a T-maze to gain a food reward. The direction of turn is indicated by a barrier which moves from the left to the right arm on a pseudo-random schedule. On the subsequent run the rat must turn in a direction opposite to the barrier, this time with the barrier removed and a total absence of cues. Normal rats will learn, over a period of days and repeated testing, to gain some 80–90% correct responses. As will be seen, this ability to learn deteriorates dramatically during old age and also when memory is impaired by the use of scopolamine or by lesioning of the nucleus basalis magnocellularis (see Barnes *et al.*, 1990a; Costall *et al.*, 1989a, 1989b). The protocol is to train male Lister-Hooded rats (250–300 g, 11–15 weeks old, termed 'young adults') on the food reinforced alternation task according to a strict regime. Food is withdrawn two days prior to testing and animals are subsequently deprived of food for 23 hours per day, but with water available ad libitum: body weight can be maintained at 85% of normal using this feeding regime.

During test, animals were taken from the dark holding room to a dimly-lit test room and they were allowed 30 minutes to adapt to the new environment. The experiments were always carried out between 08.00 and 15.00 h.

The construction of the T-maze was important and the performance on several 'models' was determined before the size and construction of the T-maze was selected for a large series of experiments. The maze was elevated 30 cm above the ground, and only a small lip formed the surround to each arm. The start arm measured 80 × 10 cm and the side arms each measured 60 × 10 cm with food wells set 3 cm deep at each end.

On day 1 each rat was allowed 10 minutes to habituate to the maze. During this habituation phase both food wells were baited with banana flavoured pellets (which the rats found to be most desirable) and the same pellets were also scattered along the approach arm to encourage the rat to explore up to the two baited arms. Rats were then placed through a series of training sessions for reinforced alternation: days 2–3 were designated 'pre-training' days. All reinforced alternation training consisted of paired trials (each pair being termed a 'run'). The first trials were the 'forced' trials in which one arm was blocked by a metal barrier whilst the other arm was baited with the banana-flavoured pellets. The second trial of the pair was the 'choice' trial in which reward pellets were placed in the cup at the end of the arm opposite to that reinforced in the first trial of the pair. A correct choice was when the rat entered the arm containing the food reward on the choice trial, passing a point marked 20 cm along the arm. Correct and incorrect choices were noted: in addition the latency to reward was recorded for both the forced and choice trials. Whilst, overall, the latter measure provides valuable information on rat behaviour on the T-maze, the most valuable measure of improvements in impaired performance was found to be the percentage of correct responses, and it is these data which are shown in Fig. 4, which actually takes the fifth day of test as being indicative of normal and impaired performance, and shows the influence on the impairments of the 5HT$_3$ receptor antagonists.

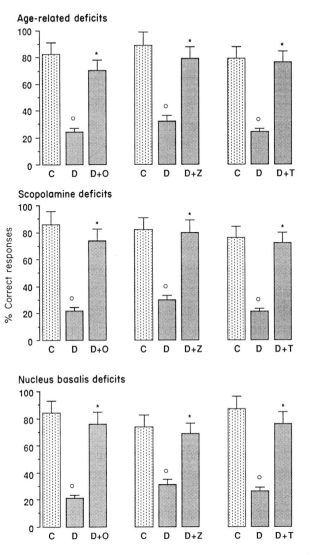

Figure 4. Influence of ageing, scopolamine treatment (Scop. 0.25 mg/kg i.p. b.d.) and lesions of the nucleus basalis magnocellularis on performance in a T-maze food reinforced alternation task, and influence on the deficits (D) of treatment with ondansetron (O, 100 ng/kg i.p. b.d.), zacopride (Z, 100 ng/kg i.p. b.d.) or tropisetron (T, 1 μg/kg i.p. b.d.). C = control animals (vehicle treated, and sham operated for lesions of the nucleus basalis). $n = 6$. ○ = $p<0.001$ for deficits, * = $p<0.01$–$p<0.001$ for reduction in these deficits by ondansetron, zacopride or tropisetron. See Barnes *et al.* (1990a), and Costall *et al.* (1989a, b) for experimental details.

Four runs were carried out on the pre-training days (intertrial interval 0 s, interrun interval 30 s) and six runs were carried out each day during training (intertrial interval 30 s, interrun interval 60 s). The way in which the barrier was placed on the forced run, i.e. the number of lefts and rights was determined on a pseudo-random basis following a Gellerman schedule, and the location between left and right was balanced across the test groups. Whilst the mouse data were analysed by one-way ANOVA followed by Dunnett's test, the rat data obtained from the T-maze were analysed by two-way ANOVA followed by Dunnett's test.

A number of interventions were used to effect impairments in performance using the T-maze. One was the use of old age animals, another the use of scopolamine and the third the stereotaxic destruction of the nucleus basalis magnocellularis. To effect destruction of this nucleus, rats were anaesthetized using sodium pentobarbitone before being placed in a stereotaxic frame for the injection of 5 μg in 5 μl of ibotenic acid (or vehicle, to provide the sham operation) at a location of Ant. 5.8 mm, Lat. ±2.6 mm and Vert. –8.2 mm (according to the atlas of Paxinos and Watson, 1982). Those rats which were used had survived for 14 days in good health. In a further series of experiments a more generalized destruction of forebrain acetylcholine function was achieved by the chronic infusion of hemicholinium-3 (HC-3), 2.5 μg/day, into the ventricular system throughout the nine day test period. A correct placement of the lesions was confirmed histologically and/or biochemically (determination of ChAT levels).

As stated above, in addition to the nucleus basalis lesions a more generalized destruction of cortical cholinergic function was achieved by use of infused HC-3. A further approach to memory impairment was to use chronically administered diazepam (a dose of 2.5 mg/kg i.p. b.d. was selected as a cognitive impairing dose which did not unduly sedate). It was interesting that none of the $5HT_3$ receptor antagonists tested, at ng/kg or μg/kg doses, could inhibit the memory impairments caused by HC-3 or diazepam. This would indicate that the $5HT_3$ receptor antagonists require some functional cholinergic activity in order to exert their beneficial effects on memory (at least from the HC-3 data). If this were to be so, then the $5HT_3$ receptor antagonists could only be expected to inhibit impaired memory when there is some mesocortical/cortical function on which to exert their neuromodulatory action: an action via a neuromodulation of acetylcholine function is also indicated by biochemical experiments showing an effect of the $5HT_3$ receptor antagonists to antagonize an inhibited acetylcholine release from cortical tissues (as will be discussed later, but see Barnes et al., 1989). The memory deficits caused by the benzodiazepines have long been recognized, and that they are not amenable to intervention with a $5HT_3$ receptor antagonist is an indication that the mechanism of the memory impairment is far more complex than may be corrected by a cholinergic enhancement. This is borne out by experiments showing that diazepam impairments in cognitive function are not amenable to therapeutic intervention from the cholinomimetics (for example, persistent infusions of arecoline fail to reverse the impairments caused by diazepam in mouse or rat performance in memory tests).

Against these failures stands the clear therapeutic efficacy of the 5HT$_3$ receptor antagonists, ondansetron, zacopride, tropisetron and granisetron as examples, to inhibit the impairments in rat T-maze performance caused by old age, scopolamine or nucleus basalis lesions. Whilst performance improves over the pre-training days, by days 5 and 6 of pre-training and training the rats have peaked in their normal performance and deficits are clearly visible: these are inhibited by ondansetron, zacopride and tropisetron. This can be seen clearly on inspection of data in Fig. 4 where control animals for the experiments for the aged-deficits, scopolamine-induced deficits or lesion-induced deficits have reached a 76–89% level of correct responding. This performance was reduced to 24–32% by old age, to 21–30% by scopolamine, and to 21–31% by the nucleus basalis lesions. In all experiments treatment with ondansetron, zacopride or tropisetron returned the responding of the memory-deficit rats almost to control values (70–79%, 72–80% and 69–76%, respectively for aged animals, scopolamine-treated animals and lesioned animals, see Fig. 4).

USE OF A RAT MORRIS WATER MAZE

This test relies upon a rat's ability to locate a submerged island in a water bath filled with milky fluid in which the cues to the location of the island can be determined from the location of cue boards and other fixed fittings around the maze. When an animal is first placed in the bath, after being shown the location of the island, it will swim randomly until by chance it locates the island (escape). On subsequent exposures to the water maze a rat will develop a strategy for locating the correct quadrant in which the island is located and, on repeated exposures, will learn to swim from any start point in the bath to rapidly locate the submerged island. Rats are naturally good swimmers and soon acquire a good response in this task, indeed, they appear to enjoy the trials so much that on gaining access to the island they frequently dive off and will swim under-water: this frustrates the experiment in which the black head of a rat is tracked by a computer as it moves through the white fluid. Thus, this test is primarily used with scopolamine to impair performance (see Costall *et al.*, 1989c).

The experimental design was to use male Lister-Hooded rats weighing 250–350 g, which were housed in groups of five and given free access to food and water. For test, the rats were placed in a square (120 × 120 cm) pool of water which was rendered opaque by the addition of an emulsion. The submerged island was a white painted platform located 2 cm below the surface of the water. The rats were trained to locate and escape onto the island using spatial strategies. A two day test protocol was used: on day 1 each rat was placed on the island for 30 s immediately before testing began. For each rat the island was kept in a constant position (although the position of the island was randomized and balanced across groups) with each rat beginning each trial at a different corner of the pool. Using a timer and a tracking device, the time was recorded for each animal to escape from the water onto the submerged island. The rat was allowed to remain on the island for 10 s before being placed in the pool for the second trial. On each trial the rat was allowed 100 s to find the island and the latency, swim speed and percentage of time spent in the island quadrant were measured. If the rat failed to locate the island within the 100 s allowed it was manually taken from the pool and placed on the island for 10 seconds, to reinforce its location, before being removed from the bath and placed, if appropriate, in the second trial. Each rat was subject to six trials on day 1 and on day 2 the rats were subject to the same procedure as day 1 on the basis that the test was designed to allow the rats to form a strategy for locating the island on day 1 which could be modified by drug intervention. It was important on each day to carry out a seventh trial in which a black visible island was used to ensure that no visual/locomotor effects were influencing performance.

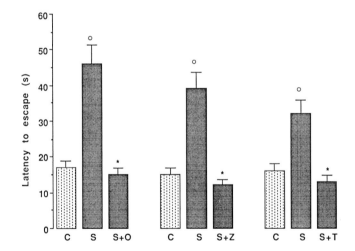

Figure 5. Impairment by scopolamine (S, 0.25 ng/kg i.p.) of performance of rats in a Morris water maze, and inhibition of such impairments by ondansetron (O), zacopride (Z) or tropisetron (T), each given at 1 µg/kg i.p. C = vehicle control. $n = 6$. $\bigcirc = p<0.001$ (impairment by scopolamine), $* = p<0.001$ (inhibition of scopolamine impairment). See Costall *et al.* (1989c) for experimental details.

On the first day of testing scopolamine, at a dose of 0.25 mg/kg i.p., could be shown to increase escape latency, but this did not achieve significance and, therefore, scopolamine challenges were always made on day 2. As in other experiments using scopolamine, it is important to emphasize that the dose was carefully selected as the maximum which could be used without impairment in visual function or other overt autonomic effect. On the second day of test the scopolamine challenge significantly impaired the escape latency by up to 50% (Fig. 5). It was this deficit which was sensitive to treatment with ondansetron, zacopride or tropisetron, each of which returned the escape latency to near normal values (Fig. 5). The 5HT$_3$ receptor antagonists which were each given at a dose of 1 µg/kg, antagonized the actions of scopolamine both on escape latency (shown) and on time spent in the correct island quadrant (Costall et al., 1989c). It is important that the lack of effect of the drug treatments on swim speed and on ability to locate the black visible island indicated the specificity of the responses recorded in that there was clearly no effect on visual performance or on locomotor performance.

USE OF A MARMOSET OBJECT DISCRIMINATION AND REVERSAL LEARNING TASK

In this test procedure, where cholinergic function appears crucial (Ridley et al., 1984), marmosets are required to select between two presented objects or stimuli, one of which is food baited. Marmosets will naturally work for a sweet food reward and it is not necessary to deprive them of food in any way before entering them into this test. Marmosets are particularly nervous of objects with arms or projections so two junk objects are used, for example a bottle stopper, a bottle cap, a syringe case, a pen top. After training, they will learn a strategy for selecting the food rewarded object and then, after they have reached a fixed criterion of a certain number of correct choices on the first object then they are required to change the learned contingency and select the second, previously unrewarded object, which is now food rewarded. Marmosets find it particularly difficult, as do humans, to abandon a learned contingency and find the second so-called reversal task far more difficult, and they take a significantly larger number of trials between reaching criterion on the second object (see Barnes et al., 1990a; Domeney et al., 1991).

The experimental protocol for use of the object discrimination and reversal learning tasks required the use of a Wisconsin General Test Apparatus (WGTA). The time of day in which testing is carried out is particularly important for a primate species and all tests were carried out between 10.00 and 15.30 h in a room where temperature and lighting conditions were identical to those of the holding rooms. Following the initial object discrimination training using two junk objects, to 90% correct performance, the task set for the marmosets was to select between two different objects (from those used for training) which covered two food wells, one of which, as on the training sessions, contained a food reward. The food rewarded object was presented to the marmoset on either the left or the right hand side, according to the pseudo-random schedule of Gellerman. On completing six consecutive correct responses (criterion) on the first food rewarded object (initial discrimination task) the reward paradigm was changed such that the marmoset was required to select the second, initially unrewarded object, to the same criterion of six consecutive correct responses (reversal task). Objects remained constant throughout the 5 day test periods: the last

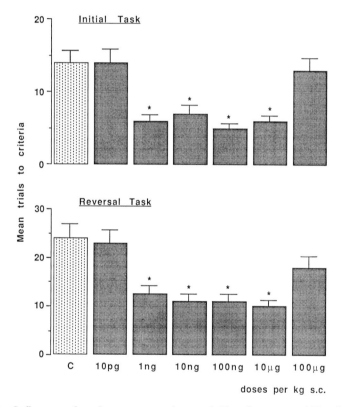

Figure 6. Influence of ondansetron, at doses of 10 pg/kg s.c. to 100 μg/kg s.c. on marmoset performance in an object discrimination reversal task using a Wisconsin General Test Apparatus. Performance is indicated for the initial object discrimination task and for the reversal learning task. $n = 4$. $p < 0.05$ for improved performance determined as number of trials to criterion (six consecutive correct responses). See Barnes *et al.* (1990a) and Domeney *et al.* (1991) for experimental details.

rewarded object of one day always became the first rewarded object of the following day. Marmosets received ondansetron (or other 5HT$_3$ receptor antagonists) or vehicle twice daily (morning and evening) of a five day test session. A blind randomized crossover design was used for drug or vehicle administration. The mean and SEM between drug and vehicle controls for the number of trials to criterion for all marmosets within a dose group on all days was analysed using a paired t test.

Treatment with ondansetron, 1 ng/kg, 10 ng/kg, 100 ng/kg and 10 µg/kg, throughout the five day test period was shown to significantly decrease the number of trials to criterion in both the object discrimination and reversal tasks. As stated previously, marmosets found the object reversal task the more difficult and improvement in the performance of this under the influence of ondansetron was most marked (Fig. 6). Other 5HT$_3$ receptor antagonists, such as zacopride and tropisetron, also improved marmoset performance, particularly on the reversal task. In each case the maximally effective dose was shown to be 10 ng/kg. It is important to note that in all of the tests described which used the described protocol in the Wisconsin General Test Apparatus, marmosets returned to pre-drug performance levels within two days of ceasing treatment with a 5HT$_3$ receptor antagonist.

ARE THERE ANY BIOCHEMICAL OR CLINICAL CORRELATES FOR THE ABILITY OF THE 5HT$_3$ RECEPTOR ANTAGONISTS TO INHIBIT AN IMPAIRED MEMORY?

Whilst it is frequent for psychotherapeutic agents to be defined by their radioligand binding profile, it was unusual that the development of suitable radioligands for the 5HT$_3$ binding site followed consequent to many of the behavioural studies. Indeed, there was some discussion in the early days of 5HT$_3$ receptor antagonist development as to whether their behavioural effects linked with an action on specific brain receptor sites. As the radioligands for the 5HT$_3$ site were developed, tritiated zacopride being one of the prototypes, they were used to define specific locations in the brain. Densities tended to be low, but the location of the specific binding sites proved to link with knowledge of those brain areas which are keys to the control of emotion, motivational and cognitive behaviour. Major loci were, therefore, the hippocampus, the amygdala, entorhinal, parietal and frontal cortex (Barnes et al., 1990b; Kilpatrick et al., 1990).

With the discovery of 5HT$_3$ receptor sites in brain areas strongly linked with cognitive performance, the next challenge was to determine how such sites may influence cholinergic function. It is crucial that the cholinergic hypothesis of the dementias or memory impairments has remained the cornerstone for determining new therapeutic approaches, and for any new drug to be accepted for a therapeutic role in memory impairments it is an asset to link its function directly or indirectly with an enhancement of the action of acetylcholine. This does not preclude the role of other neurotransmitters but does give a first indication of relevance to the dementias in the absence of any other acceptable working hypothesis. The work of Barnes *et al.* (1989), reported in *Nature*, therefore set the scene for the acceptance of the $5HT_3$ receptor antagonists as potential agents to influence memory. The technique was to use ^3H.choline loaded slices of rat entorhinal cortex and to stimulate the release of acetylcholine (checked using high performance liquid chromatography) using pulses of potassium stimulation. By comparing the responses to the first and second pulses of potassium (termed S1 and S2) and placing drug intervention between S1 and S2, it could be shown that (provided 5HT tone was manipulated by inclusion of ritanserin, influencing $5HT_2$ or $5HT_{1C}$ sites) a $5HT_3$ receptor agonist, 2-methyl-5-HT, could inhibit acetylcholine release: this inhibition of acetylcholine release could be antagonized by $5HT_3$ receptor antagonists such as ondansetron or zacopride.

Thus a biochemical basis for the influence of $5HT_3$ receptor antagonists on memory evolved, and was consistent with a hypothesis that $5HT_3$ receptor antagonists are able to facilitate an inhibited acetylcholine release. When acetylcholine function is totally impaired, as discussed previously using hemicholinium-3, then the $5HT_3$ receptor antagonists are without effect on the memory impairments. Therefore, as a working hypothesis, it is suggested that the $5HT_3$ receptor antagonists are able to improve memory by enhancing a deficient cholinergic system: when the cholinergic system is rendered non-operational then the $5HT_3$ receptor antagonists are no longer able to influence memory. If one were to take an extreme liberty in extrapolating this concept to man, then one may predict that the $5HT_3$ receptor antagonists may only enhance memory when there is some remaining performance, and that in the terminal dementias where acetylcholine function is lost, such as in full Alzheimer's disease, the $5HT_3$ receptor antagonists may not have any beneficial effect. However, such hypotheses can only be tested in man.

It is therefore pertinent at this point to turn attention to the studies which have been carried out in man. It was sensible, based on the animal studies, to commence clinical trials with aged impairments. The only studies available in the literature so far are those reported in Florence by Crook and Lakin (1991). In a paper entitled 'Effects of Ondansetron in Age-Associated Memory Impairments' the authors set the scene for much speculation and publicity. The final conclusion, it must be said, is that the action of ondansetron is being pursued not only in the aged population but in the dementias of the Alzheimer's type. This, in itself, is supportive of the feelings of the clinical investigators that ondansetron may have a role in human memory impairments. However, until clear clinical data are presented, one must restrict discussion to the findings of Crook and Lakin (1991). They used patients who were suffering from Age-Associated Memory Impairment (AAMI), a diagnostic term applied to healthy non-demented persons over 50 years of age who have experienced memory loss over the course of adult life. The term AAMI was adopted and specific diagnostic criteria proposed by a National Institute of Mental Health (NIHM) work group in the United States.

In the clinical study described by Crook and Lakin, 232 patients who met the criteria for AAMI were randomly assigned to a 0.01, 0.25 or 1.0 mg b.i.d. dose of ondansetron, or to placebo. Patients were treated double-blind for 12 weeks, followed by a two week washout period. Assessments were performed at the initiation and termination of treatment, at four week intervals during treatment, and at the conclusion of the washout period. Cognitive assessments included a computerized battery of neuropsycholog-ical tests related to learning and memory tasks of daily life, as well as behavioural rating scales. Prior to study, five test scores were selected as primary outcome measures, and the effects of ondansetron were deter-mined on these: viz. for example, name–face association — acquisition; name–face association — delayed recall; facial recall — number recognized before first error. The findings can be summarized as follows: whilst the 0.01 mg dose did not have any significant effect, compared with placebo, on any of the outcome measures, the 0.25 mg and 1.0 mg doses did have some effect. The effects of the 0.25 mg dose were most apparent towards the end of treatment, whilst the effects of the 1.0 mg dose were apparent earlier. There were points of genuine significance and the authors concluded, with caution, that ondansetron was 'of considerable interest and merits further study as a putative treatment for AAMI and perhaps other adult-onset cognitive disorders'.

OVERALL CONCLUSIONS OF PRECLINICAL AND CLINICAL STUDIES ON THE ABILITIES OF THE 5HT$_3$ RECEPTOR ANTAGONISTS TO INHIBIT MEMORY IMPAIRMENTS

This chapter summarizes data that indicate an important action of the 5HT$_3$ receptor antagonists to improve performance in memory tests in mouse, rat and primate models. It is to be presumed that such memory enhancing action relates to the 5HT$_3$ receptor antagonist action of agents such as ondansetron, zacopride or tropisetron since a common feature of these compounds is a highly selective and specific antagonism at the 5HT$_3$ receptor (Butler et al., 1988; Richardson et al., 1985; Smith et al., 1988). Whilst it is now known that very high doses of zacopride and tropisetron may influence the 5HT$_4$ recep-tor, this is unlikely to be of relevance to the present studies where doses for memory improvement are at least 1000-fold lower, occurring at the nano- or microgramme per kilogramme dose levels.

It can be hypothesized, from the biochemical work, that improvements in memory deficits caused by the $5HT_3$ receptor antagonists may link to an ability to prevent the inhibition effects of 5HT on acetylcholine release (Barnes *et al.*, 1989). It must be presumed that in the lesion studies the residual cholinergic function is sufficient to allow an attenuation of memory performance deficits, and it is obvious from the studies using hemicholinium-3 that some residual cholinergic performance is important for the $5HT_3$ receptor antagonists to exert their actions to inhibit an impaired performance in the memory tests across the species used.

Overall, the present data would indicate an important involvement of $5HT_3$ receptors in the control of memory processes. It is probable that the most important sites for improvement in memory are those which have been located for the $5HT_3$ receptor antagonist ligands in the limbic and cortical systems, and it is therefore important that in both the entorhinal cortex and hippocampus 5HT has been shown to reduce acetylcholine release (Barnes *et al.*, 1989; Bianchi *et al.*, 1990). The antagonist properties of agents such as ondansetron, zacopride and tropisetron at such cortical and limbic sites would be expected to contribute to an ability to improve performance in memory tests.

As indicated by the breadth of preclinical findings reported briefly in this chapter, it was the strength of the animal findings which prompted studies to assess the actions of $5HT_3$ receptor antagonists in man. Ondansetron has been the leader in this regard and the encouraging findings of Crook and Lakin (1991) in AAMI have encouraged further clinical work. Ondansetron has, of course, already been used in man for the treatment of emesis as well as in clinical trials for psychotherapeutic indications. Such studies, including many thousands of patients, have indicated that ondansetron can be used without unwanted side effects and with no overt changes in normal behaviour (see Crook and Lakin, 1991, and other contributions to the same symposium).

The immense complexity of events referred to under the heading of 'memory processes', encompassing a myriad of processes such as attention, discrimination, storage and retrieval of information, and the selection of an appropriate response, is likely to depend upon the functioning of highly complex neurotransmitter interactions. It is therefore not surprising that, over the years, a vast number of so-called cognitive enhancers have been described (see Sarter, 1991), but cognitive enhancers, nootropic agents and agents which inhibit memory impairments should be carefully separated. The $5HT_3$ receptor antagonists, for example, inhibit impairments in memory performance but the so-called nootropic agents, which include the piracetam-type drugs and hydergine, do not. Careful definitions are required to avoid confusion in the literature with the advent of a completely new type of compound which influences memory impairments, the $5HT_3$ receptor antagonists being the archetypical compounds.

Whatever the future may hold, the 5HT$_3$ receptor antagonists provide a beginning to an understanding of the role of 5HT$_3$ receptors in memory. It is not disputed that the future may see the preclinical and clinical development of agents affecting cholinergic, adrenergic, peptidergic, sigma, enzymatic or other systems. However, the major hope for a therapeutic interaction in memory disorders must at the present lie with the 5HT$_3$ receptor antagonists.

REFERENCES

Barnes, J.M., Barnes, N.M., Champaneria, S., Costall, B. and Naylor, R.J. (1990b). Characterisation and autoradiographic localisation of 5-HT$_3$ receptor recognition sites identified with [^{3}H]-S-zacopride in the forebrain of the rat. *Neuropharmacology*, **29**, 1037–1045.

Barnes, J.M., Barnes, N.M., Costall, B., Naylor, R.J. and Tyers, M.B. (1989). 5-HT$_3$ receptors mediate inhibition of acetylcholine release in cortical tissue. *Nature*, **338**, 762–763.

Barnes, J.M., Costall, B., Coughlan, J., Domeney, A.M., Gerrard, P.A., Kelly, M.E., Naylor, R.J., Onaivi, E.S., Tomkins, D.M. and Tyers, M.B. (1990a). The effects of ondansetron, a 5-HT$_3$ receptor antagonist, on cognition in rodents and primates. *Pharmacol. Biochem. Behav.*, **35**, 955–962.

Bartus, R.T., Dean, R.L., Beere, B. and Lippa, A.S. (1982). The cholinergic hypothesis of geriatric memory dysfunction. *Science* **217**, 408–417.

Bianchi, C., Siniscalchi, A. and Beani, L. (1990). 5-HT$_{1A}$ agonists increase and 5-HT agonists decrease acetylcholine efflux from the cerebral cortex of freely-moving guinea pigs. *Br. J. Pharmacol.*, **101**, 448–452.

Bockaert, J., Fagni, L., Sebben, M. and Dumuis, A. (1991). Pharmacological characterisation of brain 5-HT$_4$ receptors: relationship between the effects of indole, benzamide and azabicycloalkylbenzimidazolone derivatives. In: Fozard, J.R. and Saxena, P.R. (Eds), *Serotonin, Molecular Biology, Receptors and Functional Effects*, Birkhäuser, Basel, pp. 220—231.

Butler, A., Hill, J.M., Ireland, S.J., Jordan, C.C. and Tyers, M.B. (1988). Pharmacological properties of GR38032F, a novel antagonist at 5-HT$_3$ receptors. *Br. J. Pharmacol.*, **94**, 397–412.

Candy, J.M., Perry, E.K., Perry, R.H., Court, J.A., Oakley, A.E. and Edwardson, J.A. (1986). The current status of the cortical cholinergic system in Alzheimer's disease and Parkinson's disease. In: Swab, D.F., Fliers, E., Mirmiran, M., Van Gool, W.A. and Haaren, F. (Eds), *Progress in Brain Research Vol. 70. Ageing of the Brain and Alzheimer's Disease*, Elsevier, Amsterdam, pp. 106–132.

Costall, B., Coughlan, J., Kelly, M.E., Naylor, R.J. and Tyers, M.B. (1989a). Scopolamine-induced deficits in a T-maze reinforced alternation task are attenuated by 5-HT$_3$ receptor antagonists. *Br. J. Pharmacol.*, **98**, 636P.

Costall, B., Coughlan, J. and Kelly, M.E. (1989b). Continuous ICV infusion of hemicholinium-3 disrupts performance of rats in a T-maze reinforced alternation task. *Br. J. Pharmacol.*, **96**, 47P.

Costall, B., Coughlan, J., Horovitz, Z.P., Kelly, M.E., Naylor, R.J. and Tomkins, D.M. (1989c). The effects of ACE inhibitors captopril and SQ29852 in rodent tests of cognition. *Pharmacol. Biochem. Behav.*, **33**, 573–579.

Costall, B., Domeney, A.M., Farré, A.J., Kelly, M.E., Martinez, L. and Naylor, R.J. (1992). Profile of action of a novel 5-hydroxytryptamine receptor ligand E-4424 to inhibit aversive behaviour in the mouse, rat and marmoset. *J. Pharmacol. Exp. Ther.*, **262**, 90–98.

Craig, D.A. and Clarke, D.E. (1990). Pharmacological characterisation of neuronal receptor for 5-hydroxytryptamine in guinea pig ileum with properties similar to the 5-HT$_4$ receptor. *J. Pharmacol. Exp. Ther.*, **252**, 1378–1386.

Crook, T. and Lakin, M. (1991). Effects of ondansetron in age-associated memory impairments. In: *The Role of Ondansetron, a Novel 5-HT$_3$ Antagonist, in the Treatment of Psychiatric Disorders*, Satellite Symposium, 5th World Congress of Biological Psychiatry, Florence, 9 June 1991, pp. 21–23.

Domeney, A.M., Costall, B., Gerrard, P.A., Jones, D.N.C., Naylor, R.J. and Tyers, M.B. (1991). The effect of ondansetron on cognitive performance in the marmoset. *Pharmacol. Biochem. Behav.*, **38**, 169–175.

Euvrard, C., Javoy, F., Herbert, A. and Glowinski, J. (1978). Effect of quipazine, a serotonin-line drug, on striatal cholinergic interneurones. *Eur. J. Pharmacol.*, **155**, 380–396.

Fibiger, H.C., Lepiane, F.G. and Phillips, A.G. (1978). Disruption of memory produced by stimulation of the dorsal raphe nucleus: mediation by serotonin. *Brain Res.*, **155**, 380–386.

Gillett, G., Ammor, S. and Fillion, G. (1985). Serotonin inhibits acetylcholine release from rat striatum slices: evidence for a presynaptic receptor mediated effect. *J. Neurochem.*, **45**, 1687–1691.

Heise, G.A. (1987). Facilitation of memory and cognition by drugs. *Trends Pharmacol. Sci.*, **8**, 65–68.

Jackson, D., Bruno, J.P., Stachowiak, M.K. and Zigmond, M.J. (1988). Inhibition of striatal acetylcholine release by endogenous serotonin. *Brain Res.*, **457**, 259–266.

Kensner, R.P., Adelstein, T. and Crutcher, K.A. (1987). Rats with nucleus basalis magnocellularis lesions mimic mnemonic symptomatology observed in patients with dementia of the Alzheimer's type. *Behav. Neurosci.*, **101**, 451–456.

Kilpatrick, G.J., Butler, A., Hagan, R.M., Jones, B.J. and Tyers, M.B. (1990). [^{3}H]-GR67330, a very high affinity ligand for 5-HT$_3$ receptors. *Naunyn-Schmiedebergs Arch. Pharmacol.*, **342**, 22–30.

Olton, D.S. and Papas, B.C. (1979). Spatial memory and hippocampal function. *Neuropsychologia*, **17**, 669–682.

Paxinos, G. and Watson, C. (1992). *The Rat Brain in Stereotaxic Coordinates*, Academic Press, New York.

Richardson, B.P., Engel, G., Donatshe, P. and Stadler, P.A. (1985). Identification of serotonin M-receptor subtypes and their specific blockade by a new class of drugs. *Nature*, **316**, 126–131.

Ridley, R.M., Bowes, P.M., Baker, H.G. and Crow, T.J. (1984). An involvement of acetylcholine in object discrimination learning and memory in the marmoset. *Neuropsychologia*, **22**, 253–263.

Robinson, S.E. (1983). Effect of specific serotonergic lesions on cholinergic neurons in the hippocampus, cortex and striatum. *Life Sci.*, **32**, 345–353.

Sahakian, B.J. (1988). Cholinergic drugs and human cognitive performance. In: Iversen, L.L., Iversen, S.D. and Snyder, S.H. (Eds), *Handbook of Psychopharmacology Vol. 20, Psychopharmacology of the Aging Nervous System*, Plenum Press, New York, pp. 393–424.

Salamone, J.D., Channell, S.L., Welner, S.A., Gill, R., Robbins, T.W. and Iversen, S.D. (1987). Nucleus basalis lesions and anticholinergic drugs impair spatial memory and visual discrimination performance in the rat. In: Dowdall, M.J. and Hawthorne, J.D. (Eds), *Cellular and Molecular Basis of Cholinergic Function*, Ellis Horwood, Chichester, pp. 834–840.

Sarter, M. (1991). Taking stock of cognition enhancers. *Trends Pharmacol. Sci.*, **12**, 456–461.

Smith, W.L., Sancilio, L.F., Naylor, R.J., Owera-Atepo, J.B. and Lambert, L. (1988). Zacopride: a potent 5-HT$_3$ antagonist. *J. Pharm. Pharmacol.*, **40**, 301–302.

Vizi, E.S., Harsin, L.G. and Zsilla, G. (1981). Evidence of the modulatory role of serotonin in acetylcholine release from striatal interneurones. *Brain Res.*, **212**, 89–99.

Treatment and Care in Old Age Psychiatry
Edited by R. Levy, R. Howard and A. Burns
©1993 Wrightson Biomedical Publishing Ltd

10

How Benign is Benign Senescent Forgetfulness?

ROBERT HOWARD

Section of Old Age Psychiatry, Institute of Psychiatry, London, UK

Complaints of memory difficulties are common among the elderly (Livingstone *et al.*, 1990) and the apparent universality of the symptoms of age-associated memory impairment (Crook *et al.*, 1986) are depressing for anyone over the age of 30. Happily the vast majority of memory complainers identified in community surveys produce reassuringly normal performances on psychometric testing (Rabbitt and Abson, 1990; Bolla *et al.*, 1991). Memory complaints may sometimes, however, have an objective basis and be reflected in poor performance on psychometric testing. This seems to be the case for patients who have a poorer memory than would be predicted from their IQ or who feel that their memory is worse than that of their peers (Christensen, 1991).

Kral (1958) distinguished between the normal elderly, those with dementia and those with what he called 'benign senescent forgetfulness' (BSF). Although Kral did not measure memory impairment in his subjects in an objective manner, he reported that individuals with BSF had difficulty in remembering names and dates from the past. In a comparison of BSF patients with dementia sufferers, mortality was reduced in the BSF group at four year follow-up (Kral, 1962). Later workers have confirmed Kral's observation that BSF is generally non-progressive (Reisberg *et al.*, 1986; Larrabee *et al.*, 1986), although the lack of any clear defining criteria for the syndrome makes any such research difficult to carry out and interpret.

Little is known about the prognosis for cognitive function in those individuals who actively seek medical help for a complaint of failing memory but are found to perform normally on cognitive testing. Such patients are regularly seen in the Maudsley Hospital Memory Clinic (Philpot and Levy, 1987) and are given a diagnosis of BSF (although they are probably closer to Crook's AAMI than to Kral's original description of BSF). We reassure these individuals that they are not demented and tell them that we do not believe they are beginning to slide into a dementia syndrome, the symptoms of which are still so subtle that they are not yet detectable by clinical examination or conventional testing. In order to gather evidence to support such a reassuring position, we carried out a follow-up study of all those individuals who had been given a clinic diagnosis of BSF. The form of the Maudsley Hospital Memory Clinic is described elsewhere (Philpot and Levy, 1987). In short, patients who attend are self-, relative- or doctor-referrals and are given an exhaustive battery of tests including the CAMCOG component of the CAMDEX examination, a full physical and psychiatric examination, a screen of routine blood tests and a CT brain scan. At the end of a day-long assessment, each patient is given a diagnosis. Between 1984 and the beginning of this year we identified 68 individuals, from a total of 418 patients seen, who had been given a diagnosis of BSF and were considered to be memory complainers who were to all appearances normal. Some characteristics of these people are given in Table 1. Their high mean premorbid IQs reflect the socioeconomic catchment of our clinic which extends beyond the borough in which the hospital is sited.

Table 1.   Characteristics of BSF patients ($n = 64$).

	Mean	SD	Range
Age (years)	67.2	± 8.4	50–83
MMSE	28.7	± 1.3	25–30
NART IQ	120	± 5.5	99–128
Length memory problems (years)	4.1	± 2.78	1–15

Of the 68 individuals diagnosed as having BSF, one had emigrated and three had moved to new addresses which we could not trace. Of the remaining 64, 55 were willing to attend the hospital for follow-up testing which comprized the Mini-Mental State, the Kendrick tests for the elderly and the Wechsler logical memory scale. Six patients were traced but declined to attend the hospital. They were interviewed over the telephone and their GPs contacted to assess cognitive functioning. Three patients had died during the follow-up. In each of these cases, the death certificates were inspected and the GP contacted to see if there had been any evidence of dementia before death. Diagnosis of dementia was made using the ICD-10 criteria by two independent psychiatrists who had access to all the assessment and test results. The mean follow-up period for the patients was 37.2 months, and during that time six had developed a clinically recognizable dementia.

Table 2. Clinical features by diagnosis at follow up.

	Demented (n = 6)	Not demented (n = 58)	p
Age (years)	72.2 ± 8.7	66.9 ± 8.3	NS
Sex M/F	3/3	16/42	NS
Initial MMS	28.3 ± 0.8	28.7 ± 1.3	NS
Follow up MMSE	25.0 ± 2.2	28.1 ± 1.4	$p < 0.05$
Length memory problems (years)	3.8 ± 1.9	4.1 ± 2.8	NS
BP systolic mmHg	157 ± 22	139 ± 21	NS
BP diastolic mmHg	88 ± 17	84 ± 11	NS
Length f/u (months)	31.2 ± 23.4	37.8 ± 19.4	NS
Noticed by others	50% 3/6	18% 10/55	NS
FH dementia	17% 1/6	47% 27/57	NS
CT scan abnormal	50% 3/6	36% 21/58 NS	
Smokers	0% 0/6	24% 11/45	NS
NART IQ	121 ± 3.2	120 ± 5.7	NS
KOLT	18.2 ± 2.9	38.4 ± 7.9	$p < 0.001$
WLM del	2.5 ± 2.1	9.8 ± 3.2	$p < 0.002$

The patients who did become demented were older, more likely to be male than female, and were more likely to have had their memory problem noticed by someone else as well as themselves at the initial assessment (Table 2).

Six out of 68 patients developing dementia in three years is higher than the number that would be predicted from actuarial scales derived from age-matched community samples, from whom only 2.4 new cases of dementia would have been expected. The number of observed new cases of dementia among the BSF follow-up population, however, lies within the 95% confidence limits of the expected number. Thus the figures show that there is no clear evidence of a statistically significant increase in the incidence of dementia among such a population of memory complainers at three year follow-up.

After exclusion of the six patients who went on to develop dementia from analysis, we went on to look for evidence of a more modest cognitive decline among the remainder of the memory complainers. We found a very small but statistically significant fall in Mini-Mental State score (28.7 ± 1.3 compared with 28.0 ± 1.8) which we consider to be no more than would be expected to accompany normal ageing.

So is BSF benign? The conclusion of this follow-up is that in most cases it certainly is. The medium term prognosis for the development of dementia is no worse than among the normal elderly and the degree of cognitive decline observed in patients with BSF appears to be consistent with what would be expected in normal ageing.

ACKNOWLEDGEMENTS

John O'Brien,   Barbara Beats, Katie Hill and Raymond Levy were all involved in the follow-up and repeat assessments of the BSF patients.

REFERENCES

Bolla, K., Lindgren, K., Bonaccorsy, C. and Bleeker, M. (1991). Memory complaints in older adults. *Arch. Neurol.*, **48**, 61–64.

Christensen, H. (1991). The validity of memory complaints by elderly persons. *Int. J. Geriatr. Psychiatry*, **6**, 307–312.

Crook, T., Bartus, R., Ferris, S., Whitehouse, P., Cohen, G.D. and Gershon, S. (1986). Age associated memory impairment: proposed diagnostic criteria and measures of clinical change. Report of NIMH work group. *Dev. Neuropsychol.*, **2**, 261–276.

Kral, V. (1958). Neuropsychiatric observations in an old people's home. J. Gerontol., **13**, 169–176.

Kral, V. (1962). Senescent forgetfulness: benign and malignant. *Can. Med. Assoc. J.*, **86**, 257–260.

Larrabee, G., Levin, H. and High, W. (1986). Senescent forgetfulness: a quantitative study. *Dev. Neuropsychol.*, **2**, 373–385.

Livingstone, G., Hawkins, A., Graham, N., Blizzard, B. and Mann, A. (1990). The Gospel Oak Study: Prevalence rates of dementia, depression and activity limitation among elderly residents in inner London. *Psychol. Med.*, **20**, 137–146.

Philpot, M. and Levy, R. (1987). A memory clinic for the early diagnosis of dementia. *Int. J. Geriatr. Psychiatry*, **2**, 195–200.

Rabbitt, P. and Abson, V. (1990). 'Lost and Found': some logical and methodological limitations of self-report questionnaires as tools to study cognitive ageing. *Br. J. Psychol.*, **81**, 1–16.

Reisberg, B., Ferris, S., Shulman, E., Steinberg, G., Buttinger, C. and Sinaik, O. (1986). Longitudinal course of normal ageing and progressive dementia of the Alzheimer type: a prospective study of 106 subjects over a 3.6 year mean interval. *Prog. Neuropsychopharmacol. Biol. Psychiatry*, **10**, 571–578.

Treatment and Care in Old Age Psychiatry
Edited by R. Levy, R. Howard and A. Burns
©1993 Wrightson Biomedical Publishing Ltd

11

Can We Train the Brain?

CHARLES TWINING

Whitchurch Hospital, Cardiff, UK

INTRODUCTION

The prospect of mental decline is one of the most threatening aspects of ageing. Perhaps, therefore, it is not surprising that there is considerable enthusiasm for approaches which suggest how such decline may be avoided or ameliorated. The effects of physical exercise on bodily function are well established and accepted and by analogy it has been a long tradition for us to assume that mental exercise could have similar benefits on our cognitive functions. Unfortunately, the evidence from psychological research is less than convincing in this regard. One of the main reasons why I and many of my contemporaries will have spent happy hours trudging through Latin text is because it is thought that this would have some general effect on improving one's cognitive skills. The brain however does not appear to behave like a muscle, either physiologically or psychologically. Learning Latin does not have a general benefit to the brain.

Nonetheless, it is reasonable to ask the question whether it is possible to produce changes in behaviour, in particular cognitive behaviour, as a result of experience. Producing desired changes in behaviour as a result of experience is a perfectly reasonable definition of training. There is plenty of evidence that behaviour can be altered as a result of experience.

When it comes to 'training the brain' we are ultimately seeking to alter cognitive structures and strategies which are presumed to underlie human behaviour. These would include such areas as memory, which is that on which I shall focus in this chapter, thinking, as illustrated by the increasingly proven benefits of cognitive therapy for affective disorder (Morris and Morris, 1991), and affect itself. There is even scope for changing thinking and affect in the presence of memory dysfunction (Teri and Gallagher-Thompson, 1991).

139

AIMS AND OBJECTIVES

As we shall see later on, the attraction of such prospects has meant that enthusiasm can outstrip evidence (Powell-Proctor and Miller, 1982). It is therefore as well to pause before considering specific examples and remind ourselves of what we are seeking to achieve by any process of cognitive training.

The distinctions in the World Health Organisation definition between disease, disability and handicap, can be particularly useful here. We have in respect of memory problems and ageing clear evidence that there is disability in the form of memory impairment. We do, of course, largely infer this from the effects that it has on activities of daily living, namely the handicap which is produced. At the other end of the definition dimension there are the various constructs for underlying disease which may, or perhaps may not, be said to exist. These include age associated memory impairment and benign senescent forgetfulness, both of which, of course, figure within the title of this symposium. They are perhaps less established neuropathologically than primary degenerative dementia, for which there is clear evidence for abnormal memory impairment being the result of neurological disease. Finally, there is a curious, but sometimes popular concept, of minimal memory impairment (Yesavage et al., 1989) which seems to be something between normal ageing and benign senescent forgetfulness. Those of us who are familiar with the debate surrounding minimal brain damage in children will perhaps recognize the pitfalls inherent in such concepts.

There are very obvious differences between the effects of normal ageing on the one hand and those of degenerative dementia on the other. In evaluating the various treatments and retraining approaches, we need therefore to ask how it might reasonably be applied to the wide range of people who could be said to be suffering some form of memory impairment. In asking questions about efficacy we need to further delineate a number of more specific issues.

Does it work?

Clearly it is as important for psychological approaches as for any other treatment that we ascertain whether it is having a genuine effect and indeed whether it has both good effects and possibly ill effects. It is possible to produce positive effects on patients at the cost of increasing the distress of carers (Zarit et al., 1982).

How big is the effect?

We know that across the spectrum of memory impairment in later life, the nature of the deficit varies hugely in quantity and, incidentally, probably in quality as well. We need to have some idea whether the magnitudes of the effects produced by a particular intervention are comparable to the sorts of deficits that the intervention is intended to address. In the case, for example, of senile dementia, we are looking for clinically significant effects, not simply a statistically reliable result which has no bearing on people's day to day life.

Does it generalize?

If we are genuinely producing a therapy or treatment it seems appropriate to expect that it should have wider effects than simply producing change on the material which was included in the training programme. Thus we would expect a psychological treatment for depression not simply to alter thinking with respect to depressive ideation, but to have positive benefits in terms of reported mood, psychomotor activity and so on. Thus we would expect something addressing memory impairment at a disability level at least to have some effect on a range of tasks which appear to involve memory function. We are not just interested in how to produce change in very specific areas by training those particular items.

Does it last?

Finally, we are interested in something that is relatively permanent. The very nature of memory impairment is such that the past is not adequately influencing the present and if we are doing something to overcome this the reverse might be true. Changes in behaviour which only endure while the 'training' procedure is in operation cannot really be said to have undergone any lasting therapeutic improvement at least with respect to the internal strategies.

Let us now, therefore, turn to look at some examples where brain training appears to have been the object of intervention and where there is some evidence for evaluation.

REALITY ORIENTATION

This is the most obvious and widespread example of the application of changing behaviour to address the problems of memory impairment. Holden and Woods (1988) in the standard British text on reality orientation trace the origins of reality orientation (RO) back to the late 1950s and early 1960s. There does not appear to be a clear definition of what RO is. It is described, for example, as 'a technique to rehabilitate elderly and brain damaged patients with a moderate to severe degree of disorientation'. This does not actually tell us, of course, what that technique involves, and indeed that is not particularly addressed in any of the literature with which I am familiar. For our present purposes we might define RO as being a series of techniques which use external cues to promote oriented behaviour.

The nature of these cues can vary considerably. They include environmental prostheses (such as the commonly found RO board) and other signs indicating the location and timing of important places and events. But they also include staff prompts, particularly when we look at the two techniques of 'classroom RO' where specific sessions are devoted to focusing on orientation and encouraging appropriate interaction and '24 hour RO' which is intended to guide staff behaviour towards patients throughout the day. Finally, there are elements within RO procedures which are clearly intended to encourage self-prompting, so that individuals become better able to use, for example, the environmental cues which are around them or perhaps to externalize some of those cues themselves using diaries or similar techniques. The evidence for the effectiveness of RO is well summarized in Holden and Woods (1988). There are now quite a number of studies looking at the effectiveness of reality orientation, indeed, they manage to list 17 controlled trials of RO.

The evidence suggests that RO does have benefits compared with no treatment and indeed with non-contingent attention. So there does seem to be a positive answer to whether the treatment has any effect. However, the size of the effect is relatively modest, although, of course, such behaviours as finding one's way to the toilet, may have extremely positive benefits in terms of the quality of life of those residents or patients.

The evidence for generalization is really fairly depressing. The best summary seems to be that you get changes in behaviour with respect to the areas that you train and there is not much evidence for general improvements in memory function. The notion therefore that this is a 'therapy' is perhaps not entirely accurate. Indeed, the term 'therapy' seems largely to have disappeared from the RO literature and this is perhaps not just because the initials ROT make such an unfortunate acronym.

With respect to the permanence of effects, again the evidence does seem to suggest that the effects are lost, at least in respect of the patient to whom it has been applied, fairly quickly after the treatment programme ceases. Lasting changes are more to be found in staff attitudes and behaviour. Again, this argues against describing it as a therapy and brings us back to the earlier definition of its use as a way of structuring external cues to promote oriented behaviour. Returning to the distinction between disability and handicap, it seems that we are here addressing the handicap area by improving activities of daily living, rather than having a fundamental impact on the disability, let alone the disease.

Interestingly, perhaps again because of the importance of finding any positive approach to a very disadvantaged and demanding condition such as dementia, most of the work in RO has been directed at changing the behaviour of people suffering from progressing degenerative dementia. As noted earlier, the original definition and descriptions of RO note its application to brain damaged patients, and indeed if one goes back to the original papers (e.g. Taulbee and Folsom, 1966) it looks ver much as if many of the patients whom they were helping were those who were suffering from the effects of deprived institutions. One suspects that many did not have any organic brain damage. This would be quite consistent with what we know are differences in the use of the term 'dementia' on different sides of the Atlantic.

Of course, it is precisely the environmentally deprived patients rather than those with progressive dementia for whom one is likely to have the most dramatic effects because functional disorder is such as to make the environment the primary determinant of behaviour.

MEMORY THERAPY

Work with the brain damaged, particularly the younger patients with head injury, has been the focus for the development of memory therapy and cognitive rehabilitation in general. Clearly there are tremendous attractions for applying this kind of work to older people who, as with so many conditions, represent the greatest numbers of those with memory and other cognitive impairments.

However, all too often the potential application of these techniques is one that has been identified and enthused about but not actually carried out. This is especially the case when it comes to evaluating studies of such interventions. West (1989) summarized the position as follows: 'The overriding goal of any memory intervention programme should be to demonstrate that training strategies can be maintained and can be applied to tasks other than particular ones used in training. Few studies with older people have accomplished either of these goals'.

Clearly then the situation with regard to memory therapy is very similar with that to RO except that I think it fair to say that on the whole memory therapy with older people has had fewer studies than reality orientation. Certainly West's reference to the importance of generalization is absolutely crucial. The area of memory therapy also reveals the importance of emphasizing how we decide what should be trained. The papers which have looked at the application of such retraining to older people have focused on two main sources of information.

The first of these is self-report (e.g. Sunderland et al., 1986). The reports of normal elderly people themselves include memory problems, usually such things as forgetting words, forgetting names, failing to remember where an object had been located, losing the thread of a conversation and forgetting what they were about to do. They also include forgetting when something had happened and forgetting to recall whether or not a task had been completed.

Another source of information is in relating to experimental findings (Willis, 1989), although there are considerable problems here in that laboratory methods have tended to be rather remote from every day reality. This has begun to change, but the results of experimental work do tend more to point towards mnemonics as aids to remembering lists of items, which in fact are not particularly the problems of every day living.

Certainly it is important to decide whether we are aiming to train somebody in a specific task, or whether we are endeavouring to develop a memory strategy or technique which could be applied across a range of different tasks.

Whatever the particular approach, it is important to exercise restraint in our objectives and I would suggest that we stick close to Wilson's (1989) notion of cognitive rehabilitation, which has as its primary aim, improving the daily life of a cognitive impaired person.

If we are to be wise in our choice of cognitive rehabilitation, that is to say, both in terms of techniques and subjects, we need to think carefully of a number of features. These include identifying the underlying disease. Clearly dementia has about everything we could think of against it.

First it is a progressive disease process and therefore we are fighting what must essentially be a losing battle. Secondly, in general those who suffer from dementia tend to lack insight and awareness of their problems particularly compared with the people around them. They may therefore be less inclined to see the relevance of some rehabilitation programme.

Thirdly, the process of dementia is such as to cause diffuse deterioration in mental capacity which means that other functions such as language and visio-spacial skill are also impaired. Memory is not an isolated problem with other functions being relatively intact.

The importance of assessing strengths and disabilities is clearly crucial. We need to know not only what people find difficult (such as tasks which involve remembering) but also the things which they are relatively good at, such as verbal or visual imagery skills. We can then produce a programme which builds upon strengths as a way of overcoming disabilities and thereby tackling the handicaps.

In reality there is very little to guide us in terms of controlled evaluation of cognitive rehabilitation with older subjects. However, a summary of what evidence there is might be that we do best to look at those with specific and static problems, for example, those who have memory impairment following a stroke, or indeed those who report memory problems themselves.

The only problem with the latter is that whilst it is a very real 'market', it very much looks like the worried well, rather than those with more serious difficulty. It does bring to mind serious questions about whether the consumer is always in the most altruistic position to make judgements about publicly-funded service priorities.

The evidence we have suggests that the magnitude of effect to be produced by cognitive retraining in the elderly is roughly comparable to the sorts of deficits which result from normal ageing (Willis, 1989). There is therefore a lot to be said apparently for applying techniques to the normal elderly population who do report the sorts of problems that we have techniques to improve. This is not the same as saying that a thorough and wide ranging analysis of the opportunities for health gain would necessarily generate this as being the best area for intervention. Perhaps it rather depends upon the health care system within which one works.

COMPUTER-ASSISTED COGNITIVE REHABILITATION

Finally, I would like to turn briefly to the area of computer-assisted assessment and particularly rehabilitation. There has been some development of this with respect to the younger head injured patients in Britain, but in the United States there has been a veritable explosion of software directed at this area (Malucci and Eckhouse, 1988). This is so widespread that serious questions have been asked in recent years about the evidence for the effectiveness of such approaches. In a recent review of some research and discussion in relation to cognitive rehabilitation Halligan and Cockburn (1991) quote the following opinions: there appears to be a problem of 'software programs that bear no relationship to established theories of cognitive function and no clear evidence of their effectiveness'. Moreover, the view has been expressed that it may actually be the case that 'some computerized rehabilitation programs may actually do more harm than good'.

It would seem again that an element of cautious evaluation is called for rather than necessarily market-led enthusiasm.

If we look at the evidence in relation to computer rehabilitation programs, again these have been applied to a range of older subjects. The range includes those with organic dementias, the functionally ill complaining of memory loss, but who have no objective signs of abnormal decline, and those with only subjective complaints in the absence of either organic or functional illness. Not surprisingly there are major differences between these groups and we can hardly expect one approach to be applicable to all of these.

Where positive outcomes have been reported they have included firstly the learning of new skills. Obviously it is important to demonstrate that computer based systems are acceptable and appropriate for older subjects and that they make progress in learning new skills through such methods. This certainly does seem to be the case.

Perhaps more interestingly there is some evidence of improvements in intelligence scale scores and it would be interesting to look more closely at the extent to which this might reflect a generalized improvement in under-lying cognitive skills rather than specific item training. Finally, it is interest-ing to note that those who present with subjective complaints have commented, again subjectively, that they feel that their driving habits have been improved. This might suggest that there are general improvements in perhaps choice reaction time or divided attention tasks, but we need an enormous amount more work to demonstrate that this is the case.

CONCLUSIONS

Do we then have an answer to the question can we train the brain? Well it does seem some reasonable conclusions can be drawn. It certainly does seem the case that we can produce changes in behaviour, particularly cognitive behaviour, as a result of experience. The magnitude of these effects seems broadly comparable to the kinds of decline that are to be found in normal ageing and specific training can make improvements to clinically significant behaviours at least as long as the specific programme is in operation.

We need to pay very careful attention to the needs of individual subjects in terms of underlying disease, cognitive strengths and weaknesses, potential handicaps and likely benefits. The programme must be appropriate both in form and content (Moffat, 1989). The pressure on individual patients and especially their families can be enormous. We must be sensitive to this and guard against raising unrealistic expectations which we cannot fulfil.

Overall it seems reasonable to conclude that as an absolute minimum we need to look at ways in which we are developing a prosthetic environment which breaks the link between disability and handicap. There is enormous potential for benefitting large numbers of older people. A recent clinical audit carried out by one of my medical colleagues revealed that 95% of all our geriatric medical inpatients had no access to a clock or watch.

We need to start with getting the simple things right and evolve techniques which help real problems. It may be seductive but it would be premature to claim that we can dramatically awaken the parts of the brain that other treat-ments are unable to reach.

REFERENCES

Halligan, P.W. and Cockburn, J. (1991). Issues in cognitive rehabilitation: computer assisted remediation. *Neuropsychol. Rehab.*, **1**, 81–83.

Holden, V.P. and Woods, R.T. (1988). *Reality Orientation: Psychological Approaches to the 'Confused' Elderly*, Churchill Livingstone, Edinburgh.

Malucci, R.A. and Eckhouse, R.H. (1988). The use of computers in the assessment and treatment of cognitive disabilities in the elderly: a survey. *Psychopharmacol. Bull.*, **24**, 557–564.

Moffat, N. (1989). Home-based cognitive rehabilitation with the elderly. In: Poon, L.W., Rubin, D.C. and Wilson, B.A. (Eds), *Everyday Cognition in Adulthood and Late Life*, Cambridge University Press, Cambridge.

Morris, R.G. and Morris, L.W. (1991). Cognitive and behavioural approaches with the depressed elderly. *Int. J. Geriat. Psychiatry*, **6**, 407–411.

Powell-Procter, L. and Miller, E. (1982). Reality orientation: a critical appraisal. *Br. J. Psychiatry*, **140**, 457–463.

Sunderland, A., Watts, K., Baddeley, A.D. and Harris, J.E. (1986). Subjective memory assessment and test performance in elderly adults. *J. Gerontol.*, **41**, 376–384.

Taulbee, L.R. and Folsom, D. (1966). Reality orientation for geriatric patients. *Hosp. Comm. Psychiatry*, **17**, 133–135.

Teri, L. and Gallagher-Thompson, J. (1991). Cognitive-behavioural interventions for treatment of depression in Alzheimer's patients. *Gerontologist*, **31**, 413–415.

West, R.L. (1989). Planning practical memory training for the aged. In: Poon, L.W., Rubin, D.C. and Wilson, B.A. (Eds), *Everyday Cognition in Adulthood and Late Life*, Cambridge University Press, Cambridge.

Willis, S.L. (1989). Improvement with cognitive training: which old dogs learn what new tricks? In: Poon, L.W., Rubin, D.C. and Wilson, B.A. (Eds), *Everyday Cognition in Adulthood and Late Life*, Cambridge University Press, Cambridge.

Wilson, B.A. (1989). Designing memory-therapy programs. In: Poon, L.W., Rubin, D.C. and Wilson, B.A. (Eds), *Everyday Cognition in Adulthood and Late Life*, Cambridge University Press, Cambridge.

Yesavage, J.A., Lapp, D. and Sheikh, J.I. (1989). Mnemonics as modified for use by the elderly. In: Poon, L.W., Rubin, D.C. and Wilson, B.A. (Eds), *Everyday Cognition in Adulthood and Late Life*, Cambridge University Press, Cambridge.

Zarit, S.T., Zasrit, J.M. and Reever, K.R. (1982). Memory training for severe memory loss: Effects on senile dementia patients and their families. *Gerontologist*, **22**, 373–377.

Depression

Treatment and Care in Old Age Psychiatry
Edited by R. Levy, R. Howard and A. Burns
©1993 Wrightson Biomedical Publishing Ltd

12

Measuring Change in Elderly Depressives

BRICE PITT

*Psychiatry of Old Age, St Mary's and the Royal Postgraduate Medical Schools,
London, UK*

The change to be measured in elderly depressives with which this chapter is concerned is, of course, in their depression. The term 'depressive' is deemed to be equivalent to 'suffering from depressive illness', rather than to a melancholic disposition like Shakespeare's Jacques (though 'dysthymic disorder', in the American Psychiatric Association's (1987) DSM-IIIR's 'dysthymic disorder' is not necessarily excluded. 'Elderly' is taken to represent the onset of the Roman senium, the age at which Bismarck dictated that men should retire and that at which age-related psychogeriatric services usually begin, i.e. 65 (and over).

As in all depressive illnesses, the natural tendency, even in old age, is to some extent to recover. In the days before ECT and the antidepressants, it was stated of those ill enough to be admitted (perhaps compulsorily only at that time) that signs of remission might be expected after four years! (Baldwin, 1993).

Clinicians are adept at eliciting the history and symptoms of depression, both at a diagnostic interview and in monitoring the patient's subsequent course. They can interview informants as well as the patient, and get an idea of social function and behaviour. Protocols, check lists, structured interviews like the Geriatric Mental State (GMS) (Copeland *et al.*, 1976) and scales aid the process. Clinicians are also well aware that the great majority of depressed elderly patients improve substantially with treatment within a matter of weeks. Some make a full recovery while others have residual symptoms such as early waking, diurnal variation or some morbid fears, or have not returned to their former level of social function; thus, though they may have lost the criteria of 'caseness', there is not a full *restituo ad integrum*. Some patients, labelled 'refractory', are unchanged. Clinicians also know, if they have worked in the same district for more than a year or two, that recovered depressives tend to relapse; indeed, previous depression is the greatest risk factor for a depressive episode (Baldwin, 1991).

In his classic monograph *The Significance of Affective Symptoms in Old Age*, Felix Post (1962) divided his 92 patients into:

(1) Those recovering and remaining well for three years.	26%
(2) Those recovering, relapsing but recovering again during the three years.	37%
(3) Those who made incomplete recoveries; and	25%
(4) Those who remained ill with depression throughout the three years.	12%
	100%

There were also four patients who tried to kill themselves, while three actually did so.

These categories are highly relevant to the clinician but give too little information for the comparison of one treatment with another, unless the differences are very great, e.g. the use of ECT versus no treatment at all in severe acute depression. Such a study would be ethically unacceptable nowadays, and the differences between treatments, e.g. ECT and antidepressants, one antidepressant compared with another, or an antidepressant with or without complementary cognitive therapy, are rather less stark. There is therefore the need to have some numerical measure of change.

The quest for a biological measure of depression — diminished salivation, the dexamethasone suppression test (DST) (Carroll, 1982), the tyramine conjugation test (Hale *et al.*, 1986), tritiated-imipramine binding to platelets (Nemeroff *et al.*, 1988) is so far unrewarded. These tests are not even of diagnostic validity, let alone useful in monitoring change (Arnold *et al.*, 1992). (The patient's weight, however, deserves more attention than it is sometimes accorded; it is the most useful physical sign in psychiatry.) All that can be measured, therefore, is the number of depressive symptoms and their severity, or a global impression of the disorder.

The simplest such measure is the doctor or the patient's perception on a *visual analogue* scale, first developed in 1921 and usable for global or specific assessments (Hamilton, 1987). One such is a straight line, 100 mm long, between the extremes of 'depression absent' and 'extreme depression'. The degree of depression is quantified by the number of mm between where the mark is made and zero (Aitken, 1969). Little and McPhail (1973) showed that patients' self-ratings correlated with those of their psychiatrists and the Beck Depression Inventory (BDI) (Beck *et al.*, 1961). Zeally and Aitken (1969), however, showed a much closer correlation between patients' ratings and clinical judgement when the patients were admitted than during or after treatment.

In his *Observer* column John Collee reports Mihaly Czikszentmihalyi's *Experience Sampling* technique, in which a buzzer attached to the subject's clothes goes off at random several times a day, whereupon the subjects must immediately write down how they feel. While this has yet to be used for the elderly, it might have some potential. Meanwhile it has been used to assess the general mood of prostitutes in Milan (which can't, says Collee, have done much for their business, or for the mood of their customers!).

The most widely used instruments for measuring change in depressive symptoms and syndromes at all ages are rating scales, of which by far the best established is the Hamilton Depression Rating Scale (Hamilton, 1960). Hamilton himself (1987) points out the statistical problems with scales which add up different (though, it is hoped, positively correlated) symptoms and treat them as equal. (Is 'suicidal' equivalent to 'difficulty in concentration'? It must be given more weight.) Also, adjectives, describing severity (absent, trivial, mild, moderate or severe) are converted into sets of numbers in arithmetical progression, as if the scale were *interval* rather than *ordinal*: is the interval between 'trivial' and 'mild' equivalent to that between 'trivial' and 'absent'? However, he asserts that these theoretical objections become less important in practice where there are more than 10 symptoms and where the grades of severity increase.

The Hamilton Depression Scale (HDRS) (Hamilton, 1960) is completed after psychiatric interview and training is required in its use to achieve good inter-rater reliability. Of 17 items, five are concerned with somatic symptoms and three with insomnia (which theoretically limit its potential for the elderly). Ideally it should be repeated in circumstances similar to the original rating, not least time of day, to cut down other possible causes of variation. The Montgomery–Asberg Depression Rating Scale (MADRS) (Montgomery and Asberg, 1979) consists of 10 items selected as the most sensitive to changes produced by treatment. There are fewer 'somatic' items than in the HDRS, and it is probably more suitable for use with the elderly.

Questionnaires are less often used than rating scales to measure change in drug trials, perhaps because they rely more on the patient's self-appraisal (and perhaps because they have not often been put to the test), but are probably no less sensitive to change. Two worth mentioning are the 30-question Geriatric Depression Scale (GDS) (Yesavage *et al.*, 1983), which cleverly evades any somatic questions at all (and also excludes the more psychotic topics) and the Brief Assessment Scale Depression Cards (BASDEC) (Adshead *et al.*, 1992), derived from the Brief Assessment Scale (Macdonald *et al.*, 1982), which has some 'somatic' items but is fast and user-friendly. There are 'Yes/No' answers to the GDS, 'True/False' to BASDEC, which is probably better for older patients than more graded responses.

Any cognitive impairment needs to be taken into consideration when using any of these instruments. Some may be consequent on the depression, though it is more often complained of than demonstrable. It is not sufficiently often apparent to be a reliable measure of change, though 'pseudodementia' will improve if the depression resolves. Where depression is secondary to dementia ('organic' depression) then the validity of answers to the questionnaires is suspect. Katona and Aldridge's (1985) Depressive Signs Scale is a brave attempt to measure depression in the presence of dementia, but is too short to reflect all but the most dramatic change.

Change, alas, may not only be in the direction of improvement. Elderly depressives have an unfortunate tendency to relapse, as Post's (1962) and Murphy's (1983) studies showed. Other undesirable developments are (uncommonly) dementia and death: Baldwin and Jolley's (1986) prognostic study showed a slightly more encouraging outcome over a longer period than Murphy's, but there was a substantial mortality.

Prognostic studies may look at for how much of a specified period after suffering a depressive illness was an elderly person well or ill, how many relapses were there, how long did they last, what was the inter-episode interval, how complete was the recovery and what use was made of such resources as community psychiatric nurses, personal social services, out-patient appointments, day hospital days, hospital beds and what was the mortality — from suicide or other causes — and the incidence of dementia.

The timing of any relapse needs to be defined — a return to the criteria of caseness in those under regular review, a rereferral or a readmission? The techniques of *survival analysis* are valuable in comparing the outcome of one group of patients with another.

Survival analysis (Cox and Oakes, 1984) is concerned with the analysis of times to the occurrence of such an event as relapse. If the event has not happened at the time of the analysis it is said to be *censored*. Censoring also occurs if the subject dies or is otherwise lost to follow up. There may be difficulties in defining time of origin — onset or recovery from depressive illness, or time of entry into the study.

Analyses are usually based on *Life Tables or Survival Curves*, e.g. the Kaplan Meier survival curve, which proceeds in a series of small steps, indicating *conditional probability* — the probability that, having survived so long, the subject will survive that much longer. The *logrank test* is a nonparametric method for testing the null hypothesis that the groups being compared are from the same population. The *hazard ratio* indicates how different the groups are. *Cox's proportional hazards regression model* enables the effects of several variables on survival to be investigated, e.g. drug or placebo, age, sex, length of index illness, family history of affective disorder, onset of first affective illness before or after age 65, physical illness, ECT, MADRS score at indentification. All these are explored in the OADIG trial of 'How long should the elderly take antidepressants?' (Jacoby and Lunn, 1993) which is a good example of the use of survival analysis.

REFERENCES

Adshead, F., Day Cody, D. and Pitt, B. (1992). BASDEC: A novel screening instrument for depression in elderly medical in-patients. *Br. Med. J.*, **305**, 397.

Aitken, R.C.B. (1969). Measurement of feeling using visual analogue scales. *Proc. R. Soc. Med.*, **62**, 989–993.

American Psychiatric Association (1987). *Diagnostic and Statistical Manual 3rd edn, revised*, APA, Washington DC.

Arnold, E., Fineberg, N., Hannah, P., Glover, V., Pitt, B. and Sandler, M. (1992). Is the tyramine suppression test useful in elderly patients? *J. Affect. Disord.*, **26**, 1–6.

Baldwin, R.C. (1991). Depressive illness. In: Jacoby, R. and Oppenheimer, C. (Eds), *Psychiatry in the Elderly*, Oxford Medical Publications, Oxford.

Baldwin, R.C. (1993). Depressive illness in old age. In: Naguib, M. and Pitt, B. (Eds), *Practical Reviews in the Psychiatry of Old Age*, Royal College of Psychiatrists, London (in press).

Baldwin, R.C. and Jolley, D.J. (1986). The prognosis of depression in old age. *Br. J. Psychiatry*, **149**, 574–583.

Beck, A.T., Ward, C.H., Mendelson, M., Mock, J. and Erbaugh, J. (1961). An inventory for measuring depression. *Arch. Gen. Psychiatry*, **4**, 561–571.

Carroll, B.J. (1982). Dexamethasone suppression test for melancholia. *Br. J. Psychiatry*, **140**, 2292–2304.

Copeland, J.R.M., Kelleher, M.J., Kellett, J.M., Gourlay, A.J., Gurland, B.J. and Fleiss, J.L. (1976). A semi-structured clinical interview for the assessment of diagnosis and mental state in the elderly: the Geriatric Mental Status Schedule. 1: Development and reliability. *Psychol. Med.*, **6**, 439–449.

Cox, D.R. and Oakes, D. (1984). *Analysis of Survival Data*. Chapman and Hall, London.

Hale, A.S., Walker, P.L., Bridges, P.K. and Sandler, M. (1986). Tyramine conjugation test as a trait marker in endogenous depressive illness. *J. Psychiatr. Res.*, **20**, 251–261.

Hamilton, M. (1960). A rating scale for depression. *J. Neurol. Neurosurg. Psychiatry*, **23**, 56–62.

Hamilton, M. (1987). Assessment of psychopathology. In: Hindmarch, I. and Stonier, P.D. (Eds), *Hum. Psychopharmacol.*, Wiley, Chichester.

Jacoby, R. and Lunn, A.D. (1993). 'OADIG' How long should the elderly take antidepressants? A double-blind placebo-controlled study of continuation/prophylaxis therapy with dothiepin. *Br. J. Psychiatry*, (in press).

Katona, C. and Aldridge, C. (1985). The dexamethasone suppression test and depressive signs scale in dementia. *J. Affect. Disord.*, **8**, 83–89.

Little, J. Crawford, McPhail, N.I. (1973). Measures of depressed mood at monthly intervals. *Br. J. Psychiatry*, **122**, 447–452.

Macdonald, A., Mann, A., Jenkins, R., Richard, L., Godlove, C. and Rodwell, G. (1982). An attempt to determine the impact of four types of care upon the elderly in London by the study of matched groups. *Psychol. Med.*, **12**, 193–200.

Montgomery, S.A. and Asberg, M. (1979). A new depression scale designed to be sensitive to change. *Br. J. Psychiatry*, **134**, 382–389.

Murphy, E. (1983). The prognosis of depression in old age. *Br. J. Psychiatry*, **141**, 135–142.

Nemeroff, C.B., Knight, D.L., Krishman, R.R., Slotkin, T.A., Bissette, G. and Melville, M.L. *et al.* (1988). Marked reduction in platelet-tritiated imipramine binding sites in geriatric depression. *Arch. Gen. Psychiatry*, **45**, 919–923.

Post, F. (1962). *The Significance of Affective Symptoms in Old Age.* Maudsley Monograph 10. Oxford University Press, Oxford.

Yesavage, J., Brink, T., Rose, T., Lum, O., Huang, V., Adey, M. and Leira, O. (1983). Development and validation of a geriatric depression screening scale: a preliminary report. *J. Psychiatr. Res.*, **17**, 37–49.

Zealley, A.K. and Aitken, R.C.P. (1969). Measurement of mood. *Proc. R. Soc. Med.*, **62**, 993–996.

Treatment and Care in Old Age Psychiatry
Edited by R. Levy, R. Howard and A. Burns
©1993 Wrightson Biomedical Publishing Ltd

13

New Antidepressants in Elderly Patients

CORNELIUS L.E. KATONA

Department of Psychiatry of the Elderly, University College London, UK

LIMITATIONS OF CONVENTIONAL ANTIDEPRESSANT TREATMENT IN THE ELDERLY

The use of tricyclic antidepressants for elderly patients is notoriously problematic. Surprisingly few studies have examined the efficacy of these drugs against placebo in patients over the age of 60. The reviews by Gerson *et al.* (1988) and Rockwell *et al.* (1988) identified only one placebo controlled evaluation of amitriptyline (Branconnier *et al.*, 1982), two of imipramine (Gerner *et al.*, 1980; Wakelin, 1986) and none of desipramine or trimipramine. More recently Georgotas *et al.* (1987) have evaluated nortriptyline against placebo in elderly patients. Although all these studies found the active compound to be superior, it must be remembered that most of the elderly patients met with in routine clinical practice would not qualify for such clinical trials. The majority fulfil DSM-III or DSM-IIIR (American Psychiatric Association, 1980, 1987) criteria for dysthymia rather than major depressive episode (Kivela *et al.*, 1988), the latter forming the standard entry criterion for antidepressant trials in elderly as in younger subjects. Equally important, many would have one or more medical contra-indications to the use of tricyclic antidepressants. A further problem with evaluative studies of antidepressants in the elderly is that the outcome measures, like the inclusion criteria, are geared towards a young population. Rating scales like the Hamilton Depression Rating Scale (HDRS) (Hamilton, 1960), which have a heavy weighting of somatic items, are likely to be distorted in elderly patients by the coexistence of physical disease. It is unlikely that the relationship between change in scale score and true antidepressant response will be the same as in younger patients. Less age related distortion in results would be seen if global response scales such as the Clinical Global Impression (CGI); scales specifically designed to measure change in elderly depressed subjects like the Geriatric Depression Scale (GDS) (Yesavage, 1988); or scales less laden with somatic symptoms like the Montgomery–Asberg Depression Rating Scale (MADRS) (Montgomery and Asberg, 1979) were used. Evidence for long-term efficacy of tricyclic antidepressants in preventing relapse in elderly patients is also lacking. Georgotas *et al.* (1989) found nortriptyline to be no better than placebo at one year, though the monoamine oxidase (MAO) inhibitor, phenelzine, was effective.

There is also considerable evidence that elderly patients are more likely to suffer tricyclic-related side effects and to develop more serious adverse consequences as a result. In particular cognitive function is more likely to be impaired by antidepressants with powerful anticholinergic effects (Moskowitz and Burns, 1986). Elderly patients are also more vulnerable to orthostatic hypotension largely because, even in the absence of exposure to antidepressants, baroreceptor reflexes are blunted with increasing age (Woodhouse, 1992). The consequences of such orthostatic hypotension are also likely to be more severe because patients with age-related osteoporosis are more vulnerable to suffer fractures as a result of hypotension-induced falls.

Age-related pharmacokinetic changes also increase the potential of antidepressants to cause side effects. Since most tricyclics are extensively protein bound, age-associated decreases in protein synthesis can increase free plasma drug levels. The reduced creatinine clearance and reduced hepatic blood flow in older subjects may also contribute to increased blood levels of tricyclics by delaying their excretion.

At a more practical level, drugs that need to be taken many times a day and at more than one tablet per dose are more likely to be complied with poorly by elderly patients. Age-related increases both in vulnerability to other diseases and in likelihood of receiving other treatments make elderly patients more vulnerable to drug–drug and drug–disease interactions. There is also some evidence that tricyclic antidepressants may take a surprisingly long time to be effective in elderly patients, with useful effects sometimes only emerging in the seventh or eighth week of treatment (Georgotas and McCue, 1989).

In the light of this it is perhaps not surprising that primary care physicians and psychiatrists show considerable reluctance to treat elderly patients with antidepressants. MacDonald (1986) found that, although primary care physicians were able to identify most of the depressed elderly patients under their care, they hardly ever either initiated treatment themselves or made psychiatric referrals. Similarly, Copeland (1988) found that only 4% of the community sample of elderly depressed patients received treatment.

It is, therefore, clear that, theoretically at least, the 'ideal antidepressant' for elderly patients would differ considerably from the tricyclics. In particular, an ideal drug would show unchanged pharmacokinetics with ageing, be free of interactions with other drugs commonly used in the elderly, and be safely administered even to frail elderly patients with concomitant physical disease. The ideal drug would also have a simple once daily dosage regime and have proven efficacy both against established comparator drugs and placebo in intention-to-treat (ITT) as well as completer (COMP) analyses, since only the latter take drop-out rates into account. Such trials should be of epidemiologically representative samples and use clinically valid measures of antidepressant response. Further requirements for such an ideal drug would include good side effect profile, rapid onset of antidepressant action, and demonstrable efficacy in relapse prevention.

As well as the novel tricyclic antidepressant lofepramine, four serotonin specific re-uptake inhibitors (SSRIs), fluvoxamine, fluoxetine, paroxetine and sertraline, are currently available for clinical use in the United Kingdom and have been evaluated in elderly patients. The remainder of this chapter will review the controlled trial evidence concerning their efficacy in comparison with established antidepressants and where possible placebo, and seek to establish whether they represent any significant progress towards an ideal antidepressant for elderly patients. This chapter will not cover the use of the newer monoamine oxidase inhibitors as these have not yet been licensed in the UK and no results of trials of their use in the elderly have been published.

LOFEPRAMINE

Lofepramine has a conventional tricyclic structure but *in vitro* studies and trials in non-elderly subjects suggest that it is relatively free of anticholinergic side effects (Sjogren, 1980). The effects of single doses of lofepramine (70–140 mg) have been compared with 50 mg amitriptyline and placebo in drug free healthy elderly volunteers. Side effects of lofepramine and placebo did not differ significantly. Amitriptyline however was associated with more frequent subjective side effects than either lofepramine or placebo. Standing diastolic blood pressure was also reduced in comparison with lofepramine and salivary volume (an objective measure of dry mouth) reduced in comparison with both placebo and lofepramine. Though amitriptyline also impaired performance on choice reaction time, lofepramine was associated with significantly better choice recognition time than placebo (Ghose and Sedman, 1987). The same group (Ghose and Spragg, 1989) examined the pharmacokinetics of single doses of lofepramine and amitriptyline in healthy drug free elderly subjects. They found the elimination half life of lofepramine to be 2.5 h (compared with 31 h for amitriptyline), but noted very great interindividual variation in peak plasma lofepramine concentrations. These studies suggest that lofepramine has unchanged pharmacokinetics compared

Table 1. Controlled trials of newer antidepressants in old age.

	Entry criteria	Entered	Completed	Age Range	Age Mean	Drug	Dose (mg)	Duration	Outcome measures	Analysis	Results (% responder where given)	Comments
Jessel et al., 1981	CLIN	20	19	64-84	70.5	Lofepramine	105	4 Weeks	CGI	COMP	L(72%)=A(47%)	
		19	18	65-78	68	Amitriptyline	75					
Fairbairn et al., 1989	DSM-III MDE	30	24	68-88	77	Lofepramine	140	6 Weeks	MADRS	COMP	L = D	
		32	24	65-88	77	Dothiepin	100					
Wakelin, 1986	DSM-III MAD	33	24	60-71	65	Fluvoxamine	150-300	4 Weeks	HDRS CGI	COMP	F(79%)=I(65%) >P(25%)	
		29	16	60-70	66	Imipramine	150-300					
		14	12	60-68	64	Placebo	N/A					
Rahman et al., 1991	DSM-III MDE	26	17	65-86	73	Fluvoxamine	100-200	6 Weeks	MADRS CGI	NR	F(64%)=D(60%)	
		26	19	61-85	75	Dothiepin	100-200					
Phanjoo et al., 1991	DSM-III MDE	25	16	66-86	76	Fluvoxamine	100-200	6 Weeks	MADRS CGI	NR	F = M	CGI: Fluoxetine superior at 2 weeks
		25	16	66-87	77	Mianserin	40-80					
Feighner et al., 1985	DSM-III MDE	78	41	61-90	NR	Fluoxetine	20-80	6 Weeks	HDRS CGI	ITT	F(49%)=D(48%)	
		79	31	61-90	NR	Doxepin	50-200					
Altamura et al., 1989	DSM-III MDE	13	11	NR	68.5	Fluoxetine	20	5 Weeks	HDRS	COMP	F = A	Faster onset of action with amitriptyline
		15	11	NR		Amitriptyline	75					
Hutchinson et al., 1991	DSM-III MDE	58	46	NR	72	Paroxetine	30	6 Weeks	HDRS	COMP	P(55%)=A(59%)	
		32	21	(>65)	71.5	Amitriptyline	100					
Halikas, 1990	DSM-III MDE	132	92	NR	NR	Paroxetine	40	6 Weeks	HDRS CGI	ITT	P = D (P>D on depression item)	
		132	96	(>60)		Doxepin	200					
Dorman, 1990	DSM-III	29	24	NR	NR	Paroxetine	30	6 Weeks	HDRS	COMP	P(48%)>M(18%)	
		28	25	(>65)		Mianserin	60					
Cohn et al., 1991	DSM-III MDE BIP	161	82	63-85	70	Sertraline	50-200	8 Weeks	HDRS CGI	COMP/ITT	COMP (CGI): S(69%)=A(64%) ITT (HDRS): A>S	
		80	39	65-82	71	Amitriptyline	50-150					

Key: CLIN = clinical; BIP = bipolar disorder; MAD = major affective disorder; MDE = major depressive episode; NR = not recorded; L = lofepramine; D = dothiepin; A = amitriptyline; P = paroxetine; M = mianserin..

with younger subjects despite its very extensive (99%) protein binding (Dollery, 1991) and should be well tolerated by elderly people.

Two published studies have examined the efficacy of lofepramine in elderly depressed patients: against amitriptyline (Jessel *et al.*, 1981) and against dothiepin (Fairbairn *et al.*, 1989). The methods and results of these trials are summarized in Table 1. Both studies show relatively low drop out rates and although Fairbairn *et al.* (1989) included only patients with DSM-III major depressive episode, both studies used relatively appropriate outcome measures. COMP analyses only were provided, and lofepramine was found to be significantly more effective than amitriptyline and as effective as dothiepin. Analysis of side effects showed no difference from amitriptyline but less dry mouth and drowsiness than dothiepin.

Though lofepramine thus appears to be a reasonably effective antidepressant for elderly people, these results must be viewed with some caution. In particular there are no placebo controlled data and no ITT analyses; doses of both lofepramine and the comparators were relatively low (with no data on plasma levels achieved); and total numbers of subjects included were small. There are also no long-term data on the efficacy of lofepramine in preventing relapse.

FLUVOXAMINE

Fluvoxamine is chemically and pharmacologically distinct from tricyclic antidepressants and is a potent and selective inhibitor of serotonin re-uptake. Animal studies show it to be free of MAO inhibiting and anticholinergic effects and to have negligible effects on noradrenaline re-uptake (Classen *et al.*, 1977). It is rapidly absorbed, has no active metabolites and is excreted via the kidneys with a plasma half life of about 15 h that is unaffected by age (Benfield and Ward, 1986).

There have been three double-blind controlled comparisons between fluvoxamine and standard antidepressants in elderly patients. Their findings are summarized in Table 1. Only one trial (Wakelin, 1986) incorporated a placebo group. This study included subjects ranging in age between 60 and 71 and therefore did not examine a representative elderly sample. Drop out rates were relatively high in both active (fluvoxamine and imipramine) groups and the study only lasted four weeks. Clear superiority of both active drugs over placebo was demonstrated for completers. It should be noted, however, that this superiority is very much less striking if the data are subjected to ITT analysis. The studies by Rahman *et al.* (1991) and Phanjoo *et al.* (1991) compare fluvoxamine with dothiepin and mianserin, respectively. Neither of these studies has a placebo group, both have similarly high drop out rates to those in the Wakelin (1986) study, but both examined more truly elderly patients (ages ranging up to 87), had more adequate treatment durations of six weeks, and used appropriate outcome measures (MADRS and CGI). Both studies found fluvoxamine to be as effective as the comparator drugs. Rahman *et al.* (1991) also provided adequate information about response rates, which at 64% for fluvoxamine and 60% for dothiepin are similar to those reported in studies in younger patients. Surprisingly, side effect profiles were similar for fluvoxamine and comparators in all the studies although Wakelin (1986) found fluvoxamine to give rise to significantly less dry mouth than imipramine.

In the context of controlled clinical trials, fluvoxamine appears to be reasonably effective and well tolerated. Comparison against placebo is however very limited both by small numbers and high drop out rates, and there are no published data addressing the question of the drug's efficacy in relapse prevention.

FLUOXETINE

Like the other SSRIs currently available, fluoxetine has a novel pharmacological structure and is relatively free of cardiovascular, anticholinergic, antihistaminic and hypotensive effects (Feighner, 1983). Lucas and Osborne (1986) examined the pharmacokinetics of fluoxetine and its major active metabolite norfluoxetine in elderly depressed patients and found no alteration in elimination of the drug with age.

Two controlled comparisons between fluoxetine and established antidepressants have been published (Feighner and Cohn, 1985; Altamura *et al.*, 1989). The findings of these studies are summarized in Table 1. The earlier and larger study by Feighner and Cohn (1985) used doxepin as comparator and relatively high doses of both drugs, with adequate treatment duration and the CGI as main outcome measure. Patients ranged widely in age and the drop out rate was very high, approaching 50% in the fluoxetine group and exceeding it in the doxepin group. Despite the high drop out rates, reasonable ITT response rates were seen which did not differ between the two drugs.

No formal comparisons were made of emergent side effects, but adverse experiences were the reason for drop out in 32% of fluoxetine patients and 43% of doxepin patients. Anticholinergic side effects were more prominent in the doxepin group and nausea, anxiety and insomnia in the fluoxetine group. Patients in the study who responded were continued on the same drug on an open label basis for up to 48 weeks with no significant fall off in response and no emergent difference between the two drugs.

The much smaller study by Altamura *et al.* (1989) was carried out in a relatively young group (mean age 68.5 years), had a relatively short treatment period of five weeks and a fairly low dose of comparator drug (amitriptyline

75 mg). Drop out rates were low but only COMP analyses were reported, showing the two drugs to be equivalent. Amitriptyline appeared to have a faster onset of action, though this was not apparent for biological symptoms and presumably reflected the ability of amitriptyline to relieve anxiety and initial insomnia. Severity and frequency of side effects tended to be lower in the fluoxetine group, the difference reaching statistical significance for dry mouth. There was also a significant difference in weight change through the trial with amitriptyline treated patients showing significant weight gain.

On the basis of these studies, fluoxetine appears to have a distinctly different side effect profile to tricyclic antidepressants and, though the lack of placebo controlled data must be borne in mind, to be comparable in efficacy with some evidence of ability to prevent relapse.

PAROXETINE

Paroxetine is a highly selective serotonin re-uptake inhibitor which is effectively absorbed and extensively (95%) protein bound, with a complex metabolic pathway of oxidation, methylation and conjugation prior to excretion in the urine (Kaye et al., 1989). The plasma half life is approximately 24 hours but varies widely with some evidence of increased plasma half life in the elderly (Kaye et al., 1989).

Three controlled comparisons with established antidepressants in elderly patients have been published and are summarized in Table 1. Only one (Hutchinson et al., 1991) has appeared as a full length paper, the other two (Dorman, 1990; Halikas, 1990) presenting limited data in the form of extended conference abstracts. Halikas et al. (1990), comparing paroxetine with doxepin, had a large sample size but did not report their mean age. Both drugs were administered in relatively high doses over six weeks and, in an ITT analysis, were found to be equivalent, though paroxetine had a larger effect than doxepin on the depressed mood item of the HDRS. Dorman (1990), in a small study comparing paroxetine 30 mg with a relatively low dose of mianserin in a patient population again undefined by mean age, found paroxetine to be superior to mianserin. This finding must be viewed with some caution since only COMP analysis was reported and, though the response rate in the paroxetine group (48%) was reasonable, that in the mianserin group (18%) was very low. Hutchinson et al. (1991) compared paroxetine with amitriptyline in a relatively young (mean age 72) elderly group over six weeks. Drop out rates were reasonable and, in a COMP only analysis, the two drugs were found to be equally effective. All three studies showed a tendency for more anticholinergic side effects with comparator drugs than paroxetine. This reached clinical significance for anticholinergic effects overall in the study by Hutchinson et al. (1991).

Paroxetine thus appears to be of at least equal efficacy to comparator drugs with some suggestion of superiority, though the overall response rate to paroxetine was no higher than might be expected. The side effect profile of paroxetine in elderly patients closely resembles that which would be predicted from *in vitro* studies or data from younger patients.

SERTRALINE

Sertraline is a specific serotonin re-uptake inhibitor unrelated chemically to other SSRIs and relatively free of anticholinergic, antihistaminic and adverse cardiovascular side effects (Doogan and Caillard, 1988). Pharmacokinetic studies (Invicta Pharmaceuticals, data on file) suggest that in elderly volunteers, the pharmacokinetics of sertraline are similar to those in younger subjects. Its major metabolite, desmethylsertraline, is found in higher concentrations in elderly subjects. The plasma half life of sertraline in these elderly volunteers was 21.6 h and that of desmethylsertraline 83.7 h. Three out of 20 volunteers in an open study had to discontinue sertraline because of side effects such as nausea, insomnia and dizziness. Comparison of the effects of sertraline and mianserin on psychomotor performance in elderly volunteers showed sertraline (at doses up to 200 mg daily) to have a generally neutral psychomotor profile (Hindmarch *et al.*, 1990) with significant improvement in vigilance compared with placebo (Hindmarch and Bhatti, 1988).

The only controlled study of sertraline in elderly patients is a comparison with amitriptyline (Cohn *et al.*, 1990). The results of this study, which did not include a placebo group, are summarized in Table 1. The sample examined was relatively large, but the completer rate in both sertraline and amitriptyline groups was less than 50%, and though the age range was wide the mean was relatively low. Both the doses of drugs used and the duration of the trial were adequate to allow beneficial effects to emerge. The overall analysis showed equivalent efficacy for completers, though the ITT analysis indicated some superiority of amitriptyline over sertraline in magnitude of change in the HDRS. The latter finding may be due at least in part to greater responsiveness of the anxiety and sleep items of this scale to the more sedating antidepressant. Anticholinergic side effects were significantly commoner in the amitriptyline treated group and gastro-intestinal ones in the sertraline group, with similar side-effect related withdrawal rates (28% on sertraline subjects and 35% on amitriptyline). There was also a modest but statistically significant difference in weight change between the groups, amitriptyline being associated with weight gain and sertraline with weight loss. Patients achieving satisfactory response in the double-blind study continued on the same therapy for an additional 16 week period, with efficacy assessments at

12 and 24 weeks indicating no diminution in response from that at eight weeks (Invicta Pharmaceuticals, data on file).

Sertraline thus appears reasonably well tolerated by elderly patients with modest evidence for efficacy in relapse prevention. However, the high withdrawal rate and lack of placebo control limit the confidence that can be placed in these results.

CONCLUSIONS

All the antidepressant drugs reviewed above appear to be effective in 50–60% of depressed elderly patients suggesting that there is no clear difference in efficacy between them and their tricyclic predecessors. The almost complete lack of placebo controlled data remains a major problem as does the severe lack of long-term efficacy data which are of particular importance in the context of a disease as frequently recurring as depression in old age (Murphy, 1983). No single drug can be claimed to be clearly superior to the others on the basis of the evidence reviewed above, although paroxetine may be claimed to have a slight edge in terms of numbers of patients studied and evidence of superiority over comparator drug in two out of three studies.

The new antidepressant drugs probably do represent a modest step forward in the treatment of depression in elderly patients and may reasonably be seen as drugs of first choice. Their advantage lies not in greater clinical trial efficacy but in the fact that they have fewer contra-indications and a less disabling side effect profile. This may enable a higher proportion of the many depressed elderly patients in the real world who would not be eligible for entry into control clinical trials to be treated effectively. Further evidence in terms of placebo controlled efficacy and long-term relapse prevention is clearly needed. This will be aided in the next generation of clinical trials by critical cost–benefit appraisal including quality of life assessment and in which the impact on health services of poor compliance and adverse drug effects can be weighed up against that of drug cost.

REFERENCES

Altamura, A.C., Percudani, M., Guercetti, G. and Invernizzi, G. (1989). Efficacy and tolerability of fluoxetine in the elderly: a double-blind study versus amitriptyline. *Int. Clin. Psychopharmacol.*, **4**, 103–106.

American Psychiatric Association (1980). *Diagnostic and Statistical Manual of Mental Disorders (3rd edn)*, American Psychiatric Association, Washington.

American Psychiatric Association (1987). *Diagnostic and Statistical Manual of Mental Disorders (3rd edn, revised)*, American Psychiatric Association, Washington.

Benfield, P. and Ward, A. (1986). Fluvoxamine: a review of its pharmacodynamic and pharmacokinetic properties, and therapeutic efficacy in depressive illness. *Drugs*, **32**, 313–334.

Branconnier, R.J., Cole, J.O., Ghazvinian, S. and Rosenthal, S. (1982). Treating the depressed elderly patient: the comparative behavioural pharmacology of mianserin and amitriptyline. In: Costa, E. and Racagni, G. (Eds), *Typical and Atypical Antidepressants: Clinical Practice*. Raven Press, New York, pp. 195–212.

Classen, V., Davies, J.E., Hertting, G. and Placheta, P. (1977). Fluvoxamine. A specific 5-hydroxytryptamine uptake inhibitor. *Br. J. Pharmacol.*, **60**, 505–516.

Cohn, C.K., Shrivastava, R., Mendels, J., Dessain, E.G., Itil, T.M. and Lautin, A. (1990). Double-blind, multicenter comparison of sertraline and amitriptyline in elderly depressed patients. *J. Clin. Psychiatry*, **51**, 28–33.

Copeland, J.R.M. (1988). Physical ill-health, age and depression. In: Helgason, T. and Daly, R.J. (Eds), *Depressive Illness: Predictors of Course and Outcome*, Academic Press, New York, pp. 118–125.

Dollery, C. (Ed.) (1991). *Therapeutic Drugs*, Churchill Livingstone, Edinburgh, p. L53.

Doogan, D.P. and Caillard, V. (1988). Sertraline: a new antidepressant. *J. Clin. Psychiatry*, **49**, 46–51.

Dorman, T. (1990). A double-blind comparison of paroxetine and mianserin on sleep in elderly depressed patients. *Proceedings of 17th CINP Congress, Tokyo*.

Fairbairn, A.F., George, K. and Dorman, T. (1989). Lofepramine versus dothiepin in the treatment of depression in elderly patients. *Br. J. Clin. Pract.*, **43**, 55–60.

Feighner, J.P. (1983). The new generation of antidepressants. *J. Clin. Psychiatry*, **44**, 49–55.

Feighner, J.P. and Cohn, J.B. (1985). Double-blind comparative trials of fluoxetine and doxepin in geriatric patients with major depressive disorder. *J. Clin. Psychiatry*, **46**, 20–25.

Georgotas, A. and McCue, R.E. (1989). A placebo controlled comparison of nortriptyline and phenelzine in maintenance therapy of elderly depressed patients. *Arch. Gen. Psychiatry*, **46**, 783–785.

Georgotas, A., McCue, R.E., Friedman, E. and Cooper, T. (1987). The response of depressive symptoms to nortriptyline, phenelzine and placebo. *Br. J. Psychiatry*, **151**, 102–106.

Georgotas, A., McCue, R.E., Cooper, T.B., Nagachandran, N. and Friedhoff, A. (1989). Factors affecting the delay of anti-depressant effect in responders to nortriptyline and phenelzine. *Psychiatr. Res.*, **28**, 1–9.

Gerner, R., Estabrook, W., Steuer, J. and Jarvik, L. (1980). Treatment of geriatric depression with trazodone, imipramine and placebo: a double-blind study. *J. Clin. Psychiatry*, **41**, 216–220.

Gerson, S.C., Plotkin, D.A. and Jarvik, L.F. (1988). Antidepressant drug studies, 1946 to 1986: empirical evidence for aging patients. *J. Clin. Psychopharmacol.*, **8**, 311–322.

Ghose, K. and Sedman, E. (1987). A double-blind comparison of the pharmacodynamic effects of single doses of lofepramine, amitriptyline and placebo in elderly subjects. *Eur. J. Clin. Pharmacol.*, **33**, 505–509.

Ghose, K. and Spragg, B.P. (1989). Pharmacokinetics of lofepramine and amitriptyline in elderly healthy subjects. *Int. Clin. Psychopharmacol.*, **4**, 201–215.

Halikas, J.P. (1990). A double-blind comparison of paroxetine and mianserin on sleep in elderly depressed patients. *Proceedings of 17th CINP Congress, Tokyo*.

Hamilton, M. (1960). A rating scale for depression. *J. Neurol. Neurosurg. Psychiatry*, **23**, 56–62.

Hindmarch, I. and Bhatti, J.Z. (1988). Psychopharmacological effects of sertraline in normal, healthy volunteers. *Eur. J. Clin. Pharmacol.*, **35**, 221–223.

Hindmarch, I., Shillingford, J. and Shillingford, C. (1990). The effects of sertraline on psychomotor performance in elderly volunteers. *J. Clin. Psychiatry*, **51**, 34–36.

Hutchinson, D.R., Tong, S., Moon, C.A.L., Vince, M. and Clarke, A. (1991). A double blind study in general practice to compare the efficacy and tolerability of paroxetine and amitriptyline in depressed elderly patients. *Br. J. Clin. Res.*, **2**, 43–47.

Jessel, H.-J., Jessel, I. and Wegener, G. (1981). Therapy for depressive elderly patients: lofepramine and amitriptyline tested under double-blind conditions. *Z. Allg. Med.*, **57**, 784–787.

Kaye, C.M., Haddock, R.E., Langley, P.F., Mellows, G., Tasker, T.C., Zussman, B.D. and Greb, W.H. (1989). A review of the metabolism and pharmacokinetics of paroxetine in man. *Acta Psychiatr. Scand.*, **80**, 60–75.

Kivela, S.L., Pahkala, K. and Laippala, P. (1988). Prevalence of depression in an elderly population in Finland. *Acta Psychiatr. Scand.*, **78**, 401–413.

Lucas, R.A. and Osborne, D.J. (1986). The disposition of fluoxetine and norfluoxetine in elderly patients with depressive illness compared to younger subjects. *Proceedings of 16th CINP Congress, Puerto Rico*.

MacDonald, A.J.D. (1986). Do general practitioners 'miss' depression in elderly patients? *Br. Med. J.*, **292**, 1365–1367.

Montgomery, S.A. and Asberg, M. (1979). A new depression scale designed to be sensitive to change. *Br. J. Psychiatry*, **134**, 382–389.

Moskowitz, H. and Burns, M.M. (1986). Cognitive performance in geriatric subjects after acute treatment with antidepressants. *Neuropsychobiology*, **15**, 38.

Murphy, E. (1983). The prognosis of depression in old age. *Br. J. Psychiatry*, **142**, 111–119.

Phanjoo, A.L., Wonnacott, S. and Hodgson, A. (1991). Double-blind comparative multicentre study of fluvoxamine and mianserin in the treatment of major depressive episode in elderly people. *Acta Psychiatr. Scand.*, **83**, 476–479.

Rahman, M.K., Akhtar, M.J., Savla, N.C., Sharma, R.R., Kellett, J.M. and Ashford, J.J. (1991). A double-blind, randomised comparison of fluvoxamine with dothiepin in the treatment of depression in elderly patients. *Br. J. Clin. Pract.*, **45**, 255–258.

Rockwell, E., Lam, R.W. and Zisook, S. (1988). Antidepressant drug studies in the elderly. *Psychiatr. Clin. N. Am.*, **11**, 215–233.

Sjogren, C. (1980). The pharmacological profile of lofepramine: A new antidepressant drug. *Neuropharmacology*, **19**, 1213–1214.

Wakelin, J.S. (1986). Fluvoxamine in the treatment of the older depressed patient; double-blind, placebo-controlled data. *Int. Clin. Psychopharmacol.*, **1**, 221–230.

Woodhouse, K. (1992). The pharmacology of major tranquillisers in the elderly. In: Katona, C.L.E. and Levy, R. (Eds), *Delusions and Hallucinations in Old Age*. Gaskell, London, pp. 84–94.

Yesavage, J.A. (1988). Geriatric Depression Scale. *Psychopharmacol. Bull.*, **24**, 709–710.

Treatment and Care in Old Age Psychiatry
Edited by R. Levy, R. Howard and A. Burns
©1993 Wrightson Biomedical Publishing Ltd

14

ECT in the Elderly

DAVID G. WILKINSON

Old Age Psychiatry, Moorgreen Hospital, Southampton, UK

ECT

There has been a great interest in the use of ECT in the elderly in recent years, fuelled to some extent by demographic changes in the elderly population. It would be unduly repetitious to elaborate on the numerous studies which show ample evidence of the superiority of ECT over sham ECT (Johnstone *et al.*, 1980; West, 1981; Brandon *et al.*, 1984; Gregory *et al.*, 1985). In geriatric psychiatry it has been shown to be an effective treatment for affective disorders (Table 1) with good or much improved outcomes in excess of 80% of cases. It is safe despite the likelihood of multiple system disorders and medications (Gaspar *et al.*, 1982). It is well tolerated but, as will be discussed, not well liked (Malcolm, 1989). It will sometimes cause

Table 1. ECT outcome studies in the elderly.

Author	N	Electrode placement		Length of course	Outcome %	
		%Unilateral	*%Bilateral*		*Excellent/ Good*	*Poor*
Fraser and Glass (1980)	29	45	55	6.5	100	0
Gaspar *et al.* (1982)	33	0	100	8.7	79	12
Mielke *et al.* (1984)	24	57	13	13.8	75	0
Karlinsky and Shulman (1984)	33	70	9	9.3	78	21
Kramer (1987)	50	0	100	7.4	92	8
Benbow (1987)	122	3	95	8.3	80	20
Godber *et al.* (1987)	163	95	3	11.2	74	26
Magnis *et al.* (1988)	30	0	100	11	63	37
Coffey *et al.* (1988)	67	51	29	9	98	2
Figiel *et al.* (1989)	51	74	6	9	82	18

Table 2. ECT at Moorgreen Hospital Oct. 91–April 92.

	N	Average length of course	Average seizure length (s)	Total seizure length (s)
Unilateral	43 (66%)	9	31	297
Mixed	18 (27%)	17	26	328
Bilateral	5 (8%)	13	28	368
Total	66	11	28	311

or exacerbate confusion but produces no evidence of brain damage (Coffey *et al.*, 1991; Lippmann *et al.*, 1985) or lasting cognitive deficits (Devanand *et al.*, 1991). However the latter is disputed and there is some evidence that bilateral ECT can cause some lasting effects on memory (Squire, 1986). It seems that patients receiving brief pulse unilateral ECT can expect to recover fully from their depressive illness without experiencing any short- or long-term memory impairment (Weiner *et al.*, 1986). The therapeutic dilemma then is that the evidence strongly supports the view that ECT should be considered in every patient who has either failed to respond to other treatments or is so depressed as to be at risk through suicide or inanition and yet patients and the general public still regard the treatment as archaic and barbaric.

This dilemma has to be our responsibility to resolve, our silent confidence in the treatment will not be enough. Whilst we cannot ignore our patients complaining we also have to be more positive about its prescription. The allegation of barbarism has to be dealt with in the context of other medical treatments, many surgical procedures are profoundly disfiguring and yet because they offer treatment for cancer, or physical pain rather than the intolerable distress of depression they are accepted without comment. Certain procedures like episiotomy are in fact often undertaken without adequate anaesthesia with the patient entirely conscious and without any hint of consent being given. I think therefore psychiatrists should not be apologetic about ECT and should offer it positively when the established criteria for its use are satisfied. However, a positive view of its use does not automatically encourage patient acceptance. My own experience of ECT use over a recent six month period is illustrated in (Table 2). All the Consultants in the unit take part in the administration of ECT and have a great deal of therapeutic optimism but nevertheless we experience considerable patient anxiety.

TREATMENT RELATED ANXIETY

Of course anxiety is not unique to ECT, in general surgery Sheffer and Greigenstein (1960) report that 92% of their sample pre-operatively demonstrated tension and fear about the use of anaesthesia and Graham and Conley (1960) found that 34 of 70 patients on the evening before surgery acknowledged being very frightened and anxious and indeed Hughes et al. (1981) concluded that many patients found ECT less anxiety provoking than a trip to the dentist. This must not stop us addressing the problem of anxiety associated with ECT as Pippard and Ellam (1981) recommend. Heggs (1990) looked at anxiety levels associated with ECT in our unit. She used an alternating treatments design, measuring the level of anxiety using a Spielberger trait anxiety inventory (Spielberger et al., 1983) and a modified Stroop colour naming task. The tests were given before each treatment, between treatments and after discharge.

The results showed a general fall in anxiety levels with treatment but in six of nine patients showing an overall fall, there was a measurable rise in anxiety after the third or fourth treatment. One obvious point that we need to address therefore is that ECT is not a one-off operation but a repetitive procedure and this may have a bearing on anxiety. We therefore need to understand that our reassurance and persuasion is at its height before treatment starts, but we must continue to affirm the need for treatment during the course particularly perhaps after three or four treatments, when the patient is less withdrawn and disinterested and wanting to find out more about what is happening.

This study highlights something also noted by Abrams (1988) that there are some elderly patients who improve for the first three or four treatments and then get worse with further treatment and eventually fail to regain the initial improvements. ECT should not therefore be prescribed and forgotten, we should review the progress after each two or three treatments, to decide whether to continue, to increase the dose, change from unilateral to bilateral or vice versa and address any side effects that might develop such as confusion, emergence delirium, or headaches. Heggs also used a visual analogue scale for anxiety to rank the various treatment steps (Table 3).

Clearly many of the anxieties relate purely to the anaesthetic with patients fearing loss of consciousness, memory and bladder control, as well as concerns over saying embarrassing things whilst drowsy. This is at variance with the Freeman et al. (1980) study showing that only 29% of patients were afraid of waiting for or having the anaesthetic. Their study was on younger patients 12 months after treatment and yet Heggs (1990) showed at three month follow up concern about the anaesthetic was still paramount. Three of the 11 patients Heggs interviewed said they would not be prepared to have ECT again if it were necessary. This is an important factor in managing depression in the elderly who despite a good response to ECT may relapse and benefit from a further course.

Following this study a number of changes were made to practice in our unit including the provision of an information sheet; the patient being offered

Table 3. Concerns expressed by patients about ECT before and after treatment (Heggs, 1990).

Concern	Pre ECT (N = 11)	Post ECT (N = 11)	Follow-up (N = 7)
Being made unconscious	—	4	—
Losing control of bladder	1	4	—
Memory loss	1	9	—
Possible brain damage	3	2	—
Being in pain	1	—	—
Use of electricity in treatment	1	4	—
Having a convulsion or fit	1	2	—
Use of an anaesthetic	1	8	6
Not knowing what would happen	2	5	—
What others will think	1	1	—
Side effects	4	4	—
Waiting the night before	—	1	3

the chance to see the treatment room and electrodes prior to treatment, allowing patients to walk into the treatment room rather than being wheeled in on a trolley and removing the 'Nil by Mouth' notices. The latter were placed on patients' lockers seen during the afternoon before treatment and were seen as stigmatizing as well as anxiety provoking. The chief change was the establishment of an ECT users group. This group has had a significant impact in the sense of 'glasnost', giving ECT patients a positive identity and a forum for open discussion. It has allowed the other ward groups to concentrate on other issues as ECT is seldom brought up in these. The main themes are shown in Table 4 and are in general negative. Patients often need encouragement to share their positive feelings about their improvement but the group often reinforces the need for the treatment and the need to continue.

Fear of ECT is lessened by allowing patients' misconceptions to be aired; one patient thought ECT was administered through a large spiked helmet and was greatly reassured when encouraged to see the electrodes. Another

Table 4. ECT group — recurring themes.

1. How does ECT work?
2. Memory loss — reason, recovery
3. How do you decide how many?
4. 'The old days' before anaesthesia
5. Safety — has anyone died?
6. The needle
7. Would you have ECT?
8. Side effects — headache, muzziness
9. Other patients' 'horror stories'
10. The name convulsive therapy

felt the bruises on the back of her hand were due to excessive violence on the part of the anaesthetist, rather than simply extravasation of blood following the injection.

I also use a video made for teaching purposes which shows a patient before, during and after treatment together with some explanation of the procedure. This is shown to relatives and patients who are uncertain about the treatment before they give consent. No patient shown the video has subsequently refused the treatment. As it has been made by staff in the unit it adds to the sense of openness and reassurance, demystifying the procedure. Baxter *et al.* (1986) felt that videos were unhelpful. However they should be used as part of a whole anxiety reducing package.

HOW TO USE ECT

When deciding about the prescription of ECT and its continuation one must remember the initial assessment of the patient's illness, that interview is crucial to the understanding of the illness and the patient. It is the time when the patient is at his lowest ebb and yet often at his most accessible so if at that time there is enough information to suggest that the patient would respond well to ECT, this should be recorded because during trials of antidepressants and admission to hospital some of the symptoms may ameliorate and lessen one's resolve to try ECT despite lack of adequate improvement.

Two case histories underline this point.

Case one

A 73 year old married man referred a few days after moving into the catchment area of our unit in order to provide follow-up of his dementia. He was being treated with depot flupenthixol, lorazepam, and benzhexol. He had an indwelling urinary catheter and was virtually immobile due to Parkinson's disease. At interview he appeared depressed and was admitted for assessment. He recovered on amitriptyline after stopping flupenthixol and benzhexol and substituting L-dopa (Sinemet) and was able to regain continence without his catheter. However, some months later, on routine follow up I found him in his kitchen expressing quite vehemently delusions about his wife poisoning him. He never expressed these openly again but refused to take any medication, food or drink, would not dress or undress and rapidly deteriorated physically. He was admitted to hospital where his decline continued and he was undoubtedly going to die as a result of his depressive psychosis. I discussed with him and his family the use of ECT and they agreed. Nursing staff were somewhat more reticent as it is not our habit to give daily ECT to someone with an intravenous drip, nasogastric tube in order to give L-dopa and antibiotics, as well as a large sacral pressure sore. After four treatments his response was dramatic, after 19 he was returned to normal, his only complaints being the scab on his pressure sore itching and paraesthesia in his legs.

His return from the jaws of death had an immense impact on various difficult family relationships, and incidentally morale in the unit. He is still at home seven years later with evidence of cognitive impairment only recently emerging over the past year as his Parkinson's disease has progressed.

Case two

A 57 year old man referred from the general psychiatric service for long-term care with a diagnosis of progressive dementia of uncertain cause, although Pick's disease or Creutzfeldt–Jacob disease were thought more likely than Alzheimer's disease. The diagnosis was based on his rapid decline, behavioural disturbances, incontinence of urine and faeces, evidence of a left extensor plantar response, a right sided grasp reflex, EEG changes and generalized cerebral atrophy on CT scan, with normal lumbar puncture. When I met him his mutism seemed related only to emotions and feelings, he seemed orientated and aware but very depressed. He had a history of three previous depressive illnesses responding to ECT, and had one of these three months earlier after a suicide attempt by ingesting bleach and whisky. I declined to take over his care and recommended ECT. He had 10 bilateral treatments with initial remarkable improvement but discharge failed and he was readmitted in a similar state. A further 10 bilateral ECT failed this time to improve him significantly; I then admitted him and continued bilateral ECT giving a further 10 treatments, he returned to normality and six years later still has no sign of dementia. He had a brief relapse three months later for which he received 14 ECT and lithium prophylaxis and has remained well ever since.

These cases illustrate that one must always remember the initial presentation despite lengthy admissions which alter one's focus and persist with ECT if all the signs augur well; in the end it may be the only truly life saving treatment we possess.

WHO WILL RESPOND

I think it is possible to predict who will respond to ECT, it is rare for the retarded patient with delusions of guilt and suicidal intent not to respond. Unfavourable features are long standing anxiety, hypochondriasis, somatization symptoms and personality traits of hysterical or dependent nature.

Table 5. Depressive features predicting response to ECT (AHRS) (Fraser and Glass, 1980).

Guilt
Subjectively depressed mood
Psychic anxiety
Loss of interests
Agitation

Fraser and Glass (1980) (Table 5) identified five items from the Hamilton Rating Scale for depression which best predicted response to ECT: these were guilt, subjectively depressed mood, psychic anxiety, loss of interests and agitation. Others have found similar predictors and assessed the value of them (Table 6). However, despite having a clear picture of favourable and non-favourable features we have enough atypical depressives who fail to respond to other measures and respond to ECT to justify a trial of ECT as good clinical practice. In fact in an outcome study (Godber *et al.*, 1987), 27% of the sample showed predominantly neurotic features. If these have presented for the first time in late life it can well be an indication of a depressive illness and if their depressive symptoms partially resolve with antidepressants one should be encouraged to try ECT. One should also not be too distracted by a lack of vegative signs and symptoms of depressive illness. Whilst diurnal variation, weight loss, constipation, and all the other signs are useful corroborative evidence, they do not tell what the patient is thinking which I feel is always the key to whether they are depressed or not.

Table 6. Predictive factors for response to ECT.

Favourable	Unfavourable
Sudden onset	Hypochondriasis
Insight	Neurotic traits
< 1 Year duration	Intelligence
Obsessionality	
Self reproach	
(Hobson, 1953; 79% accuracy)	
Weight loss	Anxiety
Pyknic physique	Hypochondriasis
EMW	Hysterical traits
Somatic delusions	Worse in evenings
Paranoid delusions	Self pity
(Carney *et al.*, 1965; 76% accuracy)	

PARKINSON'S DISEASE AND ECT

There is now considerable evidence (Douyon *et al.*, 1989; Lebensohn and Jenkins, 1975) that ECT *per se* improves the motor symptoms of Parkinson's disease (PD) whether or not depression is present. A study by Ward *et al.* (1980) again showed some dramatic improvements in motor function but not improvement in on–off phenomena. I certainly feel that ECT can have a remarkable effect on Parkinsonian motor symptoms. However, like Abrams (1988), I feel the effect on motor performance is less long lasting than the effect on mood. I have admitted a patient with Parkinson's disease for repeat ECT who was treated with ECT previously for depression and whose mood had remained stable but whose mobility had declined. His Parkinson's disease improved rapidly after four unilateral ECT but we stopped due to incipient hypomania. Like others (Abrams, 1988), I feel maintenance ECT may be an appropriate treatment for Parkinson's disease.

When I looked at patients with Parkinson's disease referred to a psychogeriatric unit (Wilkinson, 1992) I found that 50% of the new cases were referred because of visual hallucinations. These patients are very difficult to treat as they are often completely dependent on high doses of L-dopa for mobility which may be causing the hallucinations, assuming anticholinergic agents are not being used. Some of these patients may have a Lewy body dementia which Perry *et al.* (1990) feel may be associated with hallucinations. There is a dilemma whether to reduce L-dopa or add major tranquillizers, both of which may impair mobility. ECT may be a more rational treatment than giving tranquillizers and may allow reduction in L-dopa dosage without loss of mobility.

OTHER INDICATIONS

Maintenance ECT for depression in the elderly was used by 20% of a sample of British psychogeriatricians (Benbow, 1991) and certainly has a place in the management of patients who only seem to respond to ECT and who have rapidly relapsing depressive illness, usually of a severe psychotic nature. Lithium prophylaxis should be considered first as an alternative. In the same study over half of the psychiatrists felt it appropriate to treat depression in a patient with dementia with ECT. However in my experience response can be varied with fewer than expected regaining complete remission of the depression and optimistic reports should be tempered by the knowledge that many patients with dementia will become more confused and disorientated with ECT especially if bilateral treatment is given.

There is now considerable evidence from prospective studies using magnetic resonance imaging (MRI) and computed tomography (CT) (Coffey

Table 7. Brain imaging findings in depressed patients for ECT.

	Coffey et al., 1988 N = 67	Pande et al., 1990 N = 7
Normal scans	14 (21%)	2 (28%)
Patchy white matter lesions	44 (66%)	5 (71%)
Cortical atrophy	46 (68%)	2 (28%)
Lat ventricle enlargement	45 (67%)	—

et al., 1988; Pande *et al.*, 1990) to show that there is no relationship between ECT and brain damage. Interestingly all the studies note that many of these depressed patients show significant structural brain abnormalities, often patchy white matter changes on MRI, before treatment (Table 7). This in effect means we already give ECT to a population with some degree of brain damage and extension to overt dementia need not be feared, if depression and agitation are significant features. In fact, like Parkinson's disease, it may be a more rational treatment than the usual response of escalating doses of major tranquillizers with all the possible problems of extrapyramidal side effects, and increasing confusion that these can bring. ECT has been advocated (Fogel, 1988) as an alternative to tranquillizers for the profoundly demented patient who screams or shouts and shows non-verbal signs of depression — like negativism or poor appetite. This may have advantages over medication but there may be difficulty in obtaining consent from patient and family.

ELECTRODE PLACEMENT

As I have mentioned unilateral ECT should be used in demented patients as it can produce less confusion. Fraser and Glass (1980) felt unequivocally that for the elderly unilateral treatment was as effective and carried considerably less morbidity than bilateral. Since then opinions have varied, the Royal College of Psychiatrists (1989) recommends bilateral treatment unless minimizing side effects is a major consideration and speed of action is not of paramount importance. I feel Abrams (1988) puts the vacillation over electrode placement beyond debate when he points out that unilateral ECT has a pronounced cognitive advantage over bilateral ECT and it would therefore seem foolish not to use 'substantially supra threshold, brief square wave, unilateral ECT as an initial trial in every patient' except those who are severely agitated, deluded, or suicidal, have acute mania, catatonic stupor or physically are at risk from a longer course of treatment. I completely endorse that approach except that in our unit giving bilateral treatment did not reduce the number of treatments overall (Table 2). If there is no substantial improvement after four to six unilateral treatments it should be switched to bilateral and equally bilateral treatments can be switched to unilateral after the initial improvement has been achieved. Interestingly, the first antipodean survey of ECT practice (O'Dea *et al.*, 1991) found that 63% of patients received unilateral ECT although there were some marked regional variations.

ELECTRICAL STIMULUS

I think that part of the variance in views about unilateral/bilateral electrode placement is the problem of dosing. This was epitomized by Lambourn and Gill's (1978) study where no advantage over sham ECT was shown for low energy brief pulse unilateral ECT despite their soliciting bilateral convulsions. Ictal EEGs show that grand mal seizures with full therapeutic effect are readily elicited by high intensity bilateral ECT. Low intensity stimulation particularly if unilateral produces a qualitatively different response with less generalization, less synchronicity, and less intensity, particularly over the unstimulated hemisphere, with less complete suppression of the seizure at the end. We need to ensure substantially supra-threshold stimuli if we are not to blame electrode placement for reduced efficacy rather than lack of electrical intensity.

The high risk patient has been addressed elsewhere (Abrams, 1988; Benbow, 1991). My view is that there are no absolute contra-indications to ECT only relative risks, relative that is to the morbidity or mortality of untreated depression itself. Many people are denied treatment due to irrational caution, related primarily to the perceived anaesthetic risk. Pacemakers are not barriers to treatment, neither is myocardial infarction, the greatest risk being in the first 10 days post-infarct and probably negligible at three months. Equally stroke, anaemia or anticoagulants are not contra-indications. Arterial hypertension can be controlled during treatment. Insulin dependent diabetes needs careful monitoring to ensure hydration and appropriate insulin dosage as requirements tend to reduce during treatment. In fact dehydration is probably the major problem in severely depressed retarded patients which can lead to deep vein thrombosis and pulmonary embolism if not managed carefully but this is not related to the ECT use. In fact the mortality associated with ECT according to Fink (1979) is 0.002% compared with anaesthetic induction alone of 0.003–0.04%. The main barrier to treatment is often the anaesthetist who is unsure of the procedure and the Royal College of Psychiatrists ECT committee include liaison with anaesthetists as part of its brief and hope this will encourage greater understanding. However, to return to my original theme, the concern by anaesthetists is that shared by many and the way to address it is by openness and discussion. ECT is not a universal panacea with no side effects and to pretend that it is in order to persuade patients to consent is foolish. We now have clear guidelines as to when to give ECT, how and to whom. We should use it with confidence as part of an eclectic approach to treatment and it will continue to relieve intolerable distress and save lives.

REFERENCES

Abrams, R. (1988). *Electroconvulsive Therapy*, Oxford University Press, Oxford.

American Psychiatric Association Task Force (1990). *The Practice of Electroconvulsive Therapy: Recommendations for Treatment, Training, and Privileging*. American Psychiatric Press, Washington.

Baxter, L., Roy-Burne, P. and Liston, E. (1986). Informing patients about electroconvulsive therapy: effects of a videotape presentation. *Convuls. Ther.*, **2**, 25–29.

Benbow, S.M. (1987). The use of electroconvulsive therapy in old age psychiatry. *Int. J. Geriatr. Psychiatry*, **2**, 25–30.

Benbow, S.M. (1991). Old age psychiatrists' views on the use of ECT. *Int. J. Geriatr. Psychiatry*, **6**, 317–322.

Brandon, S., Cowley, P., McDonald, C., Neville, P., Palmer, R. and Wellstood-Eason, S. (1984). Electroconvulsive therapy, results in depressive illness from the Leicestershire trial. *Br. Med. J.*, **288**, 22–25.

Carney, M.W.P., Roth, M. and Garside, R.F. (1965). The diagnosis of depressive syndromes and the prediction of ECT response. *Br. J. Psychiatry*, **125**, 91–94.

Coffey, C.E., Figiel, G.S., Djang, W.T., Cress, M., Saunders, W.B. and Weiner, R.D. (1988). Leukoencephalopathy in elderly depressed patients referred for ECT. *Biol. Psychiatry*, **24**, 143–161.

Coffey, C.E., Weiner, R.D., Djang, W.T., Figiel, G.S., Soady, S.A.R., Patterson, L.J., Holt, P.D., Spritzer, C.E. and Wilkinson, W.E. (1991). Brain anatomic effects of ECT. *Arch. Gen. Psychiatry*, **48**, 1013–1021.

Devanand, D.P., Verma, A.K., Tirumalesetti, F. and Sackheim, H.A. (1991). Absence of cognitive impairment after more than 100 lifetime ECT treatments. *Am. J. Psychiatry*, **148**, 929–932.

Douyon, R., Sorbyk, M., Kutchko, B. and Rotrosen, J. (1989). ECT and Parkinson's disease revisited; a naturalistic study. *Am. J. Psychiatry*, **146**, 1451–1455.

Figiel, G.S., Coffey, C.E. and Weiner, R.D. (1989). Brain magnetic resonance imaging in elderly depressed patients receiving electro convulsive therapy. *Convuls. Ther.*, **5**, 26–34.

Fink, M.F. (1979). *Convulsive Therapy; Theory and Practice*, Raven Press, New York.

Fogel, B. (1988). Electroconvulsive therapy in the elderly; a clinical research agenda. *Int. J. Geriatr. Psychiatry*, **3**, 181–190.

Fraser, R.M. and Glass, I.B. (1980). Unilateral and bilateral ECT in elderly patients: A comparative study. *Acta Psychiatr. Scand.*, **62**, 13–31.

Freeman, C.P.L. and Kendell, R.E. (1980). ECT: one patient's experiences and attitudes. *Br. J. Psychiatry*, **137**, 8–16.

Gaspar, D. and Samara Singhe, L.A. (1982). ECT in psychogeriatric practice — a study of risk factors, indications and outcome. *Compr. Psychiatry*, **23**, 170–175.

Godber, C., Rosenvinge, H., Wilkinson, D.G. and Smythies, J. (1987). Depression in old age: prognosis after ECT. *Int. J. Geriatr. Psychiatry*, **2**, 19–24.

Graham, L.E. and Conley, E.M. (1960). Evaluation of anxiety and fear in adult surgical patients. *Nurs. Res.*, **20**, 113–122.

Gregory, S., Shawcross, C.R. and Gill, D. (1985). The Nottingham ECT study: A double blind comparison of bilateral, unilateral and simulated ECT in depressive illness. *Br. J. Psychiatry*, **146**, 520–524.

Heggs, A., (1990). Does electroconvulsive therapy make people anxious? Unpublished BPS Dip. Clin. Psychol. dissertation, University of Southampton.

Hobson, R.F. (1953). Prognostic factors in electric convulsive therapy. *J. Neurol. Neurosurg. Psychiatry*, **16**, 275–281.

Hughes, J., Barraclough, B. and Reeve, W. (1981). Are patients shocked by ECT? *J. Roy. Soc. Med.*, **74**, 283–285.

Johnstone, E.C., Deakin, J.F., Lawler, P., Frith, C.D., Stevens, M., McPherson, K. and Crow, T.J. (1980). The Northwick Park electroconvulsive therapy trial. *Lancet*, **ii**, 1317–1320.

Karlinsky, H. and Shulman, K. (1984). The clinical use of electroconvulsive therapy in old age. *J. Am. Geriatr. Soc.*, **32**, 183–186.

Kramer, B.A. (1987). Electroconvulsive therapy use in geriatric depression. *J. Nerv. Ment. Dis.*, **175**, 233–235.

Lambourn, J. and Gill, D. (1978). A controlled comparison of real and simulated ECT. *Br. J. Psychiatry*, **133**, 514–519.

Lebensohn, Z. and Jenkins, R. (1975). Improvement of Parkinsonism in depressed patients treated with ECT. *Am. J. Psychiatry*, **132**, 283–285.

Lippmann, S., Manshadi, M., Wehry, M., Byrd, R., Past, W., Keller, W., Schuster, J., Elam, S., Meyer, D. and O'Daniel, R. (1985). 1250 ECT treatments without evidence of brain injury. *Br. J. Psychiatry*, **147**, 203–204.

Magnis, G., Fisman, M. and Helmes, E. (1988). Clinical correlates of ECT resistant depression in the elderly. *J. Clin. Psychiatry*, **49** 405–407.

Malcolm, K. (1989). Patients' perception and knowledge of electroconvulsive therapy. *Psychiatr. Bull.*, **13**, 161–165.

Mielke, D.H., Winstead, D.K. and Goether, J.W. (1984). Multiple monitored electroconvulsive therapy; safety and efficacy in elderly depressed patients. *J. Am. Geriatr. Soc.*, **32**, 180–182.

O'Dea, J.F.J., Mitchell, P.B. and Hickie, I.B. (1991). Unilateral or bilateral electroconvulsive therapy for depression? *Med. J. Aust.*, **155**, 9–11.

Pande, A.C., Grunhans, L.D., Aisen, A.M. and Haskett, R.F. (1990). A preliminary magnetic resonance imaging study of ECT treated depressed patients. *Biol. Psychiatry*, **27**, 102–104.

Perry, R., Irving, D. and Perry, E. (1990). Visual hallucinations as the presenting symptom of dementia; a type of Lewy body disease! *Int. J. Geriatr. Psychiatry*, **5**, 275–276.

Pippard, J. and Ellam, L. (1981). Electroconvulsive treatment in Great Britain. *Br. J. Psychiatry*, **139**, 563–568.

Royal College of Psychiatrists (1989). *The Practical Administration of Electroconvulsive Therapy (ECT)*, Gaskell, London.

Sheffer, M.B. and Greigenstein, F.E. (1960). Emotional responses of patients to surgery and anaesthesia. *Anesthesiology*, **21**, 502–507.

Spielberger, C.D., Gorsuch, R.L., Lushene, R.E., Vagg, P.R. and Jacobs, G.A. (1983). *Manual for the State–Trait Anxiety Inventory (STAI)*, Consulting Psychologists Press, Palo Alto.

Squire, L.R. (1986). Memory functions as affected by electroconvulsive therapy. *Ann. N.Y. Acad. Sci.*, **466**, 307–314.

Ward, C., Stern, G., Pratt, R.T.C. and McKenna, P. (1980). Electroconvulsive therapy in Parkinsonian patients with on–off syndrome. *J. Neural. Tranism.*, **49**, 133–135.

Weiner, R., Rogers, H. and Davidson, J. (1986). Effects of stimulus parameters on cognitive side effects. *Ann. N.Y. Acad. Sci.*, **462**, 315–325.

West, E.D. (1981). Electric convulsion therapy in depression; A double-blind controlled trial. *Br. Med. J.*, **282**, 355–357.

Wilkinson, D.G. (1992). The psychogeriatricians view. *J. Neurol. Neurosurg. Psychiatry*, **55**, 41–44.

Treatment and Care in Old Age Psychiatry
Edited by R. Levy, R. Howard and A. Burns
©1993 Wrightson Biomedical Publishing Ltd

15

Cognitive Therapy with the Elderly Depressed: A Rational and Efficacious Approach?

SIMON LOVESTONE

Section of Old Age Psychiatry, Institute of Psychiatry, London, UK

The shadow cast by Freud over psychotherapy with elderly patients is a long one. His view that 'near or above the age of 50 the elasticity of the mental processes . . . is as a rule lacking — old people are no longer educable', (p. 264, Freud, 1905) was widely accepted by psychoanalysts. Even recent reports by psychoanalysts on psychotherapy with elderly patients include people in their fifties. Freud's position, not to be later retracted, is curious given at that time he too was in his fifties. Seeking to understand Freud's apparent ageism, it has been suggested that at the turn of the century in Europe, the image of an 'old person' was associated with a younger age (Kahana, 1978). An alternative explanation might be Freud's personal and lifelong dislike of ageing and exaggerated fear of mortality (Weissman, 1978). It is, however, perhaps unfair to blame Freud for what is a commonly held view — that old people are rigid and less adaptable. Indeed, reviewing the effects of cognition on ageing, Morris (1991) concludes that 'fluid' cognitive abilities such as problem solving are indeed affected by age but that this is compensated for by accumulation of knowledge and the development of skills. This formulation is not dissimilar to the view of the psychoanalyst, Hildebrand (1982) that with age, defences become more rigid but that the individual learns to manage his or her resources and experiences more flexibly. If this hypothesis was accepted then it might be that psychotherapy which concentrated less on the rigid, enmeshed defensive mechanisms and instead utilized the 'fluid' resources and experiences would be more applicable in the elderly.

In recent years there has been increasing interest in psychotherapy with elderly patients with both dementia and affective disorders (Church, 1986).

Group work with the elderly is frequently used although the actual psychotherapeutic input is variable (Dobson and Culhane, 1991). Family therapy (Ratna and Davis, 1984), psychoanalytic individual psychotherapy (King, 1974; Hildebrand, 1982), and behavioural therapies (Morris and Morris, 1991) have all been employed. Psychological treatments have also been developed specifically for the elderly such as reality orientation, reminiscence therapy and validation therapy (Little, 1991). With this plethora of psychological interventions, few of which have uncontested therapeutic benefit and none of which can lay claim to an empirically based superiority it might be deemed premature to consider another psychotherapy modality for use in the elderly. However, cognitive psychotherapy has much to offer for older depressed patients. It is time limited, moderately structured and appears to be efficacious. Rather than addressing the psychodynamic triad of anxiety, defence and impulse (Malan, 1979) it addresses negative cognitions directly. In doing so it utilizes the more flexible resources of experience and wisdom rather than tackling the ingrained defensive mechanisms and impulses originating in childhood. Furthermore, it has been shown to be useful in patients with concurrent physical problems (e.g. Moorey and Greer, 1989), a situation frequently encountered in old age psychiatry.

A variety of therapies have been developed that aim to change cognitions or behaviour. Examples include rational emotive therapy (Ellis, 1962) that aims to confront irrational beliefs and self control therapy that aims to change personal behaviours (Kanfer and Karoly, 1972). However, it is cognitive behavioural therapy developed by Beck that has achieved some prominence (Beck, 1976; Beck et al., 1979). Firmly rooted in a theoretical framework, the therapy is designed to use both cognitive and behavioural strategies to identify and change maladaptive belief systems.

Three concepts are central to the theory underpinning the therapy — the cognitive model of depression. The *cognitive triad* describes a predominantly negative view of self, the future and the world. The depressed patient sees himself as useless or inadequate, his future as unremittingly bleak and his experiences, his world, as obstructive or deprived. The second concept of the model is that of *negative schemata*. Beck postulates that an individual has unique personal models with which to make sense of events. These models or schemata form relatively stable patterns. In depression, dysfunctional, negative schemata that have been dormant result in the individual no longer being able to interpret the world other than in a negative light resulting in automatic (or involuntary) negative thoughts. The final concept is that of *faulty information processing*. Patterns of thinking are adopted that fit in with the negative schemata — the patient overgeneralizes or takes out of context events that are then interpreted negatively. Many other such dysfunctional cognitive patterns are described.

Cognitive therapy based on this model aims to teach patients to identify and change these dysfunctional cognitions. Patients are encouraged to recognize the link between cognition and mood, monitor automatic and dysfunctional thoughts and to examine the logic of these, thereby challenging the validity of such thoughts. In doing so it is thought that the negative thoughts diminish or disappear entirely.

A perfectly serviceable model of depression in the younger patient may not apply to elderly depressives. However the presence of depressive negative cognitions has been demonstrated in the elderly and furthermore, as in younger patients, negative cognitions are related to depressive illness and not for example to social adversity (Lam *et al.*, 1987). As elements of the theory have demonstrable validity in the elderly, then so too might aspects of the practice of cognitive therapy. In addressing the logic of such negative cognitions the elderly patient is being encouraged to use the flexible characteristics of experience and wisdom. It can be argued that cognitive behavioural therapy uses precisely those resources most available to the elderly.

The process of cognitive therapy is described extensively elsewhere (Beck *et al.*, 1979; Emery *et al.*, 1981). In brief, after assessment the cognitive model is explained to the patient. The link between thoughts and emotions can be demonstrated using the patient's own experiences. Booklets and other literature are of great help. Following this phase, the negative automatic thoughts are identified initially with the help of the therapist and increasingly by the patient himself. A daily record of negative automatic thoughts and the cues that give rise to these is kept. Having learned to identify negative cognitions, the patient is taught to subject these to reality testing — to challenge them by matching them with available evidence from past and present experiences. For many patients this stage of the substitution of negative cognitions for more reality based thoughts will result in symptom relief. The underlying assumptions that contribute to the negative schemata can, in many cases, be identified and changed.

Therapy is brief and structured. It is helpful to identify aims or agenda at each session and for homework tasks to be set. Homework can consist of diaries of automatic thoughts kept in a systematic manner and behavioural tasks. These help to provide scenarios in which negative cognitions can be tested and more importantly can engage the patient in the process of therapy, thus providing immediate symptom relief.

A number of attempts have been made to evaluate the effectiveness of cognitive therapy in the elderly. The results of these are perhaps a little disappointing for enthusiastic proponents of cognitive psychotherapy. Although two of the three studies that had a control group showed some benefit of psychotherapy in the elderly, no study has yet shown a specific benefit of cognitive therapy. All of the studies are on small numbers of

relatively young elderly patients. Gallagher and Thompson (1982) randomized patients with research diagnostic criteria major depressive episodes to
individual cognitive, behavioural or brief insight psychotherapy with 10
patients in each group. The drop out rate was highest (50%) in the
behavioural group, with drop outs being subsequently replaced. A variety of
outcome measures including both Hamilton Depression Rating Scale
(HDRS) and Beck Depression Inventory (BDI) instruments were used with
measurements before therapy, immediately after, and at intervals up to one
year as follow up. All three groups showed improvement with therapy but
this improvement was maintained only in the cognitive and behavioural
groups. There was no difference between those patients receiving cognitive
or behavioural therapy. Gallagher and Thompson claim that the results illustrate that the gains of cognitive and behavioural therapy are because of the
acquisition of new skills and conclude that 'older depressives are more likely
to maintain clinical improvement when they have had the opportunity to
participate in therapy that provides a cogent rationale for their depression
and helps them learn specific skills for coping with it after treatment has
ended'. Unfortunately these conclusions cannot be substantiated by subsequent studies.

In a second uncontrolled study, Steur and colleagues (1984) used psychodynamic or cognitive group therapy to treat 33 patients with DSM-III major
depression. Two therapists led each group for a total of 46 90 min sessions
over a period of nine months. The drop out rate was high with 13 (39%)
patients, equally distributed between groups, not completing their therapy
course. Both types of treatment showed an improvement on both the
Hamilton Rating Scale and the Beck Depression Inventory with patients
receiving cognitive therapy showing a greater improvement in scores of the
BDI. However as this instrument is designed to measure negative cognitions
it is probable that cognitive therapy teaches patients how to score well on
the BDI. The failure to demonstrate an improvement on the Hamilton Scale
might indicate that having received cognitive therapy the BDI no longer
validly measures depression.

Three trials have compared cognitive therapy to control groups as well as
other therapies. Beutler et al. (1987) compared group cognitive therapy with
either placebo or alprazolam to alprazolam or placebo alone. Twenty-nine
patients were entered into cognitive therapy groups. The authors claim that
their findings demonstrate that alprazolam has no benefit for patients with
DSM-III major depression but that cognitive therapy is superior to non-
therapy. However their conclusions must be questioned as while all patients,
including those in placebo only condition, showed an improvement after four
to six sessions, there was a significant difference only on the BDI score
between cognitive therapy and non-cognitive therapy groups. No difference
between groups was found when the results of the Hamilton Scale were

considered. As with the study by Steur *et al.* (1984), it remains possible that cognitive therapy teaches patients correct responses to the Beck Scale without affecting all the symptoms of depression. Thompson *et al.* (1987) compared individual cognitive therapy to behavioural therapy, psychodynamic psychotherapy and waiting list controls and found after six weeks all psychotherapy group patients had improved on both their Hamilton Rating Scale of Depression and the BDI whereas delayed treatment controls remained asymptomatic as on assessment. At the end of therapy, 52% of the sample were well, and 18% had shown some improvement. There was no difference between treatment modalities.

As cognitive therapy is a skill learning exercise, it is possible that it could be taught by books. An assessment of 'bibliotherapy' of cognitive and behavioural techniques demonstrated an improvement in mood in 45 patients with depression as measured on the Hamilton Scale (Scogin *et al.*, 1989). A delayed treatment group did not improve. Although demonstrating an improvement with therapy no differences were noted between cognitive and behavioural treatment.

It seems from these studies that in moderately and non-psychotically depressed patients, therapy has a measurable effect when compared with waiting list or delayed treatment conditions. However, the question of suitable controls for psychotherapy trials is a fraught one and given that no consistent differences in efficacy between therapies has been demonstrated it remains debatable as to whether cognitive therapy is more useful than other therapies in this patient group. Similar considerations apply to cognitive therapy with younger patients. In a large meta-analysis of trials of psychotherapy, Dobson (1989) claims a clear superiority for cognitive therapy. However this widely quoted study selected trials only where the BDI was used as an outcome measure and there must be considerable doubt over whether this is an appropriate instrument in such trials. Perhaps the largest comparative trial of psychotherapy — the National Institute of Mental Health multicentre trial — failed to show substantial differences between cognitive and interpersonal psychotherapies (Elkin *et al.*, 1989). Although cognitive behavioural therapy may be useful adjunct to other treatments, easily learnt and rational, the trial data from younger depressed patients is far from convincing.

Returning to cognitive therapy in the elderly, a number of the studies reviewed here included measures of types of thought patterns in the assessment procedures and it might be that even if the efficacy of cognitive therapy is not superior to other therapies, then skills might be taught that provide a prophylactic effect. However, Thompson *et al.* (1987), Beutler *et al.* (1987) and Scogin *et al.* (1989) all failed to show that cognitive therapy differed from other therapies in the effects on either cognitive or behavioural measures. Nor can a difference between psychotherapies be seen in these studies in terms of the drop out rates. A cost–benefit analysis of the treatment of depression is beyond the scope of this chapter but it can be seen that there is a wide variability in the amount of time spent with patients by cognitive therapists. The range of direct therapist/patient contact ranges from less than 30 min of bibliotherapy to a total over the course of therapy of 24 h with individual cognitive therapy. Although described as brief therapies, clearly in some cases the amount of time spent with patients is not dissimilar to that typical of NHS dynamic psychotherapy.

To conclude, older patients with non-psychotic depression have been demonstrated to benefit from psychotherapy. Cognitive therapy is a rational, theory-based therapy that aims to teach skills that both reverse and prevent depression. The ability to utilize past experiences and knowledge suggests a particular advantage in using this therapy in older patients. However, studies to date have failed to demonstrate a clear advantage of cognitive therapy on either symptoms of depression or cognitive patterns. Older people should certainly be considered for psychotherapy but the type of therapy should be individually chosen to match both patient and therapist.

REFERENCES

Beck, A.T. (1976). *Cognitive Therapy and the Emotional Disorders*, International Universities Press, New York.

Beck, A.T., Rush, A.J., Shaw, B.F. and Emery, G. (1979). *Cognitive Therapy of Depression*. Guilford Press, New York.

Beutler, L.E., Scogin, F., Kirkish, P. *et al.* (1987). Group cognitive therapy and alprazolam in the treatment of depression in older adults. *J. Consult. Clin. Psychol.*, **55**, 550–556.

Church, M. (1986). Issues in psychological therapy with elderly people. In: Hanley, I. and Gilhoolie, M. (Eds), *Psychological Therapies for the Elderly*, Croom Helme, Beckenham, pp. 1–21.

Dobson, K.S. (1989). A meta-analysis of the efficacy of cognitive therapy for depression. *J. Consult. Clin. Psychol.*, **57**, 414–419.

Dobson, H. and Culhane, M. (1991). Family therapy. In: Jacoby, R. and Oppenheimer, C. (Eds), *Psychiatry in the Elderly*, Oxford University Press, Oxford.

Elkin, I., Shea, T., Watkins, J.J., Imber, S.D., Sotsky, S.M., Collins, J.F., Glass, D.I., Pilkonsis, P.A., Leber, W.R., Docherty, J.P., Fiester, S.J. and Parloff, M.B. (1989). National Institute of Mental Health treatment of depression collaborative research program. *Arch. Gen. Psychiatry*, **46**, 971–982.

Ellis, A. (1962). *Reason and Emotion in Psychotherapy*, Lyle Stewart, New York.

Emery, G., Holbon, S.D. and Bedrosian, R.C. (1981). *New directions in Cognitive Therapy*, Guilford Press, New York.

Freud, S. (1905). *On psychotherapy. Standard Edition Vol. 7*, London, Hogarth Press, 1956, pp. 257–268.

Gallagher, D.E. and Thompson, L.W. (1982). Treatment of major depressive disorder in older adult outpatients with brief psychotherapies. *Psychother. Theory Res. Pract.*, **19**, 482–490.

Hildebrand, H.P. (1982). Psychotherapy with older patients. *Br. J. Med. Psychol.*, **55**, 19–28.

Kahana, R.J. (1978). Psychoanalysis in later life. *J. Geriatr. Psychiatry*, **11**, 37–49.

Kanfer, F.H. and Karoly, P. (1972). Self control: a behaviouristic excursion into the lions' den. *Behav. Ther.*, **3**, 398–416.

King, P.H.M. (1974). Notes on the psychoanalysis of older patients. *J. Anal. Psychol.*, **19**, 22–37.

Lam, D.H., Brewin, C.R., Woods, R.T. and Bebbington, P.E. (1987). Cognition and social adversity in the depressed elderly. *J. Abnorm. Psychol.*, **96**, 23–26.

Little, A. (1991). Psychological treatments. In: Jacoby, R. and Oppenheimer, C. (Eds), *Psychiatry in the Elderly*, Oxford University Press, Oxford.

Malan, D.H. (1979). *Individual Psychotherapy and the Science of Psychodynamics*, Butterworth, London.

Moorey, S. and Greer, S. (1989). *Psychological Therapy for Patients with Cancer: A New Approach*, Heinemann Medical Books, Oxford.

Morris, R.G. (1991). Cognition and aging. In: Jacoby, R. and Oppenheimer, C. (Eds), *Psychiatry in the Elderly*, Oxford University Press, Oxford.

Morris, R.G. and Morris, L.W. (1991). Cognitive and behavioral approaches with the depressed elderly. *Int. J. Geriatr. Psychiatry*, **6**, 407–413.

Ratna, R. and Davis, J. (1984). Family therapy with the elderly mentally ill: some strategies and techniques. *Br. J. Psychiatry*, **145**, 311–315.

Scogin, F., Jamison, C. and Gochneaur, K. (1989). Comparative efficacy of cognitive and behavioral bibliotherapy for mildly and moderately depressed older adults. *J. Consult. Clin. Psychol.*, **57**, 403–407.

Steur, J.L., Mintz, J., Hammen, C.L., Hill, L.A., Jarvik, C.F., McCarley, T., Motoike, P. and Rosen, R. (1984). Cognitive-behavioral and psychodynamic group psychotherapy in treatment of geriatric depression. *J. Consult. Clin. Psychol.*, **52**, 180–189.

Thompson, L.W., Gallagher, D. and Breckenridge, J.S. (1987). Comparative affectiveness of psychotherapies for depressed elders. *J. Consult. Clin. Psychol.*, **55**, 385–390.

Weissman, A.D. (1978). Psychoanalysis in later life. *J. Geriatr. Psychiatry*, **11**, 51–55.

Treatment and Care in Old Age Psychiatry
Edited by R. Levy, R. Howard and A. Burns
©1993 Wrightson Biomedical Publishing Ltd

16

Sleep Disorders in the Elderly

K.W. WOODHOUSE

Department of Geriatric Medicine, University of Wales College of Medicine, Cardiff, UK

INTRODUCTION

Sleep disorders are common in the elderly; reported prevalence rates ranging from 12–50%. Altered sleep patterns may be due to the ageing process itself, psychological illness, or disease states. A thorough medical and psychological assessment of the elderly patient with disturbed sleep is mandatory. Specific therapy and non-pharmacological treatments should be tried before hypnotics are prescribed; the latter frequently have untoward effects in this vulnerable patient population.

AGE-RELATED CHANGES IN SLEEP PATTERN

The so-called 'normal' pattern of sleep does alter with ageing (Webb, 1989), although there is considerable variation between individuals, particularly in sleep latency and duration of sleep. Typical age-related changes in sleep are shown in Table 1.

The normal diurnal variation tends to change with an increased prevalence of napping, a tendency to go to sleep earlier and earlier awakening. Time taken to fall asleep is lengthened and is greater than 30 min in almost a third

Table 1. Sleep and 'normal' ageing.

Sleep onset	Delayed
Sleep 'quality'	Lighter, frequent awakenings
Sleep duration	Shorter
Time in bed	Longer
Diurnal variation	Early to bed, early to rise, napping frequent

of women and one-sixth of men. Sleep is subjectively and objectively lighter and nocturnal awakenings become more frequent, with over one half of older subjects experiencing periods of wakefulness of greater than 30 min. Total time spent asleep declines until about the age of 80 and then either stabilizes or increases slightly. However, some subjects are either particularly long (more than 9 h) or brief (less than 5 h) sleepers. Despite these changes, longer time tends to be spent in bed in the elderly, possibly reflecting changes in social environment.

Most healthy elderly patients do not seem to be worried or experience symptoms related to these changes, although they may be problematic in those with physical or psychological disturbance or who are undergoing social stress.

ABNORMAL SLEEP PATTERNS IN THE ELDERLY

The prevalence of abnormal sleep and insomnia in the elderly is a matter of some dispute, but there is no doubt that it is common. Various surveys have reported prevalence rates for insomnia varying between 12 and 50% (Ford and Kamerow, 1989; Livingstone *et al.*, 1990; Morgan *et al.*, 1988). These differences may in part be due to different definitions of insomnia used, and taken overall it would appear that between 20 and 40% of elderly people living at home experience disturbed sleep or poor sleep quality. Furthermore, there appear to be sex differences and in one of the best studies undertaken in Nottingham, UK, persistent insomnia was recorded as 28% in elderly women versus 15% in elderly men (Morgan *et al.*, 1988).

Causes of insomnia may be physical, social or psychiatric and an accurate diagnosis is essential so that rational targeted treatment may be prescribed.

Physical causes of disturbed sleep include general medical illness, respiratory disorders and a basket of diffuse neuromuscular syndromes. Social causes include stress and 'adjustment' problems and disordered sleep habit. Psychiatric causes include dementias, anxiety disorders, depression and some psychoses.

PHYSICAL DISORDERS AND SLEEP DISTURBANCE

General medical conditions

It is easy to think of many general medical conditions which may contribute to sleep disturbance. The most obvious include pain, dyspnoea, cough, nocturia and many others. Furthermore, many drugs are associated with sleep disturbance, including alcohol, xanthines, steroids, many 'alerting' psychoactive drugs, including some tricyclics and centrally acting hypoten-sive drugs.

The treatment of sleep disorder related to a general medical illness should be directed at the target disorder itself and every attempt should be made to control symptoms or withdraw offending drugs before resorting to hypnotic agents.

Snoring and sleep apnoea

Persistent snoring, even in patients who do not have true sleep apnoea (see below) not only causes disturbed sleep in both patient and spouse, but is related to such serious medical conditions as ischaemic heart disease, hyper-tension and stroke (D'Alessandro et al., 1990; Stradling and Crosby, 1990).

The definitive cure for snoring has yet to be established and would proba-bly reap significant financial rewards for the inventor. However, simple measures may help the problem. These include weight loss in overweight patients, avoidance if possible of the supine sleep position to avoid the effects of posture on pharyngeal muscles and the tongue, avoidance of excessive alcohol, tobacco and sedative use, and if necessary an otorhinolaryngeal opinion to eliminate problems such as sinusitis, nasal polyps, allergic rhinitis and so forth. Sedative drugs have no place in the treatment of snoring and may well exacerbate the condition.

Sleep apnoea

For reviews of sleep apnoea, see Bliwise et al. (1987), Kales et al. (1987) and Waldhorn (1990).

One or two episodes of apnoea during sleep may occur even in 'normal' individuals. In young patients more than five apnoeic episodes per hour is abnormal, in the elderly the tolerated level is rather greater, and over 10 episodes certainly warrant detailed investigation. Sleep apnoea may be due to nasopharyngeal obstruction, central causes or a mixture. Associated hypoxia is the rule.

The prevalence of sleep apnoea depends on the population studied and in one large survey was present in over 40% of nursing home residents, but only 4% of those living at home (Ancoli-Israel, 1989). Medical illness including heart failure, cerebrovascular disease, and degenerative neurological disease (e.g. motor-neurone disease) increases the risk of developing the condition.

Obstructive sleep apnoea is important to diagnose as it is a cause of consid-erable morbidity and is eminently amenable to treatment. The condition is much more frequent in men, particularly those who smoke and drink heavily, or have pre-existing respiratory disease such as chronic bronchitis and cor pulmonale. A typical patient will snore loudly, followed by an episode of apnoea lasting more than 10 s, accompanied by hypoxia, the episode being relieved by a loud grunt or snort as the obstruction is relieved. The patient has disturbed restless sleep, daytime sluggishness, particularly in the morning, headache and disturbed mood.

Full assessment should be undertaken involving sleep monitoring for respiratory movement and arterial oxygen desaturation. Treatment of minor forms involving under 20 apnoeic events per hour and oxygen saturation remaining above 90% may be managed conservatively in a similar way to habitual snoring.

More serious forms of sleep apnoea, particularly in patients with respiratory failure, cor pulmonale and serious arterial oxygen desaturation require specific therapy. The treatment of choice is continuous (CPAP) or by bilevel (BiPAP) positive airway pressure. This is delivered through a tight fitting facial mask and a bedside blower. The aim is to maintain airway patency. Up to 20% of patients will tolerate this poorly or not respond and in these individuals plastic surgery to nose or pharyngeal musculature may be considered.

Neuromuscular disorders

One of the commonest neuromuscular disorders causing poor sleep in the elderly is the restless legs syndrome (Montplaisir and Godbout, 1989). This is reported by almost one in 20 of the elderly population. It is a form of akathisia comprizing a creepy uncomfortable sensation in the muscles of the leg, resulting in movement to relieve the distressing symptoms. Sleep is disturbed by delayed sleep onset and frequent awakenings. In some patients the symptoms are almost intolerable leading to serious functional psychological illness.

The aetiology of the condition is a matter of debate, but almost certainly involves dopaminergic pathways in the central nervous system as similar symptoms may be precipitated by the use of various dopamine antagonists such as metoclopramide.

A variety of treatments have been tried including dopaminergic agents such as L-dopa or bromocriptine, anticonvulsants including clonazepam or carbamazepine; or even opioids such as codeine or dextropropoxyphene. Unfortunately, none of these drugs are dramatically effective, the most useful are probably clonazepam and dopamine agonists.

Myoclonic jerks may delay sleep onset or cause awakening. They are found in patients with some neurological illnesses such as neuropathy, radiculopathy, degenerative neurological conditions and also in otherwise objectively normal people. They comprise brief muscle twitchings which occur sporadically through the night and occasionally through the day. The author has found clonazepam to be a fairly useful drug in these patients.

Periodic movements of sleep are a rather more dramatic form of muscle flexion. Some authors claim that this syndrome is the most common occult medical disorder of sleep. It is characterized by a brisk flexion movement of the lower limb lasting between 20 and 40 s and causing the patient to awake. The neurological level of origin of the condition is unknown and the patients, if sleeping alone, are frequently unaware of the cause of their awakening. Treatment is similar to that of myoclonic jerks and restless legs syndrome.

SOCIAL CAUSES OF SLEEP DISORDER

The commonest 'social' causes of poor sleep are poor sleep habit (sleep hygiene), adjustment sleep disorder, and psychophysiologic insomnia. In many cases the conditions co-exist and one may progress to the other.

Irregular or poor sleep habits and behaviour patterns incompatible with good sleeping have been defined as poor sleep hygiene (Diagnostic Classification Steering Committee, 1990). Such individuals may follow irregular schedules for retiring, may spend an excessive amount of time in bed trying to sleep, and when sleep onset is delayed may rise, wander around, make a hot drink and return to bed some time (often hours) later. Poor sleep hygiene may be associated with stress, working until late, excessive use of stimulants such as caffeine and cigarettes, or alcohol abuse. Attempts at daytime napping to recoup lost sleep time may worsen the situation as may excessive consumption of xanthine containing beverages. Treatment centres around behavioural retraining and patient education including avoiding stimulants, regular daytime exercise, avoidance of naps and reinstitution of a regular sleep routine.

Adjustment sleep disorder (Diagnostic Classification Steering Committee, 1990) is experienced by between one third and one half of elderly individuals at some stage during their life. Sleep is disturbed by the advent of a social or psychological stress such as illness, hospitalization, bereavement, retirement and so on. These patients often lie awake dwelling on life events and sleep onset is considerably delayed. Adjustment sleep disorder normally resolves with time, but in some patients may progress to poor sleep hygiene or psychophysiological sleep disorder. Treatment should initially be focused on counselling and behavioural therapy, but in some intractable cases a limited course of hypnotic drugs may be deemed appropriate.

In psychophysiological insomnia (Diagnostic Classification Steering Committee, 1990) patients develop a series of learned responses whereby they associate sleep and bedtime rituals with an increased state of anxiety and arousal. It frequently follows a prolonged period of adjustment sleep disorder and poor sleep hygiene and may be particularly distressing. Although short courses of hypnotics may be prescribed, the mainstay of treatment has to be by counselling and behavioural therapy, which in experienced hands have proven to be effective in two-thirds of cases (Bootzin and Nicassio, 1978; Spielman *et al.*, 1987).

PSYCHIATRIC CAUSES OF SLEEP DISORDER

Dementia and delirium

Delirium (acute confusional state) is a frequent accompaniment of physical illness in the elderly (Lipowski, 1989). It is related to a diffuse disorder of cortical function in toxic individuals. Although affected patients may be confused and drowsy during the day, agitation, restlessness and nocturnal wakening is frequent. Treatment should be directed at the underlying physical disorder, prescription of sedative drugs may well exacerbate the problem and should as a rule be undertaken only in those whose restlessness is so severe as to constitute a medical danger to themselves or others.

Not dissimilar derangements of sleep pattern are seen in dementing patients (Rebok *et al.*, 1991) and again result from cortical disturbance. The typical demented patient who may be confused but perhaps slightly drowsy during the day, who awakes in the evening and early hours becoming restless, agitated, noisy or even aggressive is only too familiar to carers, staff of hospital geriatric wards and nursing homes. The syndrome is sometimes referred to as 'sundowning'.

As in delirious patients, changes in nursing practice such as maintaining the patient in a quiet subdued room, providing gentle comfort and possibly placing the bedding on the floor may help. In some patients however, the use of sedatives is essential, the most common drugs used being thioridazine or occasionally haloperidol. These drugs do carry significant risk of extrapyramidal disorder in these unfortunate patients and non-pharmacological therapy should be tried first.

Depression

Sleep disturbance is extremely common in depressed patients and it forms part of the DSM-III criteria (American Psychiatric Association, 1987). Sleep disorder may comprize delayed sleep onset, and particularly early awakening accompanied by low mood in the early hours.

A detailed description of insomnia in depression is beyond the scope of this chapter. Treatment should clearly be directed at the underlying psychiatric illness, antidepressant drugs, particularly those with sedative properties may be particularly helpful (Chen, 1979).

Anxiety

Elderly patients with anxiety disorders including phobic illness, obsessive compulsive phenomena and so on are frequently 'graduates' from their younger years (Ancoli-Israel, 1989). Many are already receiving appropriate treatment. If anxiety disorder develops in later life a thorough medical and psychiatric assessment is mandatory.

If physical, iatrogenic or depressive illness is diagnosed, appropriate treatment should be instituted. In selected patients judicious short-term use of hypnotic and anxiolytic drugs may be helpful, but psychological treatments should be the mainstay of therapy because of the well known dangers of long-term anxiolytic usage.

PROBLEMS OF HYPNOTIC AND SEDATIVE DRUGS IN THE ELDERLY

A variety of pharmacokinetic and pharmacodynamic changes occur with ageing which may result in the development of unacceptable side effects from this group of drugs in older patients.

Pharmacokinetic changes with ageing

Drug absorption across the gut is little altered in the elderly, but the first pass metabolism of highly extracted drugs is reduced, even in relatively healthy individuals, leading to higher plasma concentrations per unit dose (Woodhouse, 1991). This may be a problem for certain hypnotic drugs such as chlormethiazole.

Distribution volumes alter with ageing, resultant on changes on body composition. For example, body fat per kilogram body weight increases with age resulting in an increased distribution volume for fat soluble drugs; by contrast body water decreases resulting in a lower distribution volume for polar drugs. This may be particularly important for some sedatives, because increased distribution volumes lead to a prolongation of half-life in the presence of unaltered hepatic clearance. Thus, in the case of diazepam, a lipid soluble drug, distribution volume is increased and half-life is prolonged, resulting in an extended duration of action. For this type of drug a daytime 'hangover' effect is likely. Similarly, plasma albumin declines with age, resulting in higher free fraction of many benzodiazepines. As it is the free fraction of the drug which is pharmacologically active and may penetrate the blood–brain barrier, this may result in increased prevalence of type A adverse drug reactions.

The hepatic elimination of drugs falls with ageing, largely due to reduced liver mass. This will additionally prolong half-life, particularly in frail patients and may result in hangover effect. Delayed hepatic clearance of benzodiazepines is said to be more marked for oxidized drugs such as diazepam as opposed to conjugated drugs such as temazepam, and the latter group of agents may be preferable in elderly individuals.

Pharmacodynamics and homeostatic changes

Even in the presence of equivalent free plasma drug concentrations there is evidence that elderly people are inherently more susceptible to the effects of hypnotic and sedative drugs of the various kinds. This may manifest as increased somnolence, impaired postural control or even the development of acute confusional states. The exact mechanisms underlying increased sensitivity in the elderly are unclear, but may include increased penetration into the central nervous system, or changes in drug receptor numbers and/or affinity (Woodhouse, 1991).

Traditionally, homeostatic mechanisms tend to fail with ageing, particularly postural control and orthostatic blood pressure control. This may result in an increased prevalence of postural hypotension and/or falls in susceptible elderly individuals.

Specific hypnotic and sedative drugs

A large variety of hypnotic drugs are available for use in the elderly. The category of drug prescribed and the individual agent within therapeutic categories varies widely both between and within countries depending on the experience and medico-cultural background of the prescriber.

Chloral hydrate has waned in popularity, although it is still used in individual units. It is undoubtedly an effective sedative, its main drawbacks being an unpleasant taste and smell, and gastric irritation. Its derivative, *dichloralphenazone* (Welldorm) is still a popular hypnotic, has relatively minor side effects, but because the phenazone (antipyrene) moiety of the drug is an enzyme inducer, there is potential for adverse drug interactions, particularly with anticonvulsants and coumarin anticoagulants.

Chlormethiazole is both effective and widely used as an hypnotic. Its potential for habituation is relatively low and it appears to have a relatively benign side effect profile even in vulnerable patients such as those with Parkinson's disease (Tulloch *et al.*, 1991). Some patients find that this drug may cause nasal stuffiness and prickliness, but in general it is well tolerated. Its duration of action is such that hangover effects are relatively uncommon in the majority of elderly patients.

Benzodiazepines are perhaps the most widely used group of hypnotic drugs (Greenblatt *et al.*, 1991). The ultra-short acting *triazolam* which used to be frequently prescribed for delayed sleep onset has now been withdrawn in several European countries due to adverse effects. Short to medium acting drugs such as *temazepam* are now more widely used and are unquestionably effective both in inducing sleep and prolonging sleep duration. Hangover effects with *temazepam* are uncommon and this type of benzodiazepine should be used in preference to the longer acting drugs *chlordiazepoxide* and *diazepam* which are inappropriate as hypnotics in the elderly. There is now general agreement that benzodiazepines as a group may cause habituation and that withdrawal effects are frequent. For this reason it is now recommended that they should only be used in the short term if this is at all possible.

Newer hypnotic compounds such as *zopiclone* are now being introduced and are said to produce effective hypnotic effects with a relatively low prevalence of adverse effects and hangover. They are relatively more expensive than other drugs and further experience with this type of agent is required before firm recommendations on their use can be made.

SUMMARY

Sleep disorders in the elderly are frequent and may be a cause of considerable distress. An accurate physical, social and psychiatric diagnosis is essential before treatment is instituted. Simple behavioural and lifestyle changes should be made; physical and iatrogenic illness addressed before specific pharmacotherapy is instituted. If drug treatment is deemed appropriate then this should be tailored to the individual patient with regard to choice of drug in order to minimize adverse reactions and hangover effect. In general, the duration of treatment should be brief, perhaps no more than a few weeks. If these guidelines are followed, long-term hypnotic use will be required only in a small proportion of patients (Cadieux and Adams, 1992). In these individuals, careful monitoring should be undertaken for untoward events and the development of habituation. The potential for withdrawal effects should be borne in mind.

REFERENCES

American Psychiatric Association (1987). *Diagnostic and Statistical Manual of Mental Disorders, 3rd edn, revised*, American Psychiatric Association, Washington DC.
Ancoli-Israel, S. (1989). Epidemiology of sleep disorders. In: Roth, T. and Roehrs, T.A. (Guest Eds), Sleep disorders in the elderly. *Clin. Geriatr. Med.*, **5**, 347–362.
Bliwise, D.L., Feldman, D.E., Bliwise, N.G. *et al.* (1987). Risk factors for sleep disordered breathing in heterogeneous geriatric populations. *J. Am. Geriatr. Soc.*, **35**, 132–141.
Bootzin, R.R. and Nicassio, P.M. (1978). Behavioural treatments for insomnia. In: *Progress in Behaviour Modification, Vol. 6*, Academic Press, New York.

Cadieux, R.J. and Adams, D.G. (1992). Sleep disorders in older patients. Conservative treatment is usually enough. *Postgrad. Med.*, **91**, 403–416.

Chen, C.N. (1979). Sleep, depression and antidepressants. *Br. J. Psychiatry*, **135**, 385–402.

D'Alessandro, R., Magelli, C., Gamberini, G. *et al.* (1990). Snoring every night as a risk factor for myocardial infarction. *Br. Med. J.*, **300**, 1557–1558.

Diagnostic Classification Steering Committee (Thorpy, M.J., Chairman) (1990). *International Classification of Sleep Disorders: Diagnostic and Coding Manual*, American Sleep Disorders Association, Rochester, MN.

Ford, D.E. and Kamerow, D.B. (1989). Epidemiological study of sleep disturbances and psychiatric disturbances. *J. Am. Med. Assoc.*, **262**, 1479–1484.

Greenblatt, D.J., Harmatz, J.S. and Shader, R.I. (1991). Clinical pharmacokinetics of anxiolytics and hypnotics in the elderly. *Clin. Pharmacokinet.*, **21**, 165–177.

Kales, A., Vela-Bueno, A. and Kales, J.D. (1987). Sleep disorders: sleep apnea and narcolepsy. *Ann. Intern. Med.*, **106**, 434–443.

Lipowski, Z.J. (1989). Delirium in the elderly patient. *N. Engl. J. Med.*, **323**, 520–526.

Livingstone, G., Hawkins, A., Graham, N. *et al.* (1990). The Gospel Oak study: prevalence rates of dementia, depression and activity limitation among elderly residents in inner London. *Psychol. Med.*, **20**, 137–146.

Montplaisir, J. and Godbout, R. (1989). Restless legs syndrome and periodic movements of sleep. In: Kryger, M., Roth, T. and Dement, W.C. (Eds), *Principles and Practice of Sleep*, Saunders, Philadelphia, pp. 402–409.

Morgan, K., Dallosso, H., Ebrahim, S. *et al.* (1988). Characteristics of subjective insomnia among the elderly living at home. *Age Ageing*, **17**, 1–7.

Rebok, G.W., Rovner, B.W. and Folstein, M.F. (1991). Sleep disturbance and Alzheimer's disease: relationship to behavioral problems. *Aging*, **3**, 193–196.

Spielman, A.J., Saskin, P. and Thorpy, M.J. (1987). Treatment of chronic insomnia by restriction of time spent in bed. *Sleep*, **10**, 45–56.

Stradling, J.R. and Crosby, J.H. (1990). Relation between systemic hypertension and sleep hypoxaemia or snoring. *Br. Med. J.*, **300**, 75–78.

Tulloch, J.A., Ashwood, T.J., Bateman, D.N. *et al.* (1991). A single dose study of the pharmacodynamic effects of chlormethiazole, temazepam and placebo in elderly parkinsonian patients. *Age Ageing*, **20**, 424–429.

Waldhorn, R.E. (1990). Long-term compliance with nasal continus positive airway pressure therapy of OSA. *Chest*, **97**, 1272–1273.

Webb, W.B. (1989). Age-related changes in sleep. In: Roth, T. and Roehrs, T.A. (Guest Eds), Sleep disorders in the elderly. *Clin. Geriatr. Med.*, **5**, 275–287.

Woodhouse, K. (1991). Prescribing in the elderly. In: Seymour, C.A. and Summerfield, J.A. (Eds), *Horizons in Medicine*, No. 3, Royal College of Physicians, London and TransMedica Europe Ltd, Sussex, pp. 111–118.

Old Age Psychiatry and
the Law

Treatment and Care in Old Age Psychiatry
Edited by R. Levy, R. Howard and A. Burns
©1993 Wrightson Biomedical Publishing Ltd

17

Consent in Dementia: Is It Valid and Informed?

R.G. JONES

Health Care of the Elderly, University Hospital, Nottingham, UK

INTRODUCTION

The rather stark title of this chapter sharply alerts us to the ethical and legal issues surrounding the care of demented people. It is important to see this wider perspective. Treatment and care in services dealing with demented people are often hampered by the very negative unattractive stereotypes and prejudices which so many have about the elderly, the elderly mentally ill and particularly about the elderly demented. These unhelpful unattractive ideas tend to surround patients, staff and all of the service. Undoubtedly, one particular aspect is this feeling of unpleasant compulsory procedures being imposed — a feeling that there will be little choice or consent if one is in the hands of a service dealing with demented people. This is a problem against which we have to struggle.

There is perhaps also a wider struggle in medical ethics. In 1991 the American historian, Francis Fukiyama, announced the end of history. Shortly afterwards, and published in 1992, an American medical ethicist announced the end of medical ethics (Jonsen, 1992). An exaggeration, perhaps, but the real and sombre concern was that doctors were increasingly becoming so fettered and bound by measures devaluing and destroying their professional freedom that soon there would be no need of a code of medical ethics. Protocols, cost/containment and bureaucratic inspection and monitoring were increasingly hedging in the doctor so that the professional ethical code of practice, guiding the use of professional judgement, was increasingly irrelevant.

The high cost of American health care no doubt influences this perspective but it is far from totally unrecognizable in our reformed NHS, and such concerns are relevant to our struggles to deal properly with demented people.

The title of this chapter strongly raises both legal and ethical issues but clearly, in addition, it raises practical concerns. All three areas should be addressed.

CONSENT IN ENGLISH LAW

Looking first at the law, in England our title is irrelevant. Valid and informed consent are American legal concepts. In English law we deal with real consent (Law Commission, 1991). This English legal concept is enshrined in common law and has developed over centuries. The essence of it is that for consent to be real, the patient, in consenting freely, must understand in broad terms what is involved. Consent also has been developed in the concept of the duty of care owed to a patient. Through the duty of care the doctor is obliged to advise about the problem and need for treatment; to inform the patient about the treatment which may be necessary; and to warn of any significant risks associated with treatment. Most particularly the doctor does not have to fully inform the patient about every possible aspect and every conceivable side effect of treatment. But the clear implication is that the more substantial, likely and foreseeable aspects will be made known. Primarily though it is left to the doctor to decide how much disclosure of such detail, or very unlikely but possible risks, is appropriate. The court expects the doctor's practice with such disclosure to be in accordance with what would be accepted by a responsible body of medical opinion skilled and experienced in the specialty concerned. Considerable trust is placed in the proper professional practice of doctors. But at the end of the day the court reserves the right to judge for itself whether what was actually done was reasonable, and thereby produced real consent. And the court may possibly overrule the responsible body of medical opinion (Law Commission, 1991).

Thus the legal position in England and Wales leaves the doctor considerable leeway for the exercise of professional judgement.

Clearly, though, with many demented people there is no possibility of real consent. The patient cannot understand in broad terms what is involved. The doctor proposes treatment but the patient is incapable of either consenting or dissenting. Except for the special circumstances of the Mental Health Act, English law does not allow for the consent decision with adults to be taken by anyone else (Department of Health, 1990). The doctor is then left to proceed without real consent, according to appropriate professional practice. And this can leave the doctor with very difficult decisions to make.

WHAT PRACTICAL PROBLEMS ARISE

Various practical problems arise as a result of consent difficulties with demented people, many of which are very familiar to clinicians working with the elderly, but some points are well worth rehearsing.

Assessment, investigation and treatment may be refused by an incapable resistant demented person. In these cases, dementia, which is classified as a mental disorder can be used as justification under the Mental Health Act for compulsory procedures, in the interests of the health or safety of the patient, or for the prevention of harm to other persons. But this would not allow compulsory treatment of a physical disorder in its own right (Department of Health, 1990). And, there are problems of differing perceptions. A recently published textbook on geriatric medicine explicitly stated that 'dementia is not classified as a treatable mental illness for the purposes of the Act' (Bennett and Ebrahim, 1992). This is incorrect. It would equally be quite wrong if it were thought that every demented person with impaired capacity to consent should be dealt with under the Act. In fact, the Act is explicit that incapacity to consent through mental disorder should be treated in the same way as the withholding of consent. But there is scope for discussion and doubt amongst clinicians as to when compulsory procedures under the Mental Health Act are justifiable.

A reasonable approach would be to use the Act if the demented person clearly makes irrational judgements based on the effects of dementia, such as delusions, hallucinations or impaired insight, including severe memory impairment. It would not be right to use the Act with demented people who broadly understood their situation and were simply expressing long established independence linked to a desire to end their days in their own home, albeit in the setting of forgetfulness.

Frequent use of the Act with the demented would be stigmatizing and counter-productive for the good working and acceptance of community focused services, seeking to support at home. On the other hand the Law Commission has suggested that reluctance to use the Act may mean that many demented people who are incapable but who resist only weakly if at all are thereby subject to *de facto* detention without having the protection which the Act could afford (Law Commission, 1991).

In England compulsory removal from home of demented people can alternatively be achieved through Section 47 of the National Assistance Act, 1948 (Brahams, 1987). Then, they are not categorized as mentally disordered but instead as 'suffering from grave chronic disease or being aged, infirm or physically incapable . . . . (and) living in insanitary conditions, and needing care and not receiving it' (Norman, 1980). In reality, this procedure is viewed by many as too draconian and views vary greatly about how and when it should be used. In practice, it is rarely used and some feel it is an unethical infringement of civil liberty to compulsorily remove a person from home except on the grounds of formal mental disorder (Muir Gray, 1991; Greaves, 1991).

Increasing legal and ethical dilemmas are posed by demented people who lack insight into the dangers posed by their continuing driving (O'Neill, 1992). The cohort of more mobile and prosperous people now coming through into old age means that the problem is more frequent. Consent certainly may not be granted by the demented person for the breach of confidentiality often required here, though this is sanctioned by the General Medical Council and arguably is required under the wider duty of care to the community.

Dealing with financial and related affairs nearly always becomes a problem but at least ultimately there are statutory procedures available through the Court of Protection or an Enduring Power of Attorney, although concerns remain about how effective these mechanisms are (Age Concern, 1986).

Balancing the interests of the demented person against those of family carers or others can be extremely difficult. Mostly these are in harmony or at least can be reconciled but not infrequently the interests are completely contradictory. Perhaps in this situation, or perhaps with any of these problems with demented people, coercion, subterfuge or frank deception may come into play. The incapable, uncomprehending, bemused, demented patient may have all kinds of *de facto* compulsion imposed. But from a paternalistic point of view it may seem that the patient's best interests have been served whilst avoiding an unpleasant confrontation or even the need for force.

The major practical problem — the end of life

However, it is with 'how far to investigate' or 'how far to treat' that we reach the most difficult practical problem area. In practice the doctor is often left to decide this alone and at present legally this is always the case. Best practice involves consultation with the family and other team members but ultimately it remains a medical decision (Jones, 1987). And this is most particularly true in decisions on when to withdraw or withhold potentially life-saving treatment. From the doctor's point of view, the most important consideration is quality of life (Royal College of Psychiatrists, 1989). Our clinical teams, working with family carers, are skilled in assessing quality of life and should take responsibility for this. But increasingly, as we shall see, decision making in this area is complex and some fear that the cost of care may come to dominate more as a factor.

With this difficult area, brief mention should also be made of euthanasia and the liberalization of this practice in Holland. This should be something which only arises with capable patients positively seeking a good death. But the reality of the Dutch experience is that significant numbers of people were shown in a survey to have been incapable, thereby non-consenting, but nevertheless killed through 'euthanasia' (Van der Maas *et al.*, 1991). In around half of these cases, the doctors concerned admitted that they had not followed the consultation procedures which it was agreed were good practice. The worry here is the slippery slope argument. What was at first unthinkable can over a period of time become accepted and commonplace. Millard chillingly quotes Primo Levi describing how it took six months to accept stealing in a concentration camp as a normal part of life, after which it was never again questioned (Millard, 1992).

The recent *Lancet* article on assisted death — which means the deliberate medical killing of a person — similarly is a cause for concern in its possible implications for demented patients (Institute of Medical Ethics Working Party, 1990). The same authors, from the Institute of Medical Ethics, have also written on the withdrawal of life support from people with persistent vegetative states (Institute of Medical Ethics Working Party, 1991). In their work they make it clear that assisted death would be for those who were terminally ill and, clearly and appropriately, asking for medical assistance with an end to their lives. They also talk of the withdrawal of life support from those with persistent vegetative states being for those in whom previously expressed wishes are known. However, by the end of the article, this aspect is not mentioned in the conclusion and, of course, in reality there is likely to be great difficulty knowing the true nature of previous wishes. The only recently introduced Dutch liberalization suggests that doctors can quite quickly forget their guidelines. And in the eyes of many how different are our demented patients from those with persistent vegetative states?

Clearly, it would be for the doctor's professional ethical code to ensure that such procedures did not lead to the assisting into death of a stream of vulnerable, incapable and uncomprehending demented patients. But, as financial and other pressures mount, as Primo Levi found in the concentration camp, how quickly might our standards gradually and subtly, but eventually substantially, change? I suggest that assisted death has no place in dementia.

BACKGROUND ETHICAL PRINCIPLES

Looking at the legal and practical implications of the consent question quickly brings us to see there is an enormous area of ethical concern. What are the guiding ethical principles which should help us to deal with this area?

There is broad agreement (Bloch and Chodoff, 1991) that four particular considerations are paramount:

- Autonomy
- Beneficence
- Non-maleficence
- Equity

In our modern, multi-cultural and pluralist society both a multiplicity of strong, even fundamentalist, religious belief and a complete absence of any religious belief are conspicuous features. Personal choice, personal freedom, person autonomy, without causing harm to others, appears to be the principal ethical value about which most agree. For doctors, where previously we claimed our prime concern to be promoting the best interests of our patients, increasingly we now accept that our first aim has to be enabling our patients to exercize their autonomy, their choice, from an informed position.

Clearly, with the demented, exercizing autonomy is a difficult problem because of impaired capacity. But a number of mechanisms have been suggested to promote autonomy which receive a little more detailed consideration below. And we should recognize that though demented people may be incapable of making some decisions they are by no means incapable of all decisions. Most can exercize at least some choice during much of their illness. As far as possible we should allow the maximum freedom to choose whilst ensuring that no harm comes to the self or others.

But we should not deceive ourselves about the often complex and multiple care needs of demented people. If we promote the maximum choice for one demented individual this may well be at the cost of resources and staff attention for several others, thus threatening both their care and their autonomy (Jones, 1987). Ideally, there will be sufficient staff and resources but no clinician lays claim to this! And certainly the principle of autonomy then has to be placed beside other important principles, and considered together with the needs of others and of the community at large. If limitations and constraints have to be imposed it is important that we are open and explicit as to for whom and why this is so, and that this remains subject to review (Royal College of Nursing, 1986).

The other principles also merit very considerable discussion but limitation of space restricts this. Beneficence means doing the right thing — the ethically correct action. Non-maleficence essentially means 'above all do no harm'. Equity or justice clearly mean that all should be treated equally and fairly.

Equity is an interesting concept in the age of quality adjusted life years. It is clear, for instance, that the results of population surveys would consign the elderly — never mind the elderly demented — to much less health care than the younger and more economically active (Williams, 1992). Problems of ageism and of intergenerational rivalry for resource allocation in health care raise their heads.

Also relevant are Tooley's discussion of what gives an individual a serious 'right to life' (Tooley, 1972) and Brock's suggestion that the severely demented, lacking various capacities, 'lack personhood' and that they may therefore have a lesser moral status or less valid claim 'on grounds of justice to health care treatment' (Brock, 1988).

Clearly, demented people could suffer much neglect and ill treatment if we deny them status as persons. And, paraphrasing Harris (1991), in our sharp world the 'enemy' (amongst whom would be counted the demented) would become those sick unfortunates who stand between the fit, fortunate 'good guys' and their contented survival, daring to make rival claims for concern and for resources. But, of course, it would also be unethical to completely ignore the effects of the costs of treatment and care for the demented on the rest of the community (Williams, 1992).

The headings of these ethical considerations can seem quite theoretical. A helpful simple summary of what they actually mean is provided by the Stanford University Medical Centre Committee on Ethics' account of the six basic principles of medical ethics (Williams, 1992). These are:

- Preserve life
- Alleviate suffering
- Do no harm
- Tell the truth
- Respect patient autonomy
- Deal justly with patients.

These principles echo — but state more simply — the basic concerns.

Looking from the point of view of a UK clinician, there is the need to add consideration of all possible patients, both current patients and potential future patients, and the need to consider the needs of carers — and the implications of care provision for the wider community. But, in a simple brief way, this list sums up the main contradictory and clashing themes. The doctor's task is to find the appropriate ethical balance between those contrasting themes in the case of the individual patient, bearing in mind wider perspectives.

MENTAL INCAPACITY

Of central importance is the fact that the doctor assesses whether the patient is capable of giving consent. Some have even suggested that doctors veer liberally on the side of viewing the demented person as capable when they like the decision he makes and easily classify him as incapable when they dislike his decision. There is probably some truth in this rather cynical view.

It is important to recognize that the legal concept of incapacity is rather different from the medical concept. Clinicians tend to think of somebody as generally incapable by reason of a disease state producing cognitive impairment. For the law it is simply a matter of whether a person is able to make a particular decision and different criteria will be applied for different decisions. Capacity to consent to sexual intercourse, for instance, is quite different from capacity to make a valid Will and this again is quite different from capacity to consent to treatment. The law, as we have seen, leaves broad discretion to the doctor as to what may be needed. It mostly requires that there be a broad understanding, in general terms, of what is going on. And, in practice doctors probably do make very broad brush general impressionistic assessments of a demented person's capacity to consent.

Some helpful analysis has been devoted though to what sort of elements reasonably could be seen as necessary for capacity (Law Commission, 1991). These include:

● Being able to communicate a choice and being able to both communicate and maintain a stable choice
● Being able to understand (and in order to be able to do this being able to remember) relevant information necessary in order to make such a choice
● Being able to grasp the general significance of one's situation, e.g. that one is ill or in need of care
● Being able to manipulate mentally the relevant information in order to reach a rational conclusion

It is helpful to have such ideas in mind when looking at capacity but also the nature and seriousness of the decision should be considered. It would also be wrong to have so complex a concept or such complex tests that one needs to have a PhD in order to be deemed capable.

WAYS TO PROMOTE AUTONOMY

The aim must be to enable the patient to choose, to facilitate and promote autonomy as far as possible, rather than raise barriers with complex tests. This list summarizes some possible approaches to enhancing autonomy with demented patients:

● Let patients decide
● Allow freedom in safe setting
● Use views of family carers

- Make a Substitute Judgement
- Use of Living Will or Advance Directive
- Enduring Health Care Powers of Attorney
- A possible new form of Guardianship.

It can obviously be very beneficial to the quality of life of demented patients to allow them the greatest possible freedom of choice in their care, and freedom of movement in a safe environment. Care staff then try to let patients make as many decisions for themselves as possible. Clearly, there are constraints on how far this approach can go, both in their own interests and in the reasonable interests of others. Very important are the views of family carers. They may well be able to help clarify what is the patient's current wish. More often they can add to the team's awareness of what would have been the patient's approach to such decisions earlier on when capable. In this case they help to make a substitute judgement (Dyck, 1984; Veatch, 1984), to make a decision on the basis of what the patient would have decided, not on the basis of what is thought best. This really is a way of promoting autonomy rather than dealing paternalistically, in terms of best interests as judged by professionals. Of course, there must be a limit as clinicians and others cannot be by this means mandated or compelled to act unethically, ignoring the best interests.

The Living Will or advance directive (Age Concern Institute of Gerontology and the Centre of Medical Law and Ethics, 1988), formally drawn up and witnessed when capable, is, in the United States, a legally recognized way of stipulating — ahead of time — the approach one would wish in health care decisions if incapacity intervenes. Although lacking legal status here, it is thought that around 17 000 such advance directives, distributed by the Voluntary Euthanasia Society, have been completed in this country. Increasingly these will figure in the medical records of doctors dealing with demented patients.

Another approach adapts the Enduring Power of Attorney mechanism, whereby a particular person is granted power to make decisions and this power endures despite incapacity. With this adaptation the person granted power of attorney is also sanctioned to make health care decisions on behalf of the 'donor' when incapacity occurs. The major problem with both this and the Living Will approach is the overwhelming disinclination which British people feel to make even a standard Will. It seems extremely unlikely that they will go in for these more complicated legal mechanisms in the near future. With the Enduring Power of Attorney as well there must be concern arising from the Australian experience where much evidence of abuse of power was found and where 19 out of 20 cases were inappropriate or improper in various ways (Law Reform Commission of Victoria, 1990; Australian Law Reform Commission, 1988).

CURRENT PRACTICE AND SUGGESTED APPROACHES

The present position is that the doctor makes treatment decisions when the patient is incapable and in most matters the doctor's view is paramount. Consultation with the closest family carers, and sharing of discussion and perspectives with the multidisciplinary team, and with all significantly involved, are essential. In an institution the nurses or other care staff must play a key role in such discussions (Royal College of Psychiatrists, 1989).

When decisions are particularly difficult, a second opinion from a specialist or general practitioner colleague may be helpful and some have suggested the involvement of a social worker or a patient's advocate with especially hard cases. Also suggested has been the use of special bodies such as a District Ethical Committee or even Regional or National Ethical Committees. Finally, a Court could be involved, as is not unusual in the United States and is becoming more common here. But this should be exceptional. Some decision making will need to escalate up this route but the best care is likely where the great majority of decisions are taken close to the patient.

In fact the Law Commission is currently examining this whole area and it seems certain that they will propose some rationalizing of the present legal uncertainties (Law Commission, 1991). It is essential to avoid legalistic, rigid and extensive bureaucratic procedures. Swift, flexible and sensitively responsive decision making will avoid unnecessary suffering and distress to patients. Hopefully, professionals can successfully communicate this message and gain the trust and support of the community for their demonstrable good practice, so that the minimum legal interference is sought.

This is an area long overdue for review and possible reform (Law Society's Mental Health Sub-Committee, 1989). But any new mechanisms should facilitate good practice and collaboration among involved professionals. If new law is needed it seems most likely that a much reformed Guardianship would be the best mechanism, with great effort put in to make sure that this works effectively and sufficient resources to enable a Local Authority or other Guardian to be effective.

TREATING THE INCAPABLE PATIENT WITHOUT REAL CONSENT

The present legal position when giving treatment to an incapable person without real consent is summarized in the major feature of the judgement in the Re. F case (Brahams, 1989; Law Commission, 1991) where sterilization of a mature mentally handicapped girl without real consent was allowed. The main features were that treatment may proceed if it is:

- in the best interests of the person;
- necessary to save life, prevent a deterioration or ensure an improvement in the patient's physical or mental health; and
- it is accepted . . . by a responsible body of medical opinion skilled in the . . . treatment.

In exceptional circumstances the approval of the High Court should be sought.

Clearly the judgement invests a great deal of respect and trust in the professional practice of doctors. We need to continue to promote debate on these issues and to strive to ensure that the Courts, and society at large, continue to invest such faith in our practice in these very difficult situations. We should all work for this.

REFERENCES

Age Concern (1986). *The Law and Vulnerable Elderly People*, Age Concern Publications, London.

Age Concern Institute of Gerontology and the Centre of Medical Law and Ethics (1988). A Working Party Report under their auspices, *The Living Will: Consent to Treatment at the End of Life*, King's College, London.

Australian Law Reform Commission (1988). *Enduring Powers of Attorney, Third Report, No. 47*, The Australian Law Reform Commission, Canberra.

Bennett, G.J. and Ebrahim, S. (1992). *The Essentials of Health Care of the Elderly*. Edward Arnold, London.

Bloch, S. and Chodoff, P. (1991). *Psychiatric Ethics (2nd edn)*, Oxford University Press, Oxford.

Brahams, D. (1987). Involuntary Hospital Admission under Section 47 of the National Assistance Act. *Lancet*, **ii**, 406.

Brahams, D. (1989). Sterilisation of a mentally incapable woman. *Lancet*, **i**, 1275–1276.

Brock, D.W. (1988). Justice and the severely demented elderly. *J. Med. Phil.*, **13**, 73–99.

Department of Health (1990). *Mental Health Act 1983, Code of Practice*, HMSO, London.

Dyck, A.J. (1984). Ethical aspects of care of the dying incompetent. *J. Am. Geriatr. Soc.*, **32**, 661–664.

Greaves, D.A. (1991). Can compulsory removal ever be justified for adults who are mentally competent? *J. Med. Ethics*, **17**, 189–194.

Harris, J. (1991). Unprincipled QUALYs: a response to Cubbon. *J. Med. Ethics*, **17**, 185–188.

Institute of Medical Ethics Working Party (1990). Assisted death. *Lancet*, **336**, 610–613.

Institute of Medical Ethics Working Party (1991). Withdrawal of life-support from patients in a persistent vegetative state. *Lancet*, **337**, 96–98.

Jones, R.G. (1987). Problems in senile dementia. In: Elford, R.J. (Ed.), *Medical Ethics and Elderly People*, Churchill Livingstone, Edinburgh.

Jonsen, A.R. (1992). The end of medical ethics. *J. Am. Geriatr. Soc.*, **40**, 393–397.

Law Commission (1991). *Mentally Incapacitated Adults and Decision-Making: An Overview Consultation Paper No. 119*, HMSO, London.

Millard, P. (1992). Leading article: kill or care: euthanasia and the doctor in the UK. *Geriatr. Med.*, **22**, 16.

Law Reform Commission of Victoria (1990). *Enduring Powers of Attorney, Discussion Paper 18*, Law Reform Commission of Victoria, Melbourne.

Law Society's Mental Health Sub-Committee (1989). *Decision Making and Mental Incapacity. A Discussion Document*, The Law Society's Hall, London.

Muir Gray, J.A. (1991). Section 47 — Assault on or protection of the freedom of the individual? A short response to Greaves. *J. Med. Ethics*, **17**, 195.

Norman, A.J. (1980). *Rights and Risk*, National Corporation for the Care of Old People, London.

O'Neill, D. (1992). Comment — The doctor's dilemma: the ageing driver and dementia. *Int. J. Geriatr. Psychiatry*, **7**, 297–301.

Royal College of Nursing (1986). *Improving Care of Elderly People in Hospital*, Joint publication of the Royal College of Nursing, British Geriatrics Society and the Royal College of Psychiatrists, London.

Royal College of Psychiatrists (1989). *Joint Working Group on the Consent of Non-volitional Patients and de facto Detention of Informal Patients, Council Report C6*, The Royal College of Psychiatrists, London.

Tooley, N. (1972). Abortion and infanticide. *Phil. Pub. Aff.*, **2**, 37–65.

Van der Maas, P.J., van Delden, J.J.M., Pijnenborg, L. and Looman, C.W.N. (1991). Clinical Practice: Euthanasia and other medical decisions concerning the end of life. *Lancet*, **338**, 669–674.

Veatch, R.M. (1984). An ethical framework for terminal care decisions: a new classification of patients. *J. Am. Geriatr. Soc.*, **32**, 665–669.

Williams, A. (1992). Cost-effectiveness analysis: is it ethical? *J. Med. Ethics*, **18**, 7–11.

Treatment and Care in Old Age Psychiatry
Edited by R. Levy, R. Howard and A. Burns
©1993 Wrightson Biomedical Publishing Ltd

18

The Mental Health Act and Dementia

ELAINE MURPHY

*Department of Psychogeriatrics, United Medical and Dental Schools, Guy's Hospital,
London, UK*

The Mental Health Act 1983 and its forebears, right back to the Vagrancy Act of 1744, all emerged from a common concern that individuals who are ill, or handicapped in ways that render them incapable of making autonomous decisions, are especially vulnerable and therefore need special protection to ensure that any treatment and care that is given them is warranted, is of a good standard of practice and that they are not subjected to unnecessary interference and redundant medical treatment. On the other hand, there is an equally strong concern that vulnerable individuals should receive the care and treatment they need, whether they understand the need or not, and that the best available care should be afforded to them.

It is obvious that there is scope for conflict between these two principles and this has been at the root of many of the anxieties and resentments that psychiatrists and other health professionals have expressed about the 1983 Act, fuelled by a suspicion that the campaigners for the Act did not understand the needs of severely mentally ill people and were grinding axes to fight in battles other than those concerned with mentally disordered people.

We are now nearly a decade on and most of us have come to accept the need to have our own professional freedom curtailed in the interests of patients. The Act gives us a more secure way forward for treating mentally ill people who either cannot give consent as a result of mental incapacity, or who refuse treatment when they are at risk of harm. It is clear, however, that the Act was not written with mentally frail elderly people in mind. Nevertheless, dementia is a mental disorder within the meaning of the Act and in principle there should be no difficulty in using the Act for the benefit of people with dementia when that is felt to be necessary. It is worth adding that acute confusional states are also mental disorders. The fact that on occasion there are clear physiological antecedents which precipitate the disorder, or that the changes are due to cerebral organic disease, makes not a jot of difference. After all, we do not distinguish between the mental disorder of 'process' schizophrenia and the schizophrenia which arises as a consequence of long standing focal epilepsy. The origins of a mental disorder are not relevant to the Act.

The Mental Health Act covers only certain aspects of care and treatment of patients, and it must be seen in the context of the body of Common Law, which has informed professional practice before and since the Act, for all informal patients, whether they are capable of consent or not. It is worth remembering too that most common law problem areas have remained untested in a court of law and therefore it is difficult to predict what courts might decide in certain cases. A large number of the questions put to the Mental Health Act Commission by letter and telephone about the care and treatment of elderly people fall into this category. Secondly, Statute Law supersedes and replaces Common Law, so you cannot revert to Common Law principles just because you do not like Statute Law. As Commissioners travel round the country, we find that sometimes gaps in the law are being divined in what one of our lawyer colleauges, John Finch, referred to as 'multidisciplinary prayer groups'. This is, I believe, the only way we can tackle the problems until the health care professions, the Mental Health Act Commission, the Law Commission and, if necessary, the courts develop a consensus on the way forward.

The Mental Health Act is not an especially well drafted or clear piece of legislation. There are some striking gaps — provision for children is not covered well, for example, and the courts have recently made some eccentric decisions, emphasizing parental and local authority decision making about treatment of minors which seem to fly in the face of the principles of the Children Act. There are too some pretty obvious gaps, largely, I suspect, because legal drafters and parliament were not in a position to work their way through the clinical problems. For example, there is no guidance on what to do when a seriously mentally disturbed person, attending as a day patient on an in-patient ward (quite a frequent occurrence these days), turns up on the ward in a distressed state and threatens to run away and kill himself. He is not an 'admitted' patient but the nurse in charge will feel she must dissuade him from going. And yet the nurse cannot use Section 5(4), the nurses' holding power and a doctor could not use 5(2). A nurse or doctor, however, who knowingly let a suicidal person leave under these circumstances would be failing in his or her professional Duty of Care and, indeed, failing in a duty to a fellow citizen. In these circumstances the professional must take the course of action which he/she knows is in the best interests of the patient and rapidly seek assistance to get a swift assessment by an ASW and two doctors. So the Act has gaps, and if the Code of Practice also has gaps it is because of the difficulties in laying down guidelines which could well be reversed by a court case.

The clinical dilemmas psychiatrists face in caring for elderly people, especially those with dementia, usually arise out of trying to balance two entirely different and opposing sets of rights of individuals, against the risks of pushing those rights too far. The first set of rights are the rights of self determination, autonomy of action, liberty, the right to make choices; the second set of rights are the rights to protection from abuse, to receive care and treatment, the right to have someone advocate your needs. Set against those rights is the downside, the risks which arise when the balance of judgment goes awry. The freedom of someone with advanced dementia to remain alone at home in a deteriorating, unheated house, refusing meals on wheels, creates the risk of self neglect, malnutrition, starvation and the risk of lying for days in pain with a fractured femur; the risk of causing others, especially relatives, an intolerable burden of anxiety; the risk of being a grave public nuisance to neighbours as the stench of human excreta wafts over the fence and the rats move in to colonize a filthy and decaying environment. On the other hand, the paternalistic approach of many health care professionals which results in that same dementia sufferer being removed to the soul destroying anonymity of a long-stay ward or residential home, robbing her of the last shreds of human individuality, is just as grave a moral error.

Getting the balance right is exceptionally difficult for health care professionals, who are on the whole brought up in the paternalistic tradition which stresses the duty of care, and the right of patients to be protected and to receive treatment. Social workers on the other hand tend to have been educated to promote and defend the civil libertarian stance. They wish to stress the right to be autonomous and for people to be allowed to make their own decisions. Of course these are professional stereotypes but the educational background of different professions provides the context for many disputes between professionals brought to the Commission's attention in the guise of telephone questions about the Act or the Code. It is therefore crucial that professionals working alongside each other should have a common understanding of each other's philosophy and personal attitudes, or notions of where each stands on the continuum. Inevitably at times they will need to reach a compromize. The typical Friday night meeting on the doorstep of an elderly person's house, where GP, duty ASW and psychiatrist meet to decide to section or not to section and to exchange pink forms in mutual incomprehension of the other two's philosophy, is at the least undesirable, and at worst a serious failure of responsibility to the individual.

It is vital to develop an understanding of one's own and other people's philosophy if one is to deal with the kinds of problems which crop up often with elderly people and which are not covered by the Mental Health Act.

Psychiatrists who work solely with elderly people are treating patients of whom approximately two thirds will be unable to give real consent to treatment. One of the main features of dementia is that reasoning and judgment are impaired at an early stage. However, all psychiatrists are familiar with the day to day practical problems of consent to treatment in patients with a major psychosis in which suspiciousness, fear or delusional beliefs impair judgment and influence rational decision making. Dementia is no different in this respect from the other severe mental disorders.

The major difficulty for doctors is that the legal framework appears to give no guidance on the day to day practical problems which we face in real life in treating incapable patients. The current accepted position in managing mentally incapable persons is that anyone proposing to give treatment to a patient is under a duty to use reasonable care and skill. A doctor performs his duty of care if he acts in accordance with a practice rightly accepted as proper by a responsible body of skilled and experienced doctors. To fail in the duty of care to give proper treatment and care is negligence, and a patient can bring an action for negligence if he can prove he has suffered damage resulting from the doctor's failure to give adequate care. Common law then gives a good deal of latitude to the judgment of a doctor to give treatment and care to an incapable patient.

The most recent leading case to defend this approach was Re. F (mental patient: sterilization) 1990, 2.A.C.1., which was concerned with the question of what treatment could (and should) be given in the absence of valid consent. The House of Lords held that, there being no procedure for giving someone else the right to decide on behalf of a mentally incapacitated person, there was also no jurisdiction for the court to approve or disapprove the giving of treatment. But the court could grant a declaration that it would be lawful to proceed in the absence of consent, if the treatment was justified on the principle of necessity, that the treatment was deemed in the person's best interests. Well, I am not here going to go into what exactly the 'best interests' of an individual might be; they are debatable; suffice it to say that this judgment appeared to give carte blanche to the multidisciplinary discussions leading to medical decisions of the kind which were mentioned earlier.

I would like now to look at two case examples of very common situations which will be familiar to most hospital doctors, GPs and psychiatrists, but which the Mental Health Act does not cover.

Mrs Smith has always been an isolated, independent and rather testy character who was admitted to hospital for treatment of pneumonia after having been found in a collapsed state by her home help. Her insidious dementia has been coming on for the past two years and it's become increasingly obvious that she isn't coping at home alone. Mrs Smith is sometimes incontinent, the odd accident when she fails to find the ward WC. Mrs Smith does not, however, like bathing or changing. When she came into hospital it appeared she'd not changed her clothes for several months. There is no doubt that for the sake of the rest of the ward patients and staff, Mrs Smith has to be persuaded firmly, and sometimes with the nurses physically carrying her to the bathroom, to be cleaned and changed.

Now, according to some guidance I have read from health authorities, every time one of the nurses gives personal care to Mrs Smith, who is on occasions vociferously reluctant, the nurse is committing the offence of battery. The case has never been tested, but many lawyers would predict that the nurse is acting properly in the patient's best interests.

Another example:

Mrs Brown also has dementia. She believes the ward is the biscuit factory she worked in all her life; she spends her day collecting up objects from all over the ward and placing them in a box; she appears to be packing biscuits. At five o'clock every evening she wants to 'go home', home to 'cook her husband's tea'. Her husband died many years ago. She repeatedly makes for the door and would be out in the street in a flash if we let her. Every evening a nurse spends a long time persuading, cajoling, diverting her attention and sometimes physically steering her away from the door.

I could repeat a hundred instances like this where day to day treatment and care are given to reluctant patients, yes, against their will, but with the intention to fulfil the duty of care to incapable patients who are not detained formally under the Act. How should psychiatric units deal with this problem? At present, since there are no formal decision making processes to provide us with guidance, it would seem sensible then for us to adopt the 'multidisciplinary prayer group approach' mentioned earlier to devise, first, a comprehensive unit policy on *how* decisions will be made for individuals, for example *who* will be involved in decision making (staff, managers, relatives and so on) and the principles on which decisions will be made. Unit policies need to be supplemented by specific written individual care plans which outline explicitly how the policy will be translated into practice for each individual. Write decisions down in clear unequivocal language with reasons fully explained. While there are as yet few examples of litigation about the failure to provide care for elderly people or indeed many complaints about the over restrictiveness of hospital regimes, such cases are on the increase and doctors' and nurses' best defence lies in their being able to demonstrate they had discussed their practice with other doctors and professionals and have made decisions, informed by other people's views, in what they believe to be patients' best interests. Most psychiatrists believe it would be a retrograde step to detain all these incapable patients under the Mental Health Act, and would rather that an alternative, comprehensive legal framework is developed to cover all aspects of decision making for mentally incompetent adults. On the other hand, the Commission remains acutely aware that the vast majority of elderly people resident permanently in hospitals, nursing homes and registered care homes are *de facto* detained, many reluctantly so. They form one of the most vulnerable groups of patients; many of them are at far greater risk of neglect or poor treatment than the vociferous younger detained patients that do fall within the Commission's remit. Our current size and structure would not allow the Commission, however, to expand its remit into the area of '*de facto*' detained patients and, indeed, many Commission members would say we had better make sure we are doing our current job effectively before broadening our responsibilities, a view I have some sympathy with.

Turning now to another problematic topic, the treatment of physical illness, which, unless it is *directly* aimed at treating mental disorder, is not covered by the Mental Health Act. Once more it is the Common Law framework that we fall back on to provide guidance. I have already mentioned that acute confusional states are mental disorders *but* in this situation it is generally agreed that it is possible to treat under the precedent of 'Re. F'. If a physically ill, frail elderly person becomes deliriously confused, you have a duty to act in the best interests of that individual even if that means at times restricting the freedom of the individual, or physically fighting off deluded attacks of a frightened, reluctant patient and preventing them from walking out of the door. The clinical staff must get on and treat that person. They do not *need* to use the Mental Health Act, although many would say it is quite often useful to do so. These problems can sometimes be very complex. Let me take the example of an old person with dementia, living alone, rapidly deteriorating and becoming physically ill. She may well be confused as a result of a toxic state on top of her chronic dementia. Should one use the Mental Health Act to treat her if she refuses care and treatment in hospital and community services are not sufficiently developed? On the whole, if you are in doubt, it is probably better to use the safeguarding provisions of the Mental Health Act, if it is necessary to admit to hospital, than to use Common Law principles. The individual can be admitted to any hospital ward, not just a psychiatric unit. When someone is plainly in need of specialist medical care from a geriatrician, the Mental Health Act allows any hospital bed to be used and this has been done successfully in several units. It is usual in such cases for a trained psychiatric nurse from the local service to assist with receiving documents and information giving. Just because someone needs 'sectioning' doesn't mean they aren't in need of acute medical care. It is also probably better to use the Mental Health Act than that curiously 'half dead' piece of legislation, Section 47 of the National Assistance Act of 1948, which allows a local authority to apply to a magistrate, on the recommendation of a public health doctor (i.e. a proper officer), for an individual to be removed to a hospital or other place to secure necessary care and attention. Research suggests that the vast majority of people removed under Section 47, or the emergency powers enacted in 1951, are eccentric or difficult elderly people with mental disorders (Wolfson *et al.*, 1990) and the powers are used infrequently where there is an active community focused specialist care of the elderly service of medical and psychiatric specialists.

GUARDIANSHIP

Guardianship is a little used power under the Mental Health Act and one that generates a lot of phone calls and letters to the Commission from psychogeriatricians expounding angrily that their local authority won't 'remove' someone into a local authority Part III home, either from their precious acute beds or from a disgustingly neglected house. Guardianship is essentially a social services function and local authorities have sometimes perceived it as a manipulative way of clinicians attempting to acquire resources for one or two individuals, especially as a means to coerce the authority to provide residential care. There being currently no power to convey, i.e. move someone by force into a home or attend a centre for treatment, it is regarded by some local authorities as a toothless power they would rather be without. The Commission has done its best to encourage the use of guardianship in appropriate cases but the number has only risen to 120 orders per year or so even now. This is a pity since there are some local authorities using the powers very constructively and, where psychiatrists and social services work together closely as a matter of routine, it can be helpful for relatives and the local authority in implementing decisions for dementia sufferers. The Commission has recommended that the power to convey should be introduced into the section.

Clearly the present legislation for mentally incapacitated adults is a muddle. Decision making is governed by separate bits of legislation according to the kind of decision which has to be made.

Property and finance may be dealt with under the Court of Protection, through Enduring Powers of Attorney (1985), by appointees for receiving benefits from the Department of Social Security or by the supervisory powers of a court in litigation. These powers for dealing with property and finance are quite separate from the disparate provisions available for deciding on the personal care, domestic arrangements and medical treatment of an incapacitated adult. Here there is a plethora of different powers, often overlapping, from which to choose.

- Compulsory admission and treatment for mental disorder, Mental Health Act 1983
- Emergency protection powers, Section 135/136, MHA 1983
- Section 47, National Assistance Act 1948, emergency powers 1951

- Guardianship, MHA 1983
- Common Law/Re. F for physical treatments
- Declarations by High Court, on application

Currently, the Law Commission is reviewing the present unsatisfactory arrangements which lead us into so many difficulties with patients with dementia. It recently published a discussion document *'Mentally Incapacitated Adults and Decision Making'* (Law Commission, 1991) which sets out the problems and then discusses a number of options to introduce a more comprehensive, unified system of statutes to cover the issues which have great importance for those of us working with frail elderly people. The Mental Health Act is easy enough — it's just the bits that aren't in it that cause so much trouble.

REFERENCES

Law Commission (1991). *Mentally Incapacitated Adults and Decision Making: An Overview, A discussion document, LCCP No. 119*, HMSO, London.
Wolfson, P., Lindesay, J., Cohen, M. and Murphy, E. (1990). Section 47 and its use with mentally disordered people. *J. Pub. Health Med.*, **12**, 9–15.

Treatment and Care in Old Age Psychiatry
Edited by R. Levy, R. Howard and A. Burns
©1993 Gordon R. Ashton

19

Power of Attorney and Court of Protection (Handling the Affairs of the Elderly)

GORDON R. ASHTON

Gedye & Sons, Solicitors, Grange-over-Sands, UK

INTRODUCTION

The title of this chapter may sound rather technical and offputting, and may disguise the real content which is consideration of the problems that arise when an individual is incapable, by reason of mental disorder, of managing and administering his or her property and affairs. Physicians react to the phrases 'Power of Attorney' and 'Court of Protection' with the same apprehension with which I face many medical terms. An alternative title for this chapter could be 'Handling the affairs of the elderly', which is an area in which both solicitors and medical practitioners, including psychiatrists, have a role to play. We must work together, but do we understand one another?

Incapacity

For more than 25 years I have practised as a solicitor in the costa geriatrica of the Lake District — Grange-over-Sands — so I have hands-on experience of dealing with the financial affairs of the elderly, but I also have a mentally handicapped child and mix with other such parents, so am aware that mental incapacity does not only arise through old age. I have little experience of mental illness, but spend a disproportionate amount of energy explaining that this is not the same as mental handicap (or should I say 'learning disabilities'). As a lawyer I wonder if I am wasting my time? To the doctor concerned with diagnosis, treatment and prognosis, the causes of mental incapacity are of importance, and to the care worker there may be significant differences between the provision to be made for the aged, the

223

mentally handicapped and the mentally ill. But the lawyer is merely concerned with mental capacity, which means the ability to make decisions that should be recognized by others.

The distinctions that are made by the medical profession can seem illogical to lawyers. Senility, I am told, is an acquired organic brain syndrome, and whilst the circumstances and needs of a person who is senile are different to those of a person with a mental handicap, to a lawyer many of the same problems arise, in particular an inability to make decisions. However, the person with a mental handicap will never have had a greater degree of understanding than that now displayed, whereas those who have developed normally and then suffered an illness or accident causing mental disability will have at an earlier stage enjoyed a greater level of capacity. This may be relevant when it comes to making decisions for the individual, because there will be a personal pattern of decision-making to follow. It will also have an effect on the personal wealth of the individual which of course still needs to be dealt with.

Capacity or ability?

The law is concerned with the *capacity* of the individual, but this may become confused with *ability* with inappropriate consequences, e.g.:

- an individual who is not able to communicate, perhaps by reason of a stroke, may not be permitted to open a bank account although his thought processes could be unaffected;
- the individual who is able to talk coherently and sign his name may be allowed to open an account notwithstanding that he has a serious mental disability which, if realized, would establish that he did not have the capacity to do so.

Lawyers should recognize the difference between ability and capacity and ensure that the correct tests are applied especially where there are communication problems. An understanding of the nature and extent of any disability is needed if the individual's true potential is to be recognized and achieved, and the doctor can assist the lawyer in this area, because he seeks to take instructions from his client and needs to know how and when he may do so.

Types of decision

There are two fields of decision-making: (1) *personal decisions* (e.g. where to live, whether to have medical treatment); and (2) *financial decisions*.

Although there may be an urgent need to make a personal decision, English law makes no provision for delegation except in the limited range of circumstances covered by the Mental Health Act 1983. These decisions are usually made by carers, but sometimes by others on grounds of necessity or expediency, and may simply not be made at all. The law has hitherto merely concerned itself with financial decisions, and it is these that I shall discuss, but the whole issue of decision-making and mental incapacity is presently under consideration by the Law Commission (1991) and law reform is urgently needed. Appeal cases relating to medical treatment such as sterilization and abortion highlight the inadequacies of the law, but merely represent the tip of the iceberg (F v. West Berkshire Health Authority, 1989).

PROCEDURES AVAILABLE

Introduction

If the individual is incapable of handling his own affairs, someone else must do this for him, so we are concerned with the delegation of financial powers. This may be done in three different ways, and I can best illustrate this by reference to Fig. 1, looked at from the point of view of the individual. (Throughout this chapter 'he' also includes 'she'.)

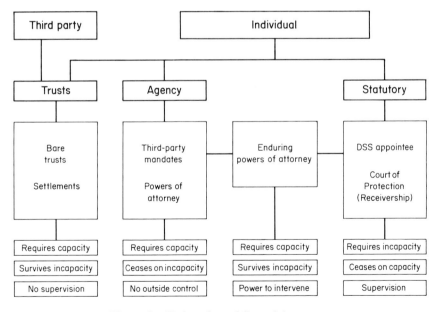

Figure 1. Delegation of financial powers.

Trusts

A trust arises when assets are held by one or more persons (called 'trustees') on behalf of other persons (known as 'beneficiaries'). A trust may be created by an individual for his own benefit in anticipation of incapacity or by someone else for his support either by a lifetime gift or under a Will. In its simplest form this may be a transfer of shares or money by an elderly person into a son or daughter's name — if a gift is not intended this creates a bare trust, but it should be confirmed in writing. A more complex form would be a settlement by or for the benefit of the elderly person (see Fig. 1).

The person who provides the money or assets must be capable of creating a trust, but if the trust is validly created it continues even if the beneficiary becomes incapable, though the trustees take a risk if they then spend money on his behalf without express power to do so. There is no outside supervision of the trustees and they only have power over the assets in trust, not any other assets of the beneficiary.

Agency

This arises where someone else is given authority to do something for you. It could be a simple mandate for a bank account or dividend, but a more elaborate form is a Power of Attorney under which an attorney is given authority to handle some or all of the donor's affairs (see Fig. 1).

The person granting the agency (the principal or donor) must be capable of appointing the agent or attorney, and the authority ceases if he becomes mentally incapable. In practice this may not be known, but the agent takes a risk if he continues to act without authority, so this is not a suitable method of handling the affairs of the elderly, though in practice it is often used. There is no outside control, but the person granting the agency has ultimate control as long as he is capable because he can cancel the authority, and in law the agency ceases when he is not capable.

Statutory

The Court of Protection has statutory powers to take over the financial affairs of an individual who becomes mentally incapable and will usually do so by appointing some suitable person as a Receiver with delegated powers to act on his behalf (Mental Health Act 1983 Part VII).

The individual must be incapable before the Court's powers arise and they cease if he again becomes capable; there is considerable supervision by the Court. The DSS Appointee procedure is also included here, but this only relates to state benefits and in practice there is no effective supervision. The affairs of those who are in private nursing or residential care homes and in receipt of Income Support residential care allowance are dealt with by an appointee who looks after the weekly benefits.

Informal methods

There are also various informal methods for dealing with the affairs of an elderly person, but these either relate to small sums of money or specific assets and I shall not go into them here. By way of example, small income tax repayments can be claimed by certain relatives, and special arrangements may be made for government pensions.

Compare procedures

When you look at Fig. 1 you will see that agency and statutory methods have attributes that are opposites — but look what appears between them — Enduring Powers of Attorney. Do these offer the best of both worlds? Do they render the use of trusts unnecessary? Let us examine this recent creature of statute.

Enduring Powers of Attorney

The Enduring Powers of Attorney Act 1985 provides a practical, inexpensive way for elderly people to anticipate incapacity. (See also the Court of Protection (Enduring Powers of Attorney) Rules 1986 and (Amendment) Rules 1990.) It creates a new form of agency document (referred to as an 'EPA') which is not revoked by subsequent mental incapacity. The individual can choose his own decision-maker, but at present his powers will only relate to financial matters. On the basis that prevention is better than cure, we should all prepare for old age and an inability to cope by signing an EPA. My firm offers a package — a Will plus an EPA, and this is attractive to clients of all ages when it is explained that mental incapacity arises from more causes than senility.

Requirements

An EPA is a special form of Power of Attorney which must be in a prescribed form. (Enduring Power of Attorney (Prescribed Form) Regulations 1990 replacing previous 1986 and 1987 regulations.) Forms may be purchased from law stationers and the current version must be used, but it is wise to employ a solicitor to deal with the formalities. The form contains explanatory information to tell the donor (that's the person appointing the attorney) its effect and the marginal notes are part of the prescribed form and must not be omitted. There are alternatives with space for additional wording so the form may be adapted to set out particular wishes of the donor, e.g. limitations on the authority given and restrictions on the manner and circumstances in which it may be exercized. There may be one or more attorneys and they may be appointed jointly or jointly and severally.

Execution

The donor signs first, and then each attorney, but any of them may make a mark if unable to sign or authorize someone else to sign on their behalf (a second witness is then needed). Signatures must be witnessed by independent persons.

Registration

Attorney(s) must apply to the Public Trust Office for registration when they have reason to believe that the donor is *or is becoming* mentally incapable. A registration fee of £50 is payable. The Power is suspended (save for essential action) pending submission of the application whereupon limited authority is restored, e.g. to pay nursing home fees. Once the EPA is registered the attorney can act fully again.

Notice of the intention to register must be given in the prescribed form to the donor by handing a form to him personally and to the closest relatives by post. There is an order of priority for these relatives (spouse, children, parents, brothers and sisters, etc.) taken class by class; at least three must be served, and if anyone from a class is included all of that class must be served. Opportunity then arises for anyone to object to registration on certain grounds.

Registration does not amount to certification that the EPA is valid but creates a procedure whereby the EPA may be challenged. There is no power over the person so the attorney cannot dictate where he shall live though control of the money inevitably gives influence.

Role of doctor

At no stage is a medical report required, but one may become important if the EPA or the need to register it is challenged.

The test of capacity to sign an EPA is not the same as the test of capacity to handle one's affairs. (Re. K, Re. F (1988) 1 All ER 358, Mr Justice Hoffmann.) The test of capacity to sign a Will is also different. An EPA will be valid if the donor understood its nature and effect notwithstanding that he was at the time of its execution incapable by reason of mental disorder of managing his property and affairs. In some cases an EPA may be validly executed even though it must immediately be registered because the donor is incapable of handling his affairs. This distinction is valuable in many cases where a person is failing — the trick is to catch them in time. I usually reassure the doctor by asking him to sign a certificate in the following terms:

'I . . . MD of . . . hereby certify that . . . of . . . who signed an Enduring Power of Attorney dated . . . in favour of . . . in my presence fully understood the nature and effect of the document he (she) was signing. In giving this certificate I offer no further opinion with regard to the mental capacity of the said . . . .'

Let us now look at the alternative procedure which must be adopted where the patient has income or assets that need to be dealt with and it is too late to have an EPA signed.

Court of Protection

The Court of Protection is an office of the Supreme Court of Judicature under the direction of a Master, and is governed by the Mental Health Act 1983, Part VII. Its operation is financed by those who use it, and unlike other courts, much of its work is done by senior officials and is carried out by correspondence. The Public Trustee, operating from the Public Trust Office in London, carries out administrative functions.

Jurisdiction

The court has authority to make orders and give directions in relation to the estates of persons who, by reason of mental disorder, are incapable of managing and administering their property and affairs (known as *patients*). This includes elderly persons who have become senile, those who suffer brain damage or become mentally ill, and persons who have a severe mental handicap.

Applications

Applications are submitted to the court by someone who considers that the affairs and property of someone else may require the protection of the court. There must be completed and submitted with the application:

- application form (Form CP1) — two copies;
- certificate of family and property (Form CP5);
- medical certificate (Form CP3);
- the commencement fee;
- copy of the patient's last Will (if available).

The applicant indicates whether he is seeking his own appointment as Receiver or that of someone else, and whether he is related to the patient.

Medical certificate

The solicitor deals with the certificate giving details of family, property, income, marital status, maintenance and other relevant information, and it is the medical certificate that you will be asked to complete. The court circulates Notes to accompany this and you should read these. Do bear in mind that you are not simply being asked to take away the patient's financial freedom; by signing the Certificate you may be preventing others from misappropriating his money. Notice of the application must be given to certain persons, including the patient, so they all have an opportunity to make representations if they do not agree.

Orders

If satisfied that it has jurisdiction, the court usually appoints a person as a Receiver to deal with the patient's financial affairs under the supervision of the Court. Specific powers will be given to the Receiver who should apply to the Court in writing if further powers are needed. A 'Short Procedure Order' is available to deal with simple matters where it is not necessary to appoint a Receiver.

Implications

Once a Receiver is appointed the patient ceases to have any personal powers over his affairs, although the court may delegate certain limited powers back to him. Fees must be paid to the court on a regular basis, and costs may also be incurred by solicitors who are often needed because of the complexity of the procedures. The expense coupled with delays and the formality involved all result in families seeking to use the court only as a last resort, and although in recent years the court has become more user friendly it still only operates in London. Dissatisfaction with these procedures coupled with increased demand for a facility of choice resulted in the EPA being introduced by Parliament.

Statutory Wills

It is worth mentioning that the court has power to authorize the signing of a Will on behalf of a patient if this is thought appropriate. Many people fail to make Wills until it is too late or allow their Wills to become out of date, and it is not generally realized that this power exists.

THE WORK IN PRACTICE

Role of lawyers

It is the role of the solicitor to deal with these procedures where needed and to ensure that there is no improper use of the assets and income of the elderly person. A solicitor must never allow himself to have a conflict of interest. He should remember that his client is the elderly person, not the attorney or receiver through whom he may receive instructions but who may not always be acting in the best interests of the elderly person. The doctor can help to identify those best interests, and should feel free to turn direct to the solicitor — or even to the Court of Protection — if he feels that they are being overlooked. For example, the money is there to be spent on the needs of the elderly person, rather than being preserved for the benefit of the next generation.

Whistle blowing

I do not believe that the legal system can provide an adequate system of supervision in all cases when dealing with the affairs of people who lack mental capacity. This would be too restrictive and too expensive. But what it can do is provide a whistle blowing procedure and an ability to intervene in those cases where something is going wrong. It is up to the professionals involved to identify these cases and to know how to blow the whistle. The solicitor represents part of this procedure although he can be by-passed by the doctor in appropriate cases.

Role of doctors

Your patient may be distressed if he cannot put his or her financial affairs in order, so you should be aware of the procedures available and those being adopted in a particular case so that you can guide and reassure the patient. You need not get further involved unless you feel that there is abuse and then you can blow the whistle.

You may be asked to witness the patient's signature to a document or to prepare a medical report, and then it is important to have some dialogue with the solicitor and to understand precisely what is involved. This is an area of practice that has not yet been fully developed between our two professions, but which is becoming increasingly important.

Medical reports

When the lawyer asks for a medical report it will be required for a particular purpose. You should not hesitate to ask what that purpose is and what are the criteria to be applied, and then word the report so that it is specifi-cally directed to those criteria rather than being general in its terms. Except in an extreme case it would be quite inappropriate to provide a report simply stating that the patient is mentally incapable, because the question is then, 'Incapable of what?'

All too often lawyers debate at great length the correct test of mental capacity for a particular transaction, and then ask the doctor for a definitive report without providing the information that is required for the doctor to form a considered view or explaining what the correct legal test is. I have already indicated that different tests apply for different purposes, but let me give you another example. The Court of Protection only has jurisdiction if the individual 'is incapable, by reason of mental disorder, of managing and administering his property and affairs' (Mental Health Act 1983, section 94(2)). This does not refer to affairs generally, but to the individual's own affairs, yet how often does the solicitor tell the doctor what these are? As a matter of law, the millionaire is far more vulnerable to having to submit to the court's jurisdiction than the pauper!

Date of report

The individual must have the necessary capacity at the time when the document is signed if it is to be valid. An unwary solicitor may seek to rely upon a report at a later date when the patient/client is no longer capable, so if capacity fluctuates or is deteriorating this should be stated. Conversely, a normally incapable patient may have a lucid interval and there is nothing wrong in obtaining a signature at such time. For these reasons it is prudent, in doubtful cases, to have the signature witnessed by the doctor.

Questions to ask

Assuming that you know the appropriate legal test, how do you assess mental capacity? Do you ask the patient questions such as 'Who is the Prime Minister?' or, better still 'Who is the Secretary of State for Health?', and then check the patient's ability to make a cup of tea? Many a successful businessman would fail such a test. Is it not more relevant to ask 'Where is your purse and how much money is in it?' and 'What bills have you received this week and how did you pay them?', followed by a test of ability to write a cheque? Do you consider ability to manage alone, or with the assistance of others? At the risk of being certified incapable (or even sectioned) by a record number of psychiatrists, dare I suggest that the typical medical practi-tioner is less qualified to form an opinion as the legal mental capaci of an elderly person than a solicitor experienced in this area of work. Perhaps the opinion of a psychiatrist should be obtained in all cases!

CONCLUSION

Although our roles and perspectives are different, doctors and the solicitors must be prepared to work together because only by attending to the patient's medical and financial needs in unison can we as professionals reassure the patient that his world is in order. Misunderstandings can easily arise due to the fact that our two professions have different priorities, but both are important to the elderly individual, and a greater understanding of what we are each seeking to achieve and how we are able to do so must surely be in the best interests of the patient/client. I hope that through this chapter I have contributed to this greater mutual understanding.

Index